HEARTLAND
MASALA

HEARTLAND MASALA

AN INDIAN COOKBOOK FROM AN AMERICAN KITCHEN

Jyoti Mukharji and Auyon Mukharji

Illustrated by Olivier Kugler

Photographs by Kevin J. Miyazaki

Ornamental motifs by Jhulan Mukharji and Aroop Mukharji

Copyright © 2025 by Jyoti Mukharji and Auyon Mukharji.

All rights reserved. No part of this book may be reproduced in any form without written permission from the publisher.

Library of Congress Cataloging-in-Publication Data available.
ISBN: 978-1-68555-328-9
Ebook ISBN: 978-1-68555-232-9
Library of Congress Control Number: 2025902872

Manufactured in China.

Editor: Amy Treadwell
Art Direction: Rachel Lopez Metzger
Illustrations by Olivier Kugler
Photographs by Kevin J. Miyazaki
Ornamental motifs by Jhulan Mukharji and Aroop Mukharji

10 9 8 7 6 5 4 3 2 1

The Collective Book Studio®
Oakland, California
www.thecollectivebook.studio

For our mothers and grandmothers

Introduction 9
- What to Expect 16
- Vocabulary, Gear & Ingredients 22
- *A Note on Pressure Cooking and Efficiency* 26
- *Spice Shopping Q & A* 29
- Tips & Techniques 32
- *The Art of Repeated Action* 35

Scratch 37
- Ghee 38
- Homemade Yogurt 40
- Hung Curd 41
- *A Note on Curry Powder* 42
- Dry-Roasted & Ground Spices 43
- Ghee Bhaat 44
- Cooked & Seasoned Chickpeas 45
- Paneer 46
- Boiled & Seasoned Potatoes 48
- *A Note on Potatoes* 49
- *The Great Curry Debate* 50
- *Masalas* 52
- Garam Masala 53
- Chaat Masala 53

Salads, Daals, and Beans 55
- Kachumbar 56
- *A Note on Courses* 57
- Tomato, Red Lentil & Ginger Soup 58
- Daal Paalak 59
- *Meet Your Beans!* 61
- Sukhi Moong Daal 62
- Daal Makhani 63
- *Daal Bubble Monsters* 66
- Arhar Daal with Green Mango 67
- Ghoogni 69
- Narkol Cholar Daal 70
- Lauki Channa Daal 72
- Channa Masala 74
- Sukha Kaala Channa 76
- Sundal 78
- Kadhi 79
- Rajma 82

Vegetables! 85
- Aloo Tamatar 87
- Bharva Bhindi 88
- Gobhi Aloo 91
- *My Mother, the Potato Wizard* 92
- Masala Brussels Sprouts 93
- *Don't Judge a Veggie by Its Crispness* 94
- Kalonji Broccoli 95
- Baingan Bharta 96
- Aloo Baingan 129
- Bharva Baingan 130
- Baghare Baingan 132
- Mattar Paneer 134
- Saag Paneer 136
- Jeera Mattar 138
- Bhutta Chaat 139

Poultry, Meat, and Fish 141
- Murgh Kaali Mirch 142
- Murgh Do Pyaaza 144
- Murgh Hariyali 146
- Murgh Rezala 148
- Murgh Makhani 151
- *There Is No Team in Tandoor* 155
- Keema Mattar 156
- *A Note on Beef* 158
- Mutton Aloo Korma 159
- Bhuna Gosht 162
- Rogan Josh 164
- Vindaloo 166
- Goan Machhli 168
- Machher Jhol 169
- Shorshe Chingri 171

Rice and Bread 175

Pulaos 176
Jeera Pulao 177
Pyaaz Pulao 178
Lemon Rice 179
Bengali Khichudi 180
The Curious Case of Kedgeree 182
Biryanis 183
Mushroom Dum Biryani 184
Kacchi Hyderabadi Biryani 186
The 70-Year-Old Roti Quesadilla 188
Roti 189
Paratha 192
Gobhi Paratha 194
Aloo Paratha 197
Lachhedaar Paratha 200
Loochi 204

This Is How We Party 207

Moongphali Aloo Chaat 208
Jhaal Mudhi 209
The Magic of Deep-Frying 210
Chire Bhaja 212
Paapdi Chaat 213
Dimer Debhil 215
Aloo Tikki 217
Sabudana Vada 220
Beguni 222
Gobhi Pakora 223
Samosa 225
Sabudana Khichudi 229
Kaathi Roll 230
Spiced Liver Toast 232
Spiced Watermelon 233
Fruit Chaat 235

Raitas, Chutneys, and a Pickle 237

Raitas 238
Kheera Tamatar Raita 239
Paalak Raita 240
Boondi Raita 241
Dhania Pudina Chutney 242
Imli Chutney 243
Tamatar Khajoor Chutney 244
Adarak Nimbu Achaar 245

Drinks and Sweets 247

When the Himalaya Give You Lemons... 248
Nimbu Pani 249
Aam Lassi 250
Masala Chai 252
A Note on Masala Chai 253
Aam Panna 254
Thandai 255
Hold Your Breath 256
Aam Panna Punch 257
Thandai Old-Fashioned 257
Sooji Halwa 258
Mishti Doi 259
Doodh Seviyan 260
Salted Caramel Almond Flan 261
Fruit Cream 263
Kulfi 264
Aam Kulfi 265
Pista Kesar Kulfi 266
Sesame Jaggery Brittle 267

Spices and Sundry 269

Spices 270
Sample Menus 278
Resources 279
Index 280
Acknowledgments 286
Recipe Testers 287

Introduction

Welcome to our cookbook. We're so excited to cook with you! Before we get started, allow us to introduce ourselves.

HELLO! MY NAME IS JYOTI. My family is from Punjab, a North Indian state known for its flatbreads, tandoori dishes, and an abiding love of dairy. Despite of my keen fondness for homestyle Punjabi fare while growing up, I never actually learned to cook as a young girl. I was much too focused on my studies and schoolwork.

All that studying landed me in medical school, where I met my husband, Jhulan, whose family is Bengali. Even though Punjab and West Bengal are both Indian states, they feel like different countries. Our courtship was a whirlwind introduction to a new cuisine, language, and culture. I soon learned to speak, read, and write Bengali, and also grew familiar with the fish, rice, and dessert preparations that Bengal is famous for.

It wasn't until Jhulan and I moved abroad to the United States in the late 1970s that I began learning to cook in earnest. Watery daals and misshapen rotis marred the early days, but I quickly improved with daily practice and the help of my mother, Nirmal, and my mother-in-law, Sumana, during their visits.

The birthplaces of our three sons—Arnob in Dallas, Texas; Auyon in Richmond, Virginia; and Aroop in Overland Park, Kansas—mark the circuitous route we took to find our home here in the Midwest. Not long before we left Virginia, we learned that Arnob, our eldest, had a moderate learning disability. I retired from medicine to be a full-time mom, a decision that I am so grateful to have made, and to have been able to make. By this point, I had also become a decent cook, having learned not only how to make the Punjabi and Bengali dishes of my youth and young adulthood, but also how to adapt them to whatever limited ingredients were available in the American supermarkets of the 1970s and '80s. (See the Masala Brussels Sprouts recipe on page 93 for an example.)

As our kids grew and started expressing opinions and desires with enthusiasm, my cooking evolved yet again. Pizzas, pastas, and sandwiches, instead of the Indian fare that Jhulan and I preferred, were the most frequent requests. We found a middle ground by alternating between Western and Indian dinners nightly (although my Western preparations admittedly featured a liberal use of Indian spices).

The current chapter of my cooking journey began in 2010, when I attempted to donate an Indian meal for eight as part of a charity auction. I was told there was already another home-cooked meal on offer, so I took an organizer's suggestion to provide a cooking class instead. By the end of that first class, I was smitten. With Jhulan's encouragement, I began teaching regularly, and I have now hosted several thousand students through my kitchen. The joy of teaching and serving as a cultural conduit has been compounded by the thrill of running my own nonprofit, something I never thought to dream of as a young hospitalist.

    The first classes I taught featured the foods of Punjab and Bengal, but my boundaries soon broadened. I began learning and teaching dishes from other states like Kerala, Goa, Gujarat, and Maharashtra. While growing up, I would only have encountered these cuisines in restaurants and at friends' houses, and there is a strong likelihood that I never would have learned to cook any of them had I stayed in India. That my classes have not only inspired countless connections with the local Kansas City community, but also strengthened and deepened my bond with India, is a curious and beautiful thing.

    The writing of this book, a collection of my favorite recipes to teach from all across India, has been a long-standing dream of mine. I'm so pleased it is finally out in the world. Thank you for your support.

Love,
Jyoti

HI! MY NAME IS AUYON, and I'm Jyoti's middle son. I was born in Richmond, Virginia, and grew up in Kansas City. These days, I live in New England, where I went to college and then stuck around. I'm a member of the indie-folk band Darlingside, in which I sing, songwrite, and play a few instruments.

My bandmates can attest that I spend most of my time thinking about food. My primary extra-musical role when we are in a recording studio is making sure everyone is fed. When we meet other touring musicians, my first questions involve restaurant-hunting strategies and dietary preferences. Side jobs, when I've had occasion to hold them, have been kitchen-adjacent, in restaurants and groceries. All to say, I love cooking and I love eating. Most of all, though, I love eating my mom's cooking, which is why I'm here.

My mom initially brought me on to test recipes and otherwise help with the writing, but my role eventually expanded into co-authorship. Cookbooks make up a significant proportion of my worldly possessions, so the prospect of having a hand in writing one was too tempting to pass up. It also proved a much larger project than I anticipated. Much of that was my own fault—as a complement to my mom's recipes and anecdotes, I wanted to present historical and cultural context, which meant diving headfirst into a field of study I was largely unfamiliar with. Despite the yearslong stress of feeling out of my depth, and after wearing my dear mother's patience down to a nub, I can now say that it all truly feels worthwhile. I am proud of what my mom and I have been able to put together, and I am grateful to you for picking up a copy.

Love,
Auyon

What to Expect

Jyoti Our cookbook is a collection of recipes I have enjoyed teaching from my classes, peppered with historical and cultural vignettes by Auyon. Many of our recipes draw from the Hindu, upper middle class kitchens of my mother and mother-in-law. Differences in religion, socioeconomic standing, and caste ancestry play a huge role in the great diversity of Indian cooking, and we acknowledge that our offering is only a narrow slice of this broad ambit.

We include dishes from all over India (with an emphasis on the cuisines of Punjab and Bengal), but our book is by no means geographically comprehensive. Nor can most of the recipes be described as fast or easy—a few even take the better part of a day, like Kacchi Hyderabadi Biryani (page 186). Since my classes are designed for newcomers and veterans alike, we included a thorough guide to the basics in the introductory materials. That said, many of the more involved recipes will take time, work, and practice, even for folks who spend a lot of time in the kitchen.

Please also be aware that we will occasionally propose things that might make you uncomfortable, or at least challenge the edicts of contemporary food writing. We will ask you, for example, to sometimes cook with a frozen vegetable regardless of whether a fresh version is available. We will encourage, even insist, that you use a nonstick pan for a broad range of dishes, not just eggs. We will even suggest that you consume mustard oil, which the FDA staunchly refuses to approve for human consumption (even though a vast swath of the Asian continent uses the stuff as its primary cooking fat, see page 171).

Be brave. Cook boldly!

ON AUTHENTICITY

Auyon There is no formal codification or seminal set of texts within Indian gastronomy. With few exceptions, seeking recipes that might properly and exclusively be deemed "authentic" is a fool's errand for the vast breadth of Indian cookery.

Even the idea of a monolithic India is a fallacy. As my mom mentioned in her introduction, to cross a state line in India is often to enter a different world. The gulf between the north and south is even broader—the Indo-Aryan languages of northern India like Hindi and Bengali are more closely related to English than they are to the Dravidian languages of South India like Tamil and Kannada. To bring it back around to food, consider the samosa: the delicate, thin-skinned iteration of Mumbai's Bohra Muslim community might not even be recognized as a samosa by a devotee of the generously built Punjabi version. A great-uncle once wrote to me, "There are many Indias." There are perhaps just as many authentic samosa recipes.

There is also the matter of diasporic cooking. My mom didn't begin learning to cook until she arrived in the United States. Many of the remembered flavors of her childhood could not be duplicated exactly, so she adapted and adjusted and made do with what she had. Her cooking is a product of both her country of origin and her new home—the story of immigrant cooking the world over. Our cookbook reflects not only this duality but also some of our own familial quirks. A deep fondness for russet potatoes, for instance, makes them a frequent addition to many of my mom's meat dishes that are typically (sadly) tuberless in restaurants and other Indian homes.

The history of Indian cooking is the history of India. The cuisine has morphed and evolved through generational retranslations, through conquests and colonizations, and through innumerable connections with foreign lands, from the Silk Road of antiquity to cooking celebrities in the age of Instagram. It is in constant flux, both within and beyond India's national borders. Any attempt to pin it down is merely a record of a moment and place. Our cookbook was written in this spirit, and our title is a nod to the same intention. The Hindustani word *masala*, which translates to "spice mixture," feels an appropriate metaphor for not only the multifaceted quality of my mother's cooking, but also the twists and turns of history that landed a daughter of Punjab here in the American heartland.

HOW TO USE THIS BOOK

Jyoti Indian cooking is not an exact science. Don't worry about adding a little extra or a little less of something. Although the recipes in this book are as specific as possible about quantitative details like ingredient measurements and cooking times, such precision is a wildly foreign concept in most Indian home kitchens.

If you like ginger or garlic, you are welcome to add more. Bigger changes (like substituting chicken for lamb) will often change the cooking time, but we've included sensory cues in addition to cooking times to allow for flexibility. We recommend making each dish as prescribed the first couple of times, taking care to note the appearance, smell, taste, and texture of the ingredients as the recipe progresses. Once you feel you have a recipe down, start to experiment and substitute. Cooking at its best is an improvisational art form.

Taste often—early on, any time you add an ingredient, and at the end. The more often you taste, the more you'll understand how each ingredient and cooking segment contributes to the whole, and how to better adjust a dish to your preferences. The only caveat here is to please forgo tasting when there are any health or safety concerns (i.e., don't try to taste hot frying oil or nibble a dish that still has uncooked meat in it).

Auyon Although the traditional way to eat most of the savory preparations in this book is warm with white basmati rice or a flatbread, don't let that limit you. Try them in tortillas as Indian tacos, over other grains like farro or brown rice, or on nachos. We sprinkled a few of our own favorite corruptions (like crushed Doritos over daal and rice!) throughout the book in the spirit of experimentation and encouragement.

Finally, while we believe that cooking from scratch produces the most delicious meals, you can always use shortcuts like pre-ground spices, store-bought achaars (Indian pickles), and canned beans if you're short on time or energy.

SALT, FAT, AND CHILI

Unlike most cookbooks, we prescribe salt measurements for most all of our recipes. "Salting to taste" is a great bit of advice if you know how the food should taste, but since you might not have cooked these dishes before, we include ballpark measurements just in case. Proper salting, which often involves adding more than you might think, is essential for making spices and flavors pop. (The few exceptional recipes that include a "salt to taste" instruction are those that involve a pre-seasoned ingredient like cooked chickpeas, potatoes, or rice.)

All of our prescriptions were calculated using Morton table salt. If you cook with flaky or kosher salt, keep in mind that those bigger crystals don't compact as well, so you may need to add a bit more to make up for the empty space. You also don't need to add all the salt at once—feel free to add a bit every time you add an ingredient, tasting at each step if possible.

Some of the recipes might also involve a larger amount of oil or ghee than you are used to. Resist any temptation to skimp on the fat, as the amount we prescribe is necessary for proper cooking and browning. While Indians have no compunctions about serving a dish with a bit of oil floating on top (and will sometimes go so far as to fold extra fat into the food at celebratory events to enrich the fare), you can certainly skim off excess fat just before serving if you desire. The flavorful oil can be refrigerated and used later.

Many people mistakenly think of Indian food as universally hot and spicy. Although there is a rich tradition of spice use across the subcontinent, chili peppers are only one component—and given that they were unknown in India until the arrival of the Portuguese, a relatively recent addition! For those who are heat-sensitive, any dish in this book can be made with the chili content reduced or removed entirely (and for color, paprika can always be substituted for cayenne).

Our recipes were written to have a mild to moderate heat content, but bear in mind that heat can vary greatly from pepper to pepper, even within the same cultivar. It's often helpful to taste a bit of any single pepper you use before cooking to get a sense of its potency. An easy way to adjust a pepper's heat is by removing its pith and seeds. Capsaicin is the compound that lends chilies their pungency, and it is most concentrated in the white pith in which the seeds are sometimes embedded. If you are worried about getting capsaicin on your fingers, try using kitchen shears to mince rather than a knife (or wear gloves).

Vocabulary, Gear & Ingredients

- The ounce measurements in this book refer to weight, not volume. Relatedly, while we primarily use volumetric measurements when listing ingredients, we also often include weights, both metric and imperial, for vegetables and legumes. Use whichever is most convenient, and do not worry if your 1 cup of blended onion proves to be heavier or lighter than our 1 cup. The recipe will be fine.

- No need to get too fussy about any of this, but "chopped" should approximate a ¼-inch (6-mm) dice, "finely chopped" an ⅛-inch (3-mm) dice, and "minced" as small as you can manage.

- For stirring instructions, "frequently" means roughly every minute or two, and "occasionally" every 3 or 4 minutes.

- Order of operations primer: "1 teaspoon cumin seeds, roasted and ground" indicates you should start with 1 teaspoon of whole cumin seeds and then roast and grind them, whereas "1 teaspoon chopped cilantro" means you should chop the cilantro first and then measure out 1 teaspoon.

- Serving sizes are a subjective matter, especially with Indian cooking. Since dishes are traditionally served simultaneously (and sometimes without any clear hierarchy) across much of the subcontinent, the side versus main distinction is often inapplicable. All to say, we've done our best to estimate serving sizes based on how we eat, but you may need to adjust based on the needs of your table. Remember also that the more dishes you serve during a meal, the more servings you'll get from each dish.

- The "+" sign between two measurements of a given ingredient in the ingredient list means that you will use those two measurements at different times within the recipe. For example, if you need 2 cups of milk early in the recipe and then 1 cup later in the recipe, it will be listed as "2 cups + 1 cup milk."

CHOPPED

FINELY CHOPPED

MINCED

ON TITLES

For the linguistically curious, the colored dots on either side of each recipe title reflect the language of origin.

HINDUSTANI   BENGALI   TAMIL   KONKANI   ENGLISH

HANDY STUFF TO HAVE AROUND

- a good, sharp knife or two, including a chef's knife (also useful for crushing spices and nuts)
- a couple of pans, one of which is large (10 to 14 inches // 25 to 36 cm in diameter), nonstick, and lidded (see page 92 for more on nonstick cookware)
- a pot or two, one of which is large, nonstick, and lidded
- a few small or medium (8 to 10 inches // 20 to 25 cm) pots and pans
- a mortar and pestle for coarse grinding or smashing
- an electric coffee grinder (that you don't use for coffee!) for finely grinding whole, dry spices
- a stand blender
- a food processor
- a rolling pin
- a deep wok or Dutch oven for deep-frying
- a digital, instant-read thermometer with a long probe and a temperature range that reaches 400°F (200°C), also for deep-frying
- a pair of tongs
- a slotted spoon or spider strainer
- a roasting rack or roasting net for stovetop dry-roasting
- butter muslin or fine cheesecloth for making paneer, ghee, and spice sachets
- a grater or Microplane (for ginger, we love the ceramic nippled plate graters)
- a digital kitchen scale
- a frying pan splatter screen
- wooden or metal skewers for kabobs
- a pressure cooker or Instant Pot (optional, see page 27)

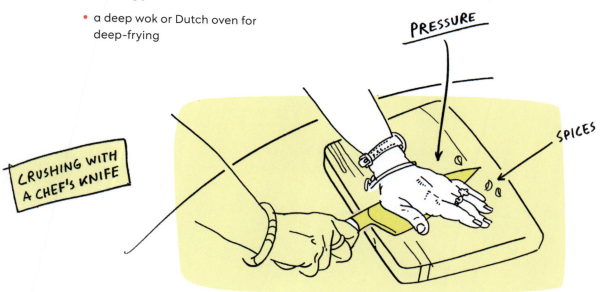

CRUSHING WITH A CHEF'S KNIFE — PRESSURE — SPICES

PRODUCE

- As you begin cooking each dish, our vegetable prep is straightforward. Wash all vegetables and fruits before using. There is no need to seed tomatoes or peel vegetables unless otherwise specified. Onions and garlic are always assumed peeled.

- To cut a vegetable lengthwise, slice it from pole to pole (along its length). To cut something crosswise, cut it through the equator.

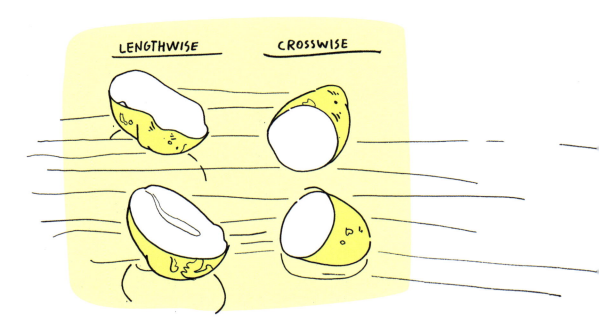

- We will call for a size for most produce (those that can vary widely). Don't worry if you end up cooking with something slightly too large or small. The dish will be fine.

- For reference, compare small onions and tomatoes to billiard balls, medium to tennis balls, and large to softballs. Small, medium, and large potatoes are roughly 2½, 3½, and 5 inches (6, 8.5, and 12.5 cm) in length, respectively.

- Use russet potatoes and yellow onions unless otherwise specified.

A Note on Pressure Cooking and Efficiency

AUYON The pressure cooker, the noisy and steam-exhausting ancestor of today's Instant Pot, has long been a standby in Indian kitchens worldwide. The technology, which makes quick work of recipes that are otherwise long-simmering, is particularly well suited to the curries and stews of Indian cuisine. That said, pressure cooking is a convenience, not a necessity—there's no need to go out and purchase a machine for the purpose of using this book.

You might ask why we are releasing a volume largely based on stovetop cooking at a time when Instant Pot blogs and cookbooks, replete with similar recipes that take just a fraction of the time, abound. Our answer? We believe the Instant Pot is a useful tool for softening legumes and meat, but much is lost when a dish is pressure cooked from start to finish. Spices don't infuse as well, while vegetables and meat don't brown as nicely. The resulting dish is often a hazy photocopy, lacking the crisp edges and subtle complexity of the original.

We understand that for many people, getting a meal to the table as quickly as possible is of the utmost importance. Relatedly, we acknowledge that the ability to take one's time to cook is a privilege. If speed and efficiency in the kitchen are crucial metrics for you, we respectfully submit that many of the recipes in this book may not be useful to you. Our goal here is to lead you to reproduce our favorite recipes just as we enjoy them in our home. Some of those recipes take time, but we feel that time is reflected in the outcome.

DAIRY

- Regarding fat content for milk and yogurt in our recipes (and in life), whole is best. It's fine to use 2 percent, but be aware that yogurt with a lower fat content can split, or curdle, when added to a hot dish. The risk of splitting can be mitigated by whisking a bit of the hot sauce or curry into the yogurt before adding the mixture to the pot. (This technique is known as tempering, but bears no relation to the spice tempering technique on page 31, at least as far as we know.) Fridge-cold yogurt is also more likely to separate when added to a hot dish. We generally prescribe using room temperature yogurt for such purposes, but the same tempering technique described above can be employed if you forget to take it out of the fridge.

- Whenever yogurt is called for, avoid store-bought Greek yogurt. Commercial varieties of Greek yogurt sometimes have additives and stabilizers that can compromise the texture of a dish once cooked. Other (non-Greek) plain, store-bought yogurts are fine to use.

- We will occasionally call for yogurt to be stirred (to incorporate the liquid, or whey, back in) or to be left unstirred. The former is helpful for curries and sauces where the yogurt needs to be incorporated into a dish, whereas the latter is useful when separating the yogurt solids from the liquid whey, as when making Hung Curd (page 41).

- Any time ghee is called for as a cooking medium (to temper spices, etc.), you can substitute canola oil in a pinch.

- Nondairy milk alternatives should not be substituted unless indicated, but lactose-free dairy milks (such as Lactaid) are generally fine to use.

SPICES AND OILS

- Spices can be intimidating. Don't feel like you need to buy every ingredient listed in the book in advance. Instead, determine a few recipes you're excited to make. Buy what you need for those, and continue to slowly acquire spices as you need them. Dried spices keep for a long time, especially if stored properly, so you don't need to worry about them going bad if you don't use them for a while. Never hesitate to get experimental with your new acquisitions, either. (As a result of building up a spice cabinet for recipe testing, Auyon started throwing fennel seeds into and onto everything—smoothies, peanut butter toast, homemade granola—and he hasn't yet looked back.)

SPICE SHOPPING Q&A

→ DIWALI DECORATIONS

Where should I buy these ingredients?

Your local Indian grocery, if you have one. It can feel like visiting another country, which is both exciting and sometimes difficult to navigate, so separating shopping and cooking by a day can be helpful if you're able to plan ahead. If you don't have a grocer close by, see our Resources (page 279) for a few online retailers we like.

Any tips on buying them?

Buy and use whole spices, grinding them as needed, since they stay fresher and taste better than pre-ground. That said, ground spices are convenient to have on hand and you can certainly use them — just buy them in smaller quantities that you'll go through more quickly.

Why can I never find curry leaves or green chilies at my local Indian grocery?

These ingredients are often unlabeled, either in open bins at the back of the store or in clear plastic bags in the corner of some cooler. Think of it as playing hide-and-seek with vegetables.

Do the store staff always seem so misanthropic? Is it me?

No. They are like that with me too.

Is there anything else I should get?

Yes! While you're at the store, we recommend stocking up on a few jars of achaar, or Indian pickle. The green mango and pachranga ("five color") varieties are great places to start.

Preparations vary widely, but achaars are usually oil-based and spice-laden — they taste like spicy-sour fireworks going off in your mouth.

My favorite way to eat them is with rice and daal, adding a tiny bit of achaar (a little goes a long way) and a small amount of yogurt to each spoonful.

We've included a recipe for a fresh ginger-lemon achaar on page 245, but the shelf-stable commercial varieties are quite different and definitely worth a try. See Resources (page 279) for brand recommendations.

← GINGER

← CURRY LEAVES

← GREEN CHILIES

- Oxygen, heat, light, and time render spices less potent. Keep spices in a cool, dark place (ideally some distance away from sources of heat like your oven and stovetop), and favor buying smaller quantities that you'll go through more quickly. Spices, both whole and ground, should be kept in airtight containers. Ground spices and spice mixes start to lose their zing after a few months, whereas whole spices will last a few years. If you have any half-filled jars that have been kicking around the back of your cupboard for the better part of a decade, dump them and invest in some fresh ingredients. It will make a difference.

- Spices are used in a variety of ways—added whole, ground into a wet paste, used as a dry powder, etc.—and a single spice is sometimes employed in multiple forms within the same dish. Each treatment draws out a different flavor, so the way in which spices are added to a dish is just as important as the types that are used.

- Part of the adventure of eating home-cooked Indian food is navigating obstacles like bones and whole spices like cinnamon sticks and bay leaves, which are necessary for proper flavor but are not themselves meant to be eaten. Use your hands to sort through things, and warn your fellow guests in case they are new to the cuisine. If you prefer, you can also remove the whole spices before serving; in that case we would reserve the cooked spices and store them with the leftovers, as they continue to impart flavor.

- We use and recommend canola or vegetable oil for most cooking and deep-frying unless otherwise specified. (Feel free to substitute other oils, but do make sure that whatever you use has a high enough smoke point for the cooking method.) Like spices, oils need to be stored in a cool, dark place to prevent them from turning rancid. Buy in quantities you'll go through in a couple of months, and store oil away from ovens and other heat sources.

- For more on spices and herbs, see our guide to Spices and Sundry (page 269).

Getting All the Good Stuff

When grinding a small amount of spices, a small brush (like an unused toothbrush) can be handy for getting all of the freshly ground goodness out of a mortar or an electric grinder.

TADKA

CUMIN PRE-TADKA   CUMIN POST-TADKA

Tadka, or the tempering of spices, is an Indian culinary technique that involves heating oil or ghee until quite hot and then adding (usually whole) spices. The spices swell, darken, sizzle, and/or pop shortly after hitting the oil, and their flavors transform and deepen. The infused oil and spices (also known as chaunk or baghaar) are then either used as a base for starting a dish or drizzled over a prepared dish to add an extra dimension of flavor. Once you get the hang of it, the process can be applied to all sorts of things, including nachos and buttered popcorn!

The process is relatively fast-paced and involves adding things to hot oil, so it's worth exercising some caution. The oil sometimes spits, most often with seeds that pop (like black mustard seeds) or ingredients that have some moisture (like curry leaves.) Try to keep hands and eyes a safe distance from the action. Activating a hood vent if you have one is generally a good idea too—especially when tempering dried chilies, which can produce a cough-inducing vapor.

The duration depends as much on the temperature of the oil as on the spices used. Pay more attention to the visual cues in the recipes (spices darkening, sizzling, or popping) than the estimated times, because it's hard to gauge the exact temperature of the oil. Something that took us 25 to 30 seconds could take as few as 5 seconds or as long as a minute for you, depending on the temperature of your oil.

Spices are delicate and can quickly burn in hot oil, so they must be monitored closely while tempering. Remove the pan from the stovetop and swirl it to cool the contents down as necessary. Sometimes things will be too far gone, though. When that happens, take a deep breath, discard the burned mixture, wash the pan, and start again. It's never worth ruining a dish over a few minutes of saved time and a handful of spices.

Tips & Techniques

step one
Be sure to give recipes a thorough read-through for any do-ahead instructions (like soaking or marinating) and to ensure that you have all the necessary gear (see page 24) before you start cooking.

be prepared
We recommend setting out, measuring, and chopping all ingredients before turning the stove on. *Mise en place* is the French term for this practice, which translates to "put in place." As you get more familiar with a dish and with Indian cooking in general, you can be a bit more freewheeling with prep and measurements. When working through a recipe for the first time, though, it will make life easier to have everything prepped and within arm's reach, especially for quicker processes like tempering spices (see page 31). Most ingredients are fine to sit while you get your prep done. Two caveats: if you cut potatoes well in advance of cooking, it is helpful to keep them submerged in water to prevent them from oxidizing and discoloring; similarly, eggplant should be cut just before cooking, not in advance.

don't undercook your onions
The longer an onion is cooked, the greater its depth of flavor. Dark, sweet, and jammy caramelized onions are the pinnacle of this transformation, which can take up to an hour on the stovetop. None of the recipes in this book involve fully caramelized onions, but it's good to keep that outcome in mind, because most cooks new to Indian cooking tend to underbrown onions for fear of burning them. As long as your heat isn't set too high, err on the side of overcooking rather than undercooking. Although some of our recipes include onions cooked only until soft and translucent, several involve cooking them until the edges are good and brown. Proper browning is crucial to getting the right flavor, texture, and color for a given dish, so be patient and stir often.

For those of you who have a lot of experience caramelizing onions, it's worth noting that Indian-style onion cookery is hotter, faster, and more fat-intensive than low-and-slow Western methods. You'll want to keep the onions moving around (more than you're used to) to make sure nothing burns. If anything does start to stick or scorch, add a spoonful of water and loosen any stuck bits.

wash your rice

To rinse rice, place the rice in a pot and cover with cold water. Give it a quick stir, then drain the rice in a colander over the sink. Repeat a few times until the surface starch has been poured off and the water runs clear. Use the same technique for legumes, which shouldn't need more than a rinse or two.

read your oil

Our recipes often begin with the instruction to heat the oil and then to add spices "once the oil starts to shimmer." If you're having trouble figuring out when that is, start by looking closely at the viscosity of the oil as you move it around in a cool pan. Look at it again once the oil has heated up for 30 seconds or so, and you will see a difference in the way it moves and ripples. (Leave it on the burner for too long and it will start to smoke, which means it's too hot.) Learning to observe physical cues will improve your cooking, and reading your oil is a great place to start.

trust us, but also trust yourself

We include approximate cooking times for individual directions (i.e., cook the onions until soft and translucent, roughly 8 minutes), but please keep in mind that these timings are only estimations. You will be using a different stove, different pans, and differently chopped ingredients, to say nothing of the variations in humidity, temperature, and atmosphere. With all that in mind, we've also included sensory cues to watch out for, so that you can focus your senses on the food and not just the clock. As you get more comfortable with a given recipe, these physical cues will begin to serve as your primary road map. Relatedly, the total cook time we prescribe at the beginning of each recipe (which accounts for prep, active, and inactive cooking time) should be taken as a rough estimate, not a precise measurement.

don't be afraid to downsize

If any recipe feels like it's a bit too much for your pan (variability in vegetable sizes is often to blame), feel free to cook in batches or halve the recipe. Frequent stirring-out-of-the-pan accidents and/or needing to cram ingredients to fit are both signs that you might want to rethink your vessel-to-ingredient ratio.

less is more

A pervasive myth is that longer marination times dependably produce a deeper penetration of flavor. In truth, the primary effect of most marinades is a surface-level treatment, and after 6 to 8 hours you reach a point of diminishing returns. (Brining, which we don't call for in this book, is a notable exception.) Since many Indian marinades include acids like lemon juice or yogurt that can denature meat proteins if left for too long (and result in an undesirable, chalky texture), it is best to keep marination times on the shorter side. Stick to our recommendations and avoid leaving dishes to marinate overnight. Doing so won't ruin the dish, but it may make the meat mushier than you want.

cut your losses

If things start to scorch, add a bit of water to the pot and then stir to keep things moving (for more on the Indian cooking technique of browning, stirring, and adding liquid known as bhunaoing, see page 162). If you see a burned crust starting to form at the bottom of the pan, stop stirring and transfer the mixture to a new pot to continue cooking, leaving the scorched bits in the old pot so that they don't ruin the dish. This problem shows up most often with starchy veggies like potatoes, and can usually be avoided by using a nonstick pan (see page 92).

à la minute

When recipes call for freshly ground black pepper or an acidic garnish like lemon juice, add them just before serving for the best flavor unless otherwise specified.

rest your sauce

Most dishes that have a sauce component will taste even better if cooked in advance and then left for an hour or two (max) at room temperature (or refrigerated for longer periods) to allow the flavors to meld. When reheating, be sure to do so slowly and gently. A full-on rolling boil may compromise the texture. If reheating from frozen, defrost the dish completely in the fridge before applying gentle heat.

water your daal

Dishes tend to thicken as they sit, especially beans and lentils. After allowing a dish to cool, you may need to add a bit of boiling water (anywhere between ¼ and 1 cup // 60 and 240 ml) to get it back to the right consistency. You can also just add tap water and bring the whole mixture to a boil, but don't skip the boiling/sterilization step.

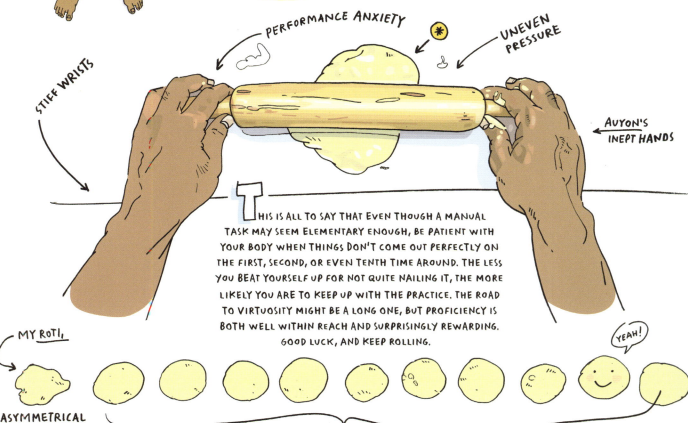

CHAPTER ONE

Scratch

• Ghee •

MAKES *roughly 1¾ cups (420 ml)*
COOK TIME: *1 hour* • **PHOTO:** *page 107*

Jyoti The subcontinent's adoration of ghee, the blue-ribbon cooking fat of Indian cuisine, goes back millennia. It is a prized medicine in Ayurveda, the traditional Indian system of health and wellness, and there are several odes and hymns dedicated to the golden stuff in the Rigveda, the most ancient of the Hindu religious texts. Once you've tried some, it's easy to understand the reverence. Ghee smells and tastes rich and nutty and wonderful, it has a higher smoke point than butter and most oils, and it keeps for weeks at room temperature (and for months in the fridge) since it contains no milk solids. On top of all of that, it's a breeze to make!

Use a cooking vessel with an enameled or otherwise light-colored interior if you have one handy, since that will make it easier to judge the color. If there's too much foam to see the color of the ghee, use a metal spoon to scoop up a bit to inspect. If you're tight for time, ghee is always available at Indian markets (and increasingly often at national supermarket chains), but the commercial varieties really don't compare to homemade.

Auyon Butter is a stable mixture, or emulsion, of water, butterfat, and milk solids. To make ghee, which is pure butterfat that has been flavored with browned milk solids, the emulsion must be broken, which happens when the butter is heated. The water boils off, and then the milk solids (proteins, sugars, and minerals) separate from the butterfat, either floating to the top as foam or sinking to the bottom.

The key to making proper, fragrant ghee, rather than just regular clarified butter, is to ensure the separated milk solids get brown and toasty before the ghee is poured off. This extra bit of cooking imparts an exquisite butterscotch-y flavor to the fat. For a golden color and milder flavor, stop cooking as soon as the milk solids are well-browned. For a deeper flavor, keep cooking for an extra 10 minutes or so, or until the melted fat looks as dark as a dark amber honey (it will lighten as it cools). Remove the pan from the heat as soon as the milk solids start to blacken, though, and ideally before they start to burn!

I also recommend experimenting with ghee outside of Indian fare. Stir in some salt and you've got an elegant salted butter upgrade for toast or pancakes. If you enjoy flavored butter, ghee's semi-solid consistency at room temperature makes it an excellent candidate for doctoring. For an especially indulgent spread, try adding a bit of acid (mustard, vinegar, lacto-ferment brine, etc.) in addition to some salt or soy sauce to complement the richness. Be warned that you might start eating it by the spoonful.

4 sticks (1 pound / 455 g) of unsalted butter, roughly chopped or left whole

1. Place a small pot over low heat. Add the butter. It is fine to give the pot a stir or two, but allow the butter to simmer gently, largely undisturbed. If your burners tend to run hot, keep a close eye on the pot and stir more often, as overcooking the browned solids is a common accident. (If that does happen and the pot starts to smell burned and acrid, don't give up hope—see Notes, opposite.) The butter will melt, foam, and then come to a boil. Once the boiling subsides, the milk solids will start to brown, both around the edges of the foam and also at the bottom of the pot as they sink and settle.

2. About 25 minutes after the butter has melted, you will have a pot of clear, golden ghee with browned milk solids at the bottom and some brown-flecked foam on top. If you can't tell what color the fat is due to the foam layer, give it a stir and follow your nose! A beguiling, nutty aroma is a telltale sign that the ghee is done. Cook a few minutes longer for a stronger flavor if desired, but be careful not to burn the milk solids.

3. Remove from the heat and allow the ghee to cool to lukewarm, about 30 minutes (longer is fine, but you may need to gently reheat the ghee if it solidifies).

4. If you plan to store the ghee outside of the fridge, strain it through a fine mesh strainer (or a more porous strainer lined with butter muslin or fine cheesecloth) into a clean, dry, airtight jar. If you plan to store the ghee in the fridge, you can afford to be a little less careful—don't worry about the strainer and just pour the ghee carefully into the jar, leaving the milk solids behind in the pot (see Notes, right).

5. Let cool to room temperature before sealing and refrigerating.

Notes

If you start to smell burning, remove the pot from the heat immediately and make sure not to stir! As soon as the fat is cool enough to safely handle, separate carefully as indicated in Step 4. Give the separated fat a sniff—we've found that the extra-browned ghee often smells and tastes delicious once isolated. If not, chalk it up to a learning experience and try again!

Don't throw away the browned solids. We love them mixed into plain rice or yellow daal, but you should try them with anything that could use a hit of brown butter (homemade ice cream, popcorn, etc.) It's worth tasting the solids first though, as they can get bitter if overbrowned. They should last for a couple of days in the fridge.

Homemade Yogurt

MAKES *2 cups (480 g)* • **COOK TIME:** *15 minutes*
FERMENTATION TIME: *at least 8 hours (ideally overnight)*
PHOTO: *page 122*

Auyon Making homemade yogurt is a magical process. In addition to allowing control over the texture, flavor, and ingredients, yogurt-making brings a delightful sense of rhythm into the kitchen—both in its dependence on the slow, steady work of active cultures and in being part of the broader, ancient tradition of home fermentation. Even though decent store-bought yogurt is readily available these days, we strongly encourage you to try your hand at it. It might take a bit of experimentation to get the flavor just right, but that is part of the fun.

I especially love sour yogurt as an accompaniment to a buttery daal or rich meat dish. If you'd like to make your yogurt more tart, just leave it out to ferment for a few hours longer before putting it into the fridge. The longer it is left in a warm spot, the more time for the bacteria in the yogurt culture to transform the sugars in the milk into lactic acid, which is what produces that delicious tang.

2 cups (480 ml) whole milk (see Notes, right)

2 tablespoons whole, unflavored yogurt (see Notes, right)

1. Put the milk in a large, microwave-safe bowl or dish, making sure the container is large enough to allow the milk to boil a bit without spilling over. Microwave the milk on high until the milk comes to a rolling boil, 3 to 5 minutes. Alternatively, rinse a medium, heavy-bottomed pot with cold water, leaving just enough water to coat the bottom in the pot (which will help prevent the milk from scorching). Add the milk to the pot. Cook over medium-high heat, stirring constantly, until it begins to seethe and foam, about 5 minutes. Remove from the heat.

2. Allow the milk to cool to around 115°F (45°C). If you don't have a thermometer handy, you can use a clean finger instead. The milk should feel comfortably hot, about as warm as a hot tub. To speed up the cooling, pour it back and forth between a couple of containers a few times.

3. Add the yogurt (the starter culture) and whisk well to fully incorporate. Transfer the mixture to a lidded container you would like the yogurt to set in. We use a ceramic yogurt pot, but the plastic tubs that store-bought yogurts come in work just as well.

4. Cover the mixture and place it in a warm spot, about 110°F (43°C) or the warmest spot you can find at home. We typically use the oven with just the oven light on and the heat off. (If you use this technique, we recommend leaving a note to warn against accidentally preheating the oven before the yogurt is removed.)

5. Leave undisturbed for at least 8 hours, and ideally overnight, to set. Store in the fridge once fully set, and reserve at least 2 tablespoons for the next batch. Homemade yogurt will keep for at least a couple of weeks in the fridge. Trust your eyes and nose—if something looks or smells off, it probably is.

Notes

This recipe will not work with plant-based milks, but it works well with lactose-free dairy milks like Lactaid.

For a starter culture, you can use your favorite unflavored commercial yogurt that has active cultures—you'll basically be making more of the same. Be warned, though, that because commercial cultures are typically bred for consistency rather than resilience, they may not last for more than a generation or two. If you're planning on making yogurt regularly, check out our Resources (page 279) for our favorite starter culture.

Hung Curd

MAKES *roughly ¾ cup (190 g)* • **REST TIME:** *2 hours*

Jyoti Hung curd is the Indian version of Greek yogurt. Use regular, store-bought plain yogurt or Homemade Yogurt (opposite) to prepare it. We discourage substituting commercial Greek yogurt for hung curd as an ingredient, though, as our experiments with it never came out quite right, perhaps due to the additives and stabilizers. For the greatest yield, use freshly opened, unstirred yogurt (but it is totally fine to use a container that has been opened and/or stirred if that is all you have).

Auyon The stuff that drains out of the curd is whey, a slightly acidic liquid rich in probiotics and electrolytes. A quick internet search will yield plenty of ways to use it, like as a liquid for cooking rice, but my favorite is to blend it with some fresh or frozen fruit and drink it as a smoothie. You won't get much whey out of just 1 cup (240 g) of yogurt, but the recipe multiplies easily.

1 cup (240 g) whole, unflavored yogurt (store-bought or homemade, page 40), unstirred if possible

Set up a fine-mesh strainer over a bowl big enough to fit the strainer. Place the yogurt into the strainer and rest for at least 2 hours to allow the whey to drain out, or up to 4 hours if you like very thick yogurt. Use right away, or transfer the hung curd to a lidded container and store in the refrigerator for a week or two. The hung curd might be a little sour due to the increased fermentation time outside of the fridge, but it should otherwise look and smell like thick yogurt. Trust your eyes and nose—if something looks or smells off, it probably is.

A NOTE ON CURRY POWDER

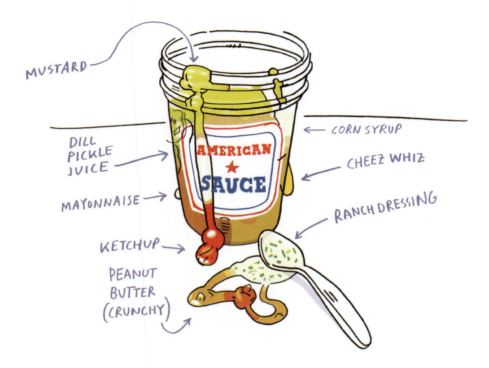

Auyon The term *curry* traces back to Portuguese and English reconfigurations of similar-sounding South Indian (Kannada, Malayalam, and Tamil) words that refer to spices and dishes of sautéed vegetables and meat. The word's first recorded use was in a 1502 Portuguese travel report, and British colonizers later adopted the term to describe the vast breadth of vegetable and meat preparations cooked in a sauce (see page 50).

Within Indian cuisine today, curry refers to the presence of a spiced gravy. Contrary to the marketing of the "curry powders" of Western manufacture, however, the word does not denote a specific flavor. There is no single blend of spices that is representative of Indian curries at large.

To bring the relationship between Western curry powder and Indian home cooking closer to home, imagine finding a jar of "American Sauce" in the foreign foods section of a grocery store in a faraway country. Although the sauce might occasionally prove useful and the individual ingredients might look familiar, you probably wouldn't put it on everything.

(Again, this discussion applies only to Indian cuisine. The landscape is markedly different in, say, Japan, where curry was first introduced in the nineteenth century by British merchant ships carrying Anglo-Indian curry powder. The Japanese modified the recipe over the following decades, but the national definition of curry would forever be tied to the convenience of a mix.)

• Dry-Roasted & Ground Spices •

COOK TIME: *less than 5 minutes*

Jyoti This technique is crucial to getting the proper flavor for certain dishes. The effect is similar to that of roasting nuts: flavors deepen and transform.

A light touch is key, as over-roasting will produce a bitter flavor. As with tadkas (see page 31), if the spices start to burn, don't hesitate to throw them out and start again. It's never worth ruining a dish over a few minutes of saved time and a handful of spices.

When a recipe calls for both cumin and coriander roasted and ground, it's fine to cook and grind the spices together (we'll include a reminder in each recipe).

As many spices as you need

1. In a heavy-bottomed pan (choose a size that will fit all the spices comfortably) over medium-high heat, add the whole spices for your recipe and cook, stirring or shaking frequently. The spices will first smoke a bit, and then start to change color.

2. Remove the pan from the heat as soon as the spices darken a shade or two and become fragrant. The cooking time is often as quick as a minute or two, but it will depend on the kind and quantity of spices and the strength of your stove, so pay close attention to the color and smell.

3. Transfer the spices to a plate and cool completely before pulverizing in a coffee grinder reserved for spices or using a mortar and pestle (if you don't have either, see Note, right).

4. Store in an airtight container and use within a few days. For the best flavor, we recommend roasting and grinding small quantities as needed. Ground spices also keep well in the freezer.

Note
Improvise with a letter-size piece of parchment paper over a cutting board. Fold the parchment in half, and then open the paper and center the roasted (and cooled) spices close to the crease. Refold the parchment in half and use a heavy object like a rolling pin to bash the spices over the cutting board. To keep the spices from spilling, use your fingers to close the parchment at the open ends while crushing (or fold the parchment paper over at the ends to keep things sealed in). Open the paper and shuffle the spices around occasionally to get a more even grind.

Ghee Bhaat

RICE with GHEE

SERVES 4 • COOK TIME: 30 minutes • PHOTO: page 110

Jyoti There is a great deal of mystique assigned to rice cookery in the West, but the fundamental techniques are straightforward. There are two basic approaches: boiling the rice in a large volume of water, as with pasta, or boiling it in just enough water to get absorbed. The benefit of the first method is that it consistently produces distinct, separate grains, but much of the nutritive value gets flushed out with the water. The second method, which cooks the rice via both boiling and steaming, retains more of the nutrients, but it involves a bit of measurement.

Our basic rice recipe follows the measured-water method. It is a simple, three-step process: cook partially covered, cook covered, and then rest. More attention-intensive procedures can involve different heat sources (i.e., parboiling the rice on the stovetop and then moving it into the oven, as with our biryanis, see pages 183–187), or briefly sautéing the raw rice with some oil and spices before boiling to imbue the grains with flavor (as with our Jeera Pulao, page 177), but in all cases, the principles remain the same.

If you need to double this recipe, reduce the water by 10% (i.e. for 3 cups // 580 g rice, use 5½ cups // 1300 ml water).

Auyon Basmati rice is an aromatic, long-grain variety traditionally grown in the foothills of the Himalaya. It is the undisputed queen of Indian rice cultivars, prized for its aroma and grain length. Its name derives from the Sanskrit roots *vas* (aroma) and *mayup* (ingrained).

1½ cups (290 g) white basmati rice, rinsed (see below)

1 teaspoon salt, plus more to taste

1 tablespoon unsalted ghee (store-bought or homemade, page 38)

1. Combine the rice, salt, and 3 cups (720 ml) water in a medium, lidded pot. Half-cover and bring the mixture to a boil over high heat.

2. Cook until the level of the water is just at or below the surface of the rice, about 5 minutes. It should look like there are soap bubbles coming out of the rice.

3. Reduce the heat to low, cover the pot completely, and cook undisturbed for an additional 10 minutes. Without cracking the lid open, remove the pot from the heat and let it sit, covered, for an additional 10 minutes.

4. Uncover, add the ghee, and let it melt into the rice before fluffing the mixture gently with a fork. Taste for salt and serve hot.

Rice Tips

1. Rinsing the rice is optional, but the grains will be more separate and have a slightly more pleasing texture if you take the time to do so. We recommend it.

2. The reason we suggest waiting until the water level is even with the rice before covering it with a lid is that if you cover it too early, the water can foam up and make a starchy mess on the stovetop. Beware.

3. Use a vessel with a tight-fitting lid, because the goal is to retain as much steam as possible. Relatedly, resist the temptation to open the lid to check on the rice as it steams.

4. Don't skimp on the resting time. Letting the rice rest for a full 10 minutes off the heat will ensure a superior texture and minimize grain breakage.

5. The ghee here is an indulgence. We typically forgo it for everyday meals, but it is a nice addition for special occasions.

Cooked & Seasoned Chickpeas

MAKES *2½ to 3 cups (450 to 540 g)*
SOAK TIME: *8 hours (ideally overnight)*
COOK TIME: *90 minutes*

Jyoti The chickpea's breadth of use, which spans sweets, doughs, thickening agents, fried foods, and savory fare, makes it a prime contender for the subcontinent's most beloved legume. To fully capture the magic, we encourage using dried beans whenever possible. While canned chickpeas are both convenient and consistent (and totally fine to use in a pinch), they lack the creaminess of the freshly cooked stuff. They also inevitably retain some of the metallic flavor of the can they were housed in.

Auyon Indian chickpea consumption is largely limited to two types: the white chickpea, also known as the garbanzo bean or Kabuli channa (and the most commonly sold variety in the United States), and the smaller, darker Bengal gram, also known as kaala channa or Desi channa. Almost all of the whole chickpea recipes in this book call for the more familiar white chickpea—Sukha Kaala Channa (page 76) is the only exception.

1 cup (200 g) dried chickpeas, rinsed

1 teaspoon salt

Pinch of baking soda

1. Place the chickpeas, salt, and 4 cups (960 ml) water in a large bowl. Stir well to combine, then soak for at least 8 hours or overnight.

2. Combine the chickpeas, soaking liquid, and baking soda in a medium lidded (but uncovered for now) pot over high heat (or see Pressure Cooker Alternative, below) and bring to a rolling boil. Reduce the heat to low and cook the mixture at a gentle boil. Any foam or scum that develops over the first few minutes of cooking should be removed (but no need to get surgical). Keep an eye on the water level during cooking, and add water if it gets lower than the level of the legumes.

3. Once the pot stops threatening to boil over, after about 20 minutes of cooking, cover the pot completely.

4. Cook until the chickpeas are meltingly tender but still hold their shape, an additional 40 to 50 minutes. If the chickpeas will be used for a recipe that requires chilled chickpeas, err on the side of extra soft because they will firm up in the fridge. The chickpeas can be stored in the refrigerator for 2 to 3 days or frozen for up to 6 months.

PRESSURE COOKER ALTERNATIVE:
You can use a pressure cooker or an Instant Pot to speed up the cooking process if desired. Combine the chickpeas, soaking liquid, and baking soda in the pressure cooker. Seal the machine and cook for 10 minutes once the pressure has built up and/or the hissing starts. Turn the heat off and leave the beans to cool in the pressure cooker for 20 minutes before opening the lid. Check the beans for tenderness and continue cooking as necessary, either on the stove or for another few minutes under pressure.

Paneer

FRESH CHEESE

MAKES *12 ounces (340 g) or 30 bite-size pieces*
COOK TIME: *75 minutes* • **REST TIME:** *6+ hours (ideally overnight)* • **PHOTO:** *page 107*

Jyoti Paneer is a widely adored acid-set fresh cheese. Regional variations abound, and what follows is an adaptation of the North Indian version that I grew up with. Tangy and soft with just a hint of chew, it is easily incorporated into a broad range of dishes because it is traditionally unflavored. Resist the temptation to add any salt—it throws off the chemistry and texture.

To make paneer, you will need some butter muslin or fine cheesecloth and something heavy to keep it weighted down. The process is otherwise simple and straightforward, and requires just two ingredients.

Keep in mind that before you use homemade paneer in any recipes, you will need to lightly fry it (see Mattar Paneer, page 134, and Saag Paneer, page 136). The browning both adds structural stability and lends the cheese a chewy-crisp crust that contrasts nicely with the pillowy interior.

Auyon Scholars disagree as to the origins of paneer. There is one mention in the Vedas, Hindu religious texts dating back to the second millennium BCE, of something that could be translated as "cheese," but it also, rather unhelpfully, could just refer to "an abundance of curds." Another school of thought puts more weight on an ancient Hindu proscription against the purposeful curdling of milk, suggesting that paneer didn't come into vogue until the arrival of the Portuguese and their cheesemaking ways in the late fifteenth century. Meanwhile, the word *paneer* is Persian in origin.

2 quarts (2 L) fresh whole milk (ideally within 24 hours of purchase)

¼ cup (60 ml) distilled white vinegar

1. Rinse a large, heavy-bottomed pot with cold water, leaving just enough water to coat the bottom of the pot. This step will help prevent the milk from scorching.

2. Add the milk to the pot. Cook over medium-high heat, stirring gently but constantly, until the milk comes to a boil, about 15 minutes. Alternatively, microwave the milk on high in a large, microwave-safe bowl or dish until the milk comes to a boil, about 20 minutes. A skin may form on the milk, which is fine to remove or stir back in. Take care not to burn yourself when removing the milk from the microwave.

3. Off the heat, gently stir in the vinegar. The mixture will separate into curds (the milk solids will become the paneer) and whey, a yellow-green liquid. Be sure to scrape any curds that are sticking to the whisk or spatula back into the mixture. Let cool for at least 45 minutes, until cool enough to handle.

4. Line a fine-mesh strainer or colander with a large (at least 16-inch // 40.5-cm) square of butter muslin or fine cheesecloth and set it over a large bowl. Carefully scoop or pour the curds into the colander, allowing the whey to collect in the bowl underneath.

5. Gather the edges of the cheesecloth to make a pouch out of the curds, and gently twist or squeeze to remove most, but not all, of the whey. Don't go overboard, as some remaining moisture is necessary for shaping. Save the nutritious whey and use it for cooking daal, beans, or rice (see page 41).

6. Place the pouch on a raised, flat surface like a small cutting board (don't use anything with an elevated edge, like a plate). Unwrap the paneer and shape it, on the cheesecloth, into a flat, even, ¾-inch- (2-cm-) thick, 5-ish-inch (12-cm) square or disk with your hands. Fold the edges of the cheesecloth back over the top of the paneer to form a flat package. All surfaces of the paneer should be encased in cheesecloth, like a wrapped present.

7. Put the whole structure, cutting board and all, onto a rimmed baking sheet (or into a dry sink if you can spare the space)—anywhere water can drain off freely without making a mess. Finally, place a large pot filled with water (or a stack of plates, or anything heavy with a flat bottom) on top of the paneer to serve as a weight. Rest for at least 4 hours at room temperature, and ideally overnight.

8. Remove the weight. Set the wrapped paneer on a plate or tray (because a bit more moisture may be released) and place the tray in the fridge for another couple of hours to chill. Once chilled, the paneer should be firm with a bit of moisture, but neither hard nor wet.

9. Open the cheesecloth and carefully flip the paneer over so that the flatter side is face-up. Use a sharp knife to cut the paneer into 1 x 1¼-inch (2.5 x 3.2-cm) pieces. Crumbly edges on the perimeter are to be expected—this is homestyle cooking. Store in the fridge for up to a week or in the freezer for up to a year.

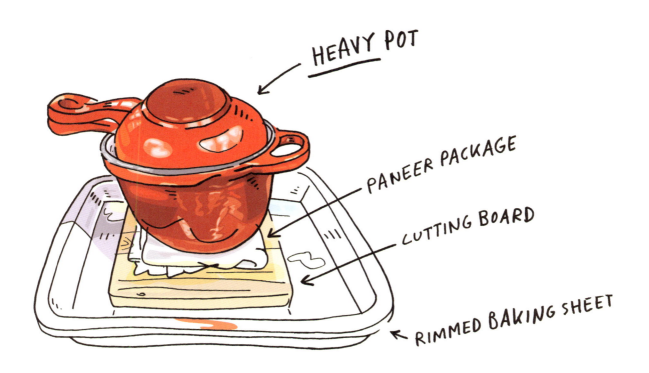

Boiled & Seasoned Potatoes

MAKES *4 potatoes* • **COOK TIME:** *1 hour*

4 large russet potatoes (2¾ pounds // 1280 g total)

2 tablespoons salt

Jyoti Always boil potatoes with their skins on to protect them from getting too waterlogged. If you need to peel them for a recipe, let them cool before using your fingers to scrape off the skin, which should come off easily after boiling.

If cooking fewer than 4 potatoes, reduce the salt and water by the same factor (i.e., for 2 large potatoes, use just 4 cups // 960 ml water and 1 tablespoon salt).

1. Combine the potatoes, salt, and 8 cups (2 L) water in a large pot. The water should cover the potatoes with room to spare. Add more if necessary. Bring to a rolling boil over high heat.

2. Reduce the heat to medium, cover, and cook until the potatoes are easily pierced by a fork, 40 to 45 minutes. Drain the potatoes and let cool to room temperature. Store in the fridge and use within a couple of days.

A NOTE ON POTATOES

Potatoes are categorized, based on their starch content, into three groups: starchy, all-purpose, and waxy. Russets, which anchor the starchy end of the spectrum, are the only kind we use at home. Their fluffy texture makes them ideal for soaking up the flavors of the sauce or curry they are embedded in, often making them the unexpected star of a dish. Unfortunately, that same absorbent quality also makes them prone to crumble and dissolve into their surroundings, or worse, form a burned crust at the bottom of the pan.

To avoid such disaster, we have four recommendations:

1. Don't skimp on the oil.

2. Use a nonstick pan (see page 92).

3. Handle cooked potatoes gently (i.e., don't stir too vigorously or too often once they are added to the dish).

4. If a recipe calls for boiled potatoes, boil the potatoes a few hours in advance (and as early as the night before) if you're able, then toss them in the fridge—they will firm up and be much less apt to break apart.

Lastly, we recommend resisting the urge to use waxy or all-purpose potatoes—the improvement in structural integrity is not worth the losses in tenderness and flavor.

For more on potato cookery, see My Mother, the Potato Wizard (page 92.)

THE GREAT CURRY DEBATE

Auyon Curry's complicated history has led some Indian-American chefs and food writers to publish statements like "You can't order a curry in India, because the word *curry* doesn't exist there." The whole concept of curry, the explanation goes, is a made-up Western imposition that cheapens the dizzying diversity of dishes that exist on the subcontinent.

Origins aside, the word *curry*, and the concept of a curry powder, are both very much alive and well in India. Restaurateurs across the country routinely use the term as a descriptor on their menus with no sense of postcolonial irony, while Indian spice shops sport rows of brightly hued masalas (some of which include both the words *curry* and *powder* on the label), reflecting the enormous variation of regional and dish-specific spice blends within Indian cookery.

English is one of the official languages used by the Indian government. Tea is one of the most widely consumed beverages on the subcontinent. *Curry* is a term used by Indians and non-Indians alike to describe Indian dishes with a sauce component. These facts are all inextricably linked to India's colonial past and should be recognized as such, but that does not make their veracity up for debate.

Our final word: curry most certainly exists in India. We have ordered it in Indian restaurants (in India!), and you can too. Just don't expect it to be curry-flavored (see page 42).

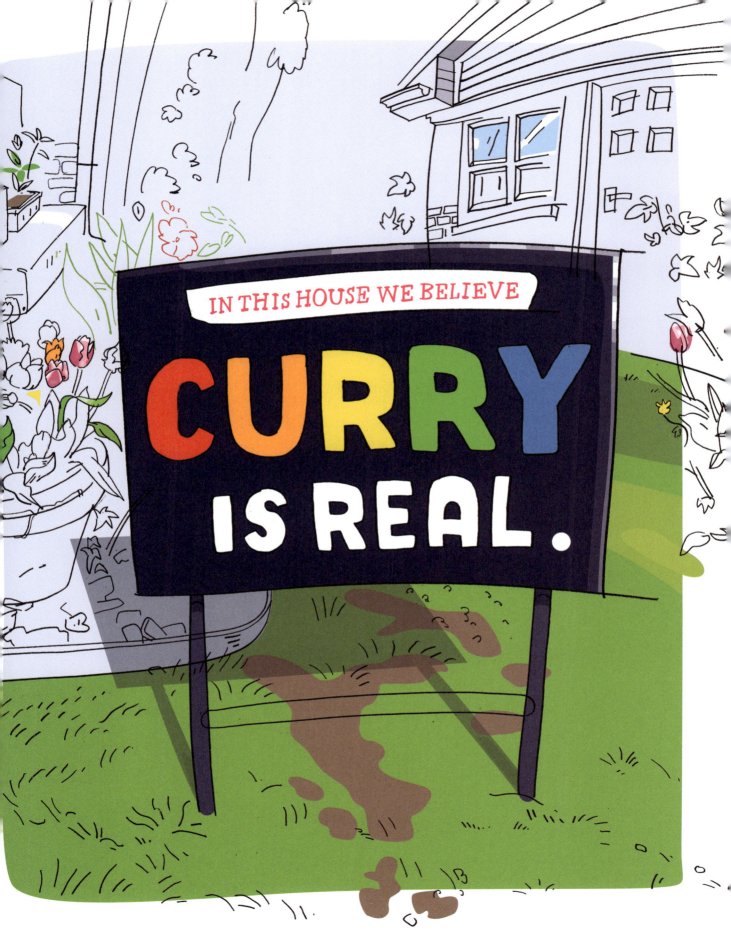

Masalas

JYOTI   The word *masala* translates to "spice mixture." While both of the recipes that follow can be easily purchased at your local Indian grocery, we encourage you to try making at least the Garam Masala ("warm spice mix") at home. The process is simple, gratifying, and scales up nicely. Experiment with different proportions and ingredients, too—recipes and compositions vary widely across the subcontinent. The only specialized equipment you will need is a coffee grinder you don't use for coffee.

Chaat Masala is a spice blend that I admittedly purchase premade more often than I make at home, but we included the recipe in case you are feeling plucky.

AUYON   Although we only included a handful of recipes that call for Chaat Masala, that should not limit you. Ground spices and spice mixes start to lose their potency after a few months, so take that as a license to experiment when you've got some of either on hand. Chaat Masala has a funky, sulfurous quality (from kaala namak, see page 249) that adds a whole new dimension to mixed fruit (Fruit Chaat, page 235) or to peanut butter toast with a drizzle of honey.

• Garam Masala •

MAKES *just over 2 tablespoons*
COOK TIME: *30 minutes plus time to cool*

- 2 teaspoons cumin seeds
- 1 teaspoon cloves
- 1 teaspoon black peppercorns
- One 3-inch (7.5-cm) cinnamon stick, broken into a few pieces
- 2 black cardamom pods

1. Preheat the oven to 200°F (95°C).

2. Place the cumin, cloves, peppercorns, cinnamon, and cardamom on a baking sheet and bake, undisturbed, until the spices darken slightly and become fragrant, about 30 minutes.

3. Let cool to room temperature before pulverizing in a coffee grinder reserved for spices. Store in an airtight container in the freezer for up to a year.

• Chaat Masala •

MAKES *roughly 3 tablespoons*
COOK TIME: *30 minutes plus time to cool*

- 1 teaspoon cumin seeds
- 1 teaspoon coriander seeds
- ¼ teaspoon black peppercorns
- 1¼ teaspoons kaala namak (black salt, see Kaala Namak, page 249)
- 1 teaspoon dried mint
- 1 tablespoon amchoor (ground dried mango, see page 271)
- ½ teaspoon anardana powder (ground dried pomegranate, see page 271)
- ¼ teaspoon ground dried ginger
- ⅛ teaspoon ground Kashmiri chili (see page 271)

1. Preheat the oven to 200°F (95°C).

2. Place the cumin, coriander, and peppercorns on a baking sheet and bake, undisturbed, until the spices darken slightly and become fragrant, about 30 minutes.

3. Let cool to room temperature, then combine the toasted spices with the kaala namak, mint, amchoor, anardana, ginger, and chili. Pulverize the mixture in a coffee grinder reserved for spices. Store in an airtight container in the freezer for up to a year.

CHAPTER TWO

Salads, Daals, and Beans

Kachumbar

CUCUMBER, TOMATO, and POMEGRANATE SALAD

SERVES 4 • PREP TIME: *15 minutes* • PHOTO: *page 119*

Jyoti Due to water quality and hygiene concerns, dishes composed of dressed raw vegetables do not feature prominently in traditional Indian fare. The most conspicuous exception is kachumbar, a relish of onion, tomato, and cucumber. Unlike Western salads, this dish should be served by the spoonful as a fresh, crunchy counterpoint to the cooked food—think salsa fresca rather than a Caesar.

Keep in mind that the kachumbar model is a flexible one. Our inclusion of pomegranate seeds, adopted from Sumayya Usmani's *Summers Under The Tamarind Tree*, is a deliciously tart (but decidedly nontraditional) variation. Chopped turnips and radishes are also lovely additions.

Auyon Cucumbers are native to India, and a wild ancestor of the domesticated variety can still be found growing in the foothills of the Himalaya. Historian Colleen Taylor Sen reports that there are over forty words for the vegetable in Sanskrit, "indicating that it may have been cultivated for shape, size, and bitterness at an early stage."

- 1½ cups (240 g) chopped cucumber (¼-inch // 6-mm dice, about 2½ Persian or mini cucumbers, see Cucumber Snobbery, below)
- 1 cup (135 g) chopped tomato (¼-inch // 6-mm dice, about 1 medium tomato)
- ¼ cup (40 g) chopped red or yellow onion, briefly rinsed in cold water and drained (¼-inch // 6-mm) dice)
- ¼ cup (15 g) finely chopped fresh cilantro, stems and leaves
- 2 tablespoons fresh pomegranate arils (see page 276)
- 1 teaspoon fresh lemon juice
- ¼ teaspoon salt
- Several generous grinds of black pepper

1. Combine the cucumber, tomato, onion, cilantro, and pomegranate in a medium bowl. Stir well.

2. Just before serving, add the lemon juice, salt, and black pepper. Taste for salt and lemon. Serve at room temperature.

Cucumber Snobbery

If you can't find Persian cucumbers, you can substitute an equivalent amount of chopped Kirby, pickling, English/hothouse, or Armenian cucumbers—really anything but the thick-skinned, waxed variety standard to American grocery stores. If that's all that's available, we recommend holding off on preparing this dish until you're able to make your way to an Indian or specialty market.

There's also no need to peel the cucumbers first. As with all our recipes, assume that fruits and vegetables should remain unpeeled unless directed otherwise.

A NOTE ON COURSES

This section roughly correlates to "soups and salads," but we should note that by and large, Indian meals are traditionally served all at once rather than split up into courses. There may be a few things to nibble on before the meal, and sweets are often served at the end, but even these aren't fixed rules. In some states, like Gujarat and Maharashtra, sweets are eaten during the meal rather than afterward.

Salads, Daals, and Beans

Tomato, Red Lentil & Ginger Soup

SERVES 6 • **COOK TIME:** *75 minutes, plus time to cool if necessary* • **PHOTO:** *page 123*

Jyoti This dish, an Indian twist on a classic tomato soup, is adapted from my mother-in-law's repertoire. She was an excellent cook with a knack for integrating Indian and Western culinary aesthetics, having grown up in the twilight of the British colonial period.

Although you might be tempted to replace the water with vegetable or chicken stock, don't. Flavored stock will overwhelm the delicate balance of spices and vegetables.

Auyon Speaking from experience, if you try to blend hot soup using a stand blender without letting it cool, the steam released will blow the lid off the machine and spatter soup everywhere. Use an immersion blender, or let the soup cool to lukewarm before transferring to a stand blender (and crack the lid ever so slightly away from you while blending). If you have a Vitamix or a similar machine with a steam vent, disregard this note—just make sure the steam vent is actually open.

¼ cup (60 ml) canola oil

4 Indian bay leaves

1 black cardamom pod, cracked open so the seeds are exposed

One 3-inch (7.5-cm) cinnamon stick

1½ cups (235 g) chopped yellow onion (¼-inch // 6-mm dice, about 1 medium onion)

2 pounds (910 g) ripe tomatoes, chopped (¼-inch // 6-mm dice, about 3 large or 6 medium tomatoes; good-quality canned tomatoes may be substituted)

1 cup (175 g) red masoor daal, rinsed

1½ teaspoons salt, plus more as needed

Boiling water (optional), as needed

2 tablespoons grated fresh ginger (peeled or unpeeled are both fine here)

Garnish

Several generous grinds of black pepper

2 tablespoons unsalted butter, softened

1 lemon, cut into 6 wedges

1. Heat the oil in a large, lidded (but uncovered for now) pot over medium heat. Once the oil starts to shimmer, add the bay leaves, cardamom pod, and cinnamon. Sizzle, giving the pan a shake or two, until the bay leaves darken a couple of shades and all the spices become more fragrant, about 1 minute.

2. Add the onion and cook, stirring occasionally, until soft and translucent, 8 to 10 minutes.

3. Add the tomatoes, daal, salt, and 3 cups (720 ml) water. Bring the mixture to a boil, removing any foam or scum that develops.

4. Cover the pot and reduce the heat to medium-low so that the mixture settles into a gentle boil. Cook, stirring occasionally, until the tomatoes start to break down and the lentils are meltingly tender, about 40 minutes.

5. Remove the bay leaves, cardamom pod, and cinnamon stick with a slotted spoon or spider, and then set the soup aside to cool for a bit. Use a stand blender (make sure the soup has cooled sufficiently) or an immersion blender to puree to a smooth consistency.

6. Reheat the soup gently over medium-low heat, if desired. (This soup may be served at any temperature, depending on the season and menu, but bear in mind that a chilled soup will require a bit more salt than a warm one in order to taste just right.)

7. The final consistency should be akin to a pureed vegetable soup. If it seems too thick, slowly add boiling water, or bring the mixture to a boil after adding tap water, until it reaches the desired consistency.

8. Press the grated ginger through a fine-mesh strainer over a bowl, being careful to extract as much juice as possible from the fiber. Stir the fresh ginger juice into the soup. Taste for salt.

GARNISH

9. Ladle the soup into bowls to serve. Garnish each bowl with a generous grind of black pepper and a small dollop of butter, with a lemon wedge on the side. The citrus really makes the flavor pop, so encourage your guests to squeeze it in.

Daal Paalak

DAAL with SPINACH

SERVES 4 • COOK TIME: 70 minutes • PHOTO: page 119

Auyon Daals are the essential Indian comfort food. They can be dressed up or served unadorned, and they take well to a variety of spice and vegetable complements.

One apocryphal tale tells of Shah Jahan, the Mughal emperor who built the Taj Mahal. In his later years, Shah Jahan was imprisoned by his son Aurangzeb, who instructed Shah Jahan to pick one food to eat for the rest of his life. The prison cook discreetly suggested daal, because the cook was confident he would be able to make a different version of it every day of the year.

In the spirit of occasionally changing things up, feel free to try this dish with a garnish of crispy onions, fried potatoes, or my childhood favorite: Nacho Cheese Doritos®. Crush them up in your fist and sprinkle haphazardly.

1 cup (215 g) yellow moong daal, rinsed

2 teaspoons grated, peeled fresh ginger

1¼ teaspoons salt, plus more as needed

5 ounces (140 g) frozen spinach, about 1½ cups when roughly broken up

Boiling water (optional), as needed

Tadka
1 tablespoon unsalted ghee (store-bought or homemade, page 38)

¾ teaspoon cumin seeds

¼ teaspoon ground cayenne (optional)

Garnish
1 tablespoon finely chopped fresh cilantro, stems and leaves

1 lemon, cut into 8 wedges

1. Combine the daal, ginger, and salt with 5 cups (1.2 L) water in a large, lidded (but uncovered for now) pot. Bring to a boil over high heat.

2. Reduce the heat to low and partially cover. Simmer, stirring occasionally, until the legumes have softened considerably and the water starts to look opaque when stirred, about 20 minutes. Any foam or scum that develops over the first few minutes of cooking should be removed (but no need to get surgical).

3. Stir in the spinach and cover the pot completely. Continue to cook, stirring a couple of times, until the daal has completely softened and begun to break down, an additional 30 minutes or so. (The actual cooking time depends on the freshness of the beans and can vary a lot. Tenderness, rather than time, should be your focus. Check the pot often, don't hesitate to add water if the level gets low, and trust your senses.) Test the daal by gently mashing it with the back of a spoon or ladle. If the liquid thickens and turns opaque, the daal is done.

4. The daal should have the texture of a pureed vegetable soup. If it's closer to pancake batter, slowly add boiling water (or bring the daal to a boil after adding tap water) until it reaches the desired consistency. Taste for salt.

TADKA

5. To prepare the tadka (see page 31), heat the ghee in a small pan over medium heat. Once the ghee is good and hot, add the cumin seeds and sizzle, giving the pan a shake or two, until the seeds darken a couple of shades and become fragrant, about 20 seconds.

6. Remove from the heat and add the cayenne (if using). Swirl the pan to combine. Pour the tadka over the daal.

7. To clean out any ghee and spices that are still sticking to the pan, add a bit of daal from the pot and swirl the pan around a few times before pouring it back into the daal.

GARNISH

8. Garnish with cilantro and serve with lemon wedges on the side. Serve hot.

Serving Tip

→ This dish may thicken as it cools, especially if left uncovered. If cooking in advance, you may need to add ¼ cup (60 ml) boiling water (or bring the daal to a boil after adding tap water) to get it back to the right consistency.

	WHOLE	HULLED + HALVED
URAD		
MOONG		
MASOOR		
ARHAR		

MEET YOUR BEANS!

Since you might encounter some legumes you haven't cooked with before, we've included some introductions below. A quick note on terminology: The Hindustani word *daal* generally refers to split, hulled legumes, either raw or cooked (the term itself is derived from the Sanskrit word for "split.") For the purposes of this book, we will specify *beans* when referring to a whole, unhulled legume and *daal* when indicating the split-and-hulled version.

(It's worth noting that *daal* is also sometimes used as a catch-all designation for hulled and whole legumes alike, which can create some confusion when navigating the aisles of your local Indian grocer. Such labels will usually include a clarifying specification, i.e. "whole masoor daal" vs "split masoor daal.")

Urad

Native to the grasslands of South India, these round beans are black-skinned in their whole form and ivory-colored when split and hulled into daal. The daal is sometimes fried alongside spices in a tadka (see page 31) to add a crunchy, earthy element to rice and vegetables, and can also be milled into a flour.

Moong

Another South Indian native, these tiny green beans are known as green gram, whole moong, or mung beans. When split and hulled into daal, they are lemon yellow. The whole beans are often sprouted for use in vegetarian preparations.

Masoor

Although *lentil* is often used as an umbrella term for all small legumes, the word technically refers to a specific species, *Lens culinaris*, named for its lens-shaped seeds (the word *lentil* derives from the Latin diminutive for "lens"). There are several varieties of true lentils. Red-orange masoor daal is the split and hulled version of brown lentils, which came to India from West Asia around the fourth millennium BCE. They are quick-cooking and generally available at Indian stores and supermarkets alike.

Arhar

Another Indian native, these green-beige beans are known as pigeon peas when whole, and as arhar daal, toor daal, tuvar daal, and split pigeon peas when split and hulled into a gold-colored daal. They hold their shape better than similarly sized legumes, and take a bit longer to cook. At Indian groceries, the daal comes in both oil-packed and dry versions. The oil functions as a preservative, and although there's no putative difference in flavor or cooking time, you do have to wash the oil off before cooking. We use and recommend the dry version.

See page 45 for a note on chickpea varieties.

Sukhi Moong Daal

DRY DAAL with TOMATO AND ONION

SERVES 4 • **COOK TIME:** *80 minutes* • **PHOTO:** *page 106*

Jyoti This was my dad's favorite daal. Its thicker texture makes it an ideal accompaniment for flatbreads like Roti (page 189) or Paratha (page 192). To eat it Indian-style, tear off a small piece of flatbread and place it over some daal. Pinch a bit of daal into the bread using the tips of your fingers, and then pop the mini-wrap into your mouth. Repeat.

Although eating with your hands can be a bit messy in the beginning, it is the traditional way to eat in much of India. I firmly believe it makes the food taste better.

Auyon Sometimes I find bits of daal in my eyebrows when I eat with my hands, but it is worth it. As with all skills, it takes some time to master.

1 cup (215 g) yellow moong daal, rinsed

1 teaspoon salt, plus more as needed

½ teaspoon ground turmeric

Tadka
¼ cup (50 g) unsalted ghee (store-bought or homemade, page 38)

¾ cup (85 g) chopped yellow onion (¼-inch // 6-mm dice, about ½ small onion)

¾ cup (90 g) chopped tomato (¼-inch // 6-mm dice, about 1 small tomato)

¼ teaspoon ground cayenne (optional)

1. Combine the daal, salt, turmeric, and 3½ cups (840 ml) water in a large, lidded (but uncovered for now) pot. Bring to a boil over medium-high heat.

2. Reduce the heat to low and partially cover. Any foam or scum that develops over the first few minutes of cooking should be removed (but no need to get surgical). Simmer, stirring occasionally, until almost all the liquid has evaporated and the legumes have softened and begun to break down, about 45 minutes. (The actual cooking time depends on the freshness of the beans and can vary a lot. Tenderness, rather than time, should be your focus. Check the pot often, don't hesitate to add water if the level gets low, and trust your senses.)

3. Cover the daal completely for the last few minutes of cooking to ensure any stubborn legumes get fully cooked. This preparation is meant to be drier than most daals, and the final texture should be akin to that of a thick, almost semisolid porridge. Taste for salt.

TADKA

4. To prepare the tadka (see page 31), heat the ghee in a small pan over medium heat. Once the ghee is good and hot, add the onion and cook, stirring occasionally, until soft and translucent, 6 to 8 minutes.

5. Add the tomato and cook, stirring occasionally, until it starts to break down, another 5 minutes or so.

6. Remove from the heat and add the cayenne (if using). Swirl the pan to combine. Pour the tadka over the daal, and to keep the presentation traditional, don't stir it in. Serve hot.

Serving Tip

→ This dish may thicken as it cools, especially if left uncovered. If cooking in advance, you may need to add ¼ cup (60 ml) boiling water (or bring the daal to a boil after adding tap water) to get it back to the right consistency.

Daal Makhani

BUTTERY BLACK DAAL

SERVES 6 • **SOAK TIME:** *8 hours (ideally overnight)*
COOK TIME: *3½ hours* • **PHOTO:** *page 128*

Jyoti This recipe is one of the handful of now-famous dishes that originated at the Moti Mahal restaurant in New Delhi in the mid-twentieth century (see page 155). The original restaurant recipe, a variant of a traditional North Indian urad preparation, was notable for its inclusion of cream and tomatoes. Our version replaces the cream with yogurt, which dials back the richness a touch while adding some tanginess. As the cook time indicates, this recipe is a commitment, but it is well worth the effort.

1 cup (200 g) dried black urad beans, rinsed

½ cup (90 g) dried red kidney beans, rinsed

4 teaspoons grated, peeled fresh ginger

1¼ teaspoons salt, plus more to taste

½ cup (120 g) whole, unflavored yogurt (store-bought or homemade, page 40), stirred to a smooth consistency and at room temperature

Tadka
3 tablespoons unsalted ghee (store-bought or homemade, page 38)

1 cup (170 g) chopped yellow onion (¼-inch // 6-mm dice, about 1 small onion)

1 cup (135 g) chopped tomato (¼-inch // 6-mm dice, about 1 medium tomato)

2 cloves garlic, finely chopped

½ teaspoon ground cayenne (optional)

Garnish
1 tablespoon (salted or unsalted) butter

1. Combine the urad beans and kidney beans with 8 cups (7.5 L) water in a large bowl. Soak overnight, or for 8 to 10 hours.

2. Transfer the urad beans, kidney beans, and soaking water to a large, lidded pot (see Pressure Cooker Alternative, page 64). Add the ginger and salt, and stir to combine. Bring the mixture to a boil, uncovered, over high heat.

3. Reduce the heat to low and partially cover, with the lid cracked open ½ inch (12 mm), stirring once or twice. After 30 minutes of partially covered cooking, cover the pot completely.

4. Continue to cook at a gentle boil, stirring a few times, until the legumes are meltingly tender, up to 2½ hours total. (The actual cooking time depends on the freshness of the beans and can vary a lot. Tenderness, rather than time, should be your focus. Check the pot often, don't hesitate to add water if the level gets low, and trust your senses.)

5. In some cases, depending on the age of the beans, getting them perfectly soft is impossible without a few minutes in a pressure cooker. Not to worry if you don't own one—the dish will still be delicious with a bit of bite to the beans. If you do happen to have a pressure cooker, though, and you find that the beans have not softened to your liking after a couple hours of cooking, transfer the daal to a pressure cooker. Seal the machine and cook for 10 minutes once the pressure has built up and/or the hissing starts. Check for tenderness and repeat if necessary.

6. Using a potato masher or the back of a ladle, mash roughly half of the legumes into the liquid. The beans should yield and break down easily, thickening the daal. The texture should be similar to that of a thin porridge.

7. Stir in the yogurt and cook, stirring occasionally, for an additional 10 minutes. Remove from the heat and set aside.

recipe continues

Daal Makhani
· continued ·

TADKA

8. To prepare the tadka (see page 31), heat the ghee in a medium pan over medium-high heat. Once the ghee is good and hot, add the onion and cook, stirring occasionally, until the onion is soft, golden, and translucent with browned edges, 8 to 10 minutes (see page 32).

9. Add the tomato and garlic and cook, stirring occasionally, until the tomato starts to break down, about 5 minutes.

10. Remove from the heat and add the cayenne (if using). Swirl the pan to combine. Pour the tadka over the daal and stir to combine. Taste for salt.

GARNISH

11. Just before serving, heat the butter over medium heat in the same pan that just held the tomato mixture. Watch carefully, as overcooking the butter will render it grainy and compromise the texture of the dish. As soon as the butter melts, pour it over the daal. To keep the presentation traditional, don't stir it in. Serve hot.

Serving Tip

→ This dish may thicken as it cools, especially if left uncovered. If cooking in advance, you may need to add ¼ cup (60 ml) boiling water (or bring the daal to a boil after adding tap water) to get it back to the right consistency.

PRESSURE COOKER ALTERNATIVE

You can use a pressure cooker or an Instant Pot for the entirety of the initial cooking of the beans if you'd prefer. Combine the urad beans, kidney beans, soaking liquid, ginger, and salt in the pressure cooker. Seal the machine and cook for 25 minutes once the pressure has built up and/or the hissing starts. Turn the heat off and leave the beans to cool in the pressure cooker for 20 minutes before releasing the steam. Check the beans for tenderness and continue cooking as necessary, either on the stove or for another few minutes under pressure. Proceed with the rest of the recipe as written, starting at Step 6.

DAAL BUBBLE MONSTERS

Be warned that if you decide to get clever and cover a pot of daal to bring it to a boil more quickly, you will inadvertently summon a bubble monster that will escape the lid and make a turmeric-yellow mess out of your stovetop. Leaving the lid cracked a bit allows you to retain more heat than an uncovered pot, but also gives the steam somewhere to go. Cover partially and with care.

Arhar Daal with Green Mango

SERVES 4 • SOAK TIME: 3 hours
COOK TIME: 1¾ hours • PHOTO: page 105

Jyoti My mother cooked this daal so often that it grew to be emblematic of her hospitality among her circle of friends. She passed the recipe down to me as her mother did to her. It is, I think, a perfect daal—it retains the cozy, warming qualities of simpler preparations, but its balance of sweet, sour, and spice lends it a beguiling complexity.

Don't let the long spice list intimidate you. Most all of them are added in one fell swoop at the end as a garnish, and the bulk of the cooking time involves the daal bubbling away happily on the stovetop, unattended. Don't cover the pot too early, though.

Auyon The unripe mango necessary for this recipe is not something you'll find in most supermarkets. You're looking for a hard, unyielding fruit, picked well before ripening, with a sour, nutty taste. This fruit is meant for cooking and pickling, not for fresh eating. You should be able to find it at most Indian markets, either fresh or frozen (if using frozen, no need to peel, unless someone in the household is sensitive to mango skin—see page 275).

1 cup (200 g) yellow arhar daal, rinsed

¼ large, peeled, unripe green mango (2 ounces // 60 g), cubed (½-inch // 12-mm), about ½ cup

2 teaspoons sugar

1½ teaspoons salt, plus more to taste

½ teaspoon ground turmeric

Boiling water (optional), as needed

Tadka

4½ teaspoons unsalted ghee (store-bought or homemade, page 38)

⅛ teaspoon heeng (ground asafoetida, see page 274)

½ teaspoon black or brown mustard seeds

½ teaspoon cumin seeds

½ teaspoon coriander seeds, coarsely crushed

3 cloves garlic, finely chopped

2 small sprigs fresh curry leaves, stripped from the stems (see page 273)

¼ teaspoon ground cayenne (optional)

Garnish

1 tablespoon finely chopped fresh cilantro, stems and leaves

1. Combine the daal with 6 cups (5.7 L) water in a large bowl. Soak for 3 to 4 hours.

2. Transfer the daal and soaking liquid to a large, lidded (but uncovered for now) pot. Add the green mango, sugar, salt, and turmeric. Stir to combine. Bring the mixture to a boil over high heat.

3. As soon as the mixture comes to a boil, reduce the heat to low. Half-cover the pot and simmer for about 20 minutes, stirring once or twice to keep the daal from sticking to the bottom of the pot. Any foam or scum that develops over the first few minutes of cooking should be removed (but no need to get surgical).

4. Cover the pot completely and cook, stirring a few times, until the daal has completely softened and begun to break down, about 1 hour. (The actual cooking time depends on the freshness of the beans and can vary a lot. Tenderness, rather than time, should be your focus. Check the pot often, don't hesitate to add water if the level gets low, and trust your senses.) Test the daal by gently mashing it with the back of a spoon or ladle. If the liquid thickens and turns opaque, the daal is done.

5. The daal should be about the same consistency as a pureed vegetable soup. If the daal is totally tender but the liquid is still thin and clear, use a potato masher to mash about a quarter of the daal to thicken the mixture. If it's too thick, slowly add boiling water (or bring the daal to a boil after adding tap water) until it reaches the desired texture. Taste for salt.

TADKA

6. To prepare the tadka (see page 31), heat the ghee in a small pan over medium heat. Once the ghee is good and hot, add the heeng and sizzle for 10 seconds.

recipe continues

Arhar Daal with Green Mango
· continued ·

7. Add the mustard seeds, cumin seeds, and coriander seeds. Cook, undisturbed, until the mustard seeds are popping vigorously, about 30 seconds (watch out for oil splatter—use a splatter screen if you have one).

8. Add the garlic and stir until the garlic barely starts to take on color, 30 to 45 seconds.

9. Add the curry leaves and watch out for oil splatter—use a splatter screen if you have one. Cook, giving the pan a shake to distribute them evenly, until the leaves crisp up, an additional 15 seconds. If it's hard to tell visually, you should be able to feel the texture change while stirring them around in the pan.

10. Immediately remove from the heat and add the cayenne (if using). Swirl the pan to combine. Pour the tadka over the daal.

11. To clean out any ghee and spices that are still sticking to the pan, add a bit of daal from the pot and swirl the pan around a few times before stirring it back into the pot.

GARNISH
12. Garnish with cilantro and serve hot.

Serving Tip

→ This dish may thicken as it cools, especially if left uncovered. If cooking in advance, you may need to add ¼ cup (60 ml) boiling water (or bring the daal to a boil after adding tap water) to get it back to the right consistency.

Ghoogni

CHICKPEA CURRY with TAMARIND

SERVES 4 • **COOK TIME:** *50 minutes (longer if cooking chickpeas from scratch)* • **PHOTO:** *page 100*

Jyoti Ghoogni is a street food beloved in the eastern state of Bengal. It has also become a fan favorite in my classes, especially among my vegan and vegetarian students. Tamarind is the key ingredient here—its sour punch and rich color truly transform the familiar chickpea. For two of our favorite recipe combinations, see Aloo Tikki (page 217) and Samosa (page 225).

¼ cup (60 ml) canola oil

2 Indian bay leaves

2 black cardamom pods, cracked open so the seeds are exposed

½ teaspoon cumin seeds

1 cup (170 g) chopped yellow onion (¼-inch // 6-mm dice, about 1 small onion)

4 teaspoons grated, peeled fresh ginger

¾ teaspoon ground coriander

2½ cups (430 g) Cooked & Seasoned Chickpeas (see page 45), or canned chickpeas, with 1½ cups (360 ml) cooking or can liquid reserved (if you don't have that much, just make up the volume with water)

1 teaspoon tamarind paste (see page 277)

¼ teaspoon ground cayenne (optional)

Boiling water, as needed

Salt, to taste

Garnish

2 tablespoons finely chopped ripe tomato

1 tablespoon finely chopped fresh cilantro, stems and leaves

1 tablespoon chopped yellow onion (¼-inch // 6-mm dice)

¼ teaspoon garam masala (store-bought or homemade, page 53)

1. Heat the oil in a medium, lidded (but uncovered for now) pot over medium heat. Once the oil starts to shimmer, add the bay leaves, cardamom pods, and cumin seeds. Sizzle, giving the pan a shake or two, until the spices darken a couple of shades and become fragrant, about 30 seconds.

2. Add the onion. Cook, stirring occasionally, until the onion is soft and golden with plenty of well-browned edges, 10 to 12 minutes (see page 32).

3. Add the ginger and ground coriander. Stir to incorporate as they cook for a minute or two.

4. Add the chickpeas, tamarind, and cayenne (if using) and mix well. Lastly, add 1½ cups (360 ml) chickpea cooking broth. Partially cover the pot and cook at a gentle boil, stirring occasionally to make sure nothing sticks to the bottom of the pot, until the ghoogni thickens, 10 to 12 minutes. Don't boil off all of the liquid—there should be a bit of gravy remaining. Remove from the heat.

5. Thicken the ghoogni further by using a potato masher or the back of a ladle to mash about a third of the chickpeas into the liquid. The consistency should be akin to that of a thick vegetarian chili. Add a bit of boiling water to adjust the texture if the ghoogni seems too thick after mashing.

6. Season with salt.

GARNISH

7. Garnish with tomato, cilantro, onion, and garam masala. Serve hot.

Serving Tip

→ This dish may thicken as it cools, especially if left uncovered. If cooking in advance, you may need to add ¼ cup (60 ml) boiling water (or bring the mixture to a boil after adding tap water) to get it back to the right consistency.

Salads, Daals, and Beans

Narkol Cholar Daal

SPLIT and HULLED CHICKPEAS with COCONUT

SERVES 4 • **SOAK TIME:** *4 hours*
COOK TIME: *1½ hours* • **PHOTO:** *page 101*

Jyoti The next two recipes are regional variations on a theme. Channa daal, the common factor, is the split and hulled version of Bengal gram, the smaller, darker cousin of the familiar garbanzo bean. It should be available at any Indian grocery.

This preparation, which features coconut, is from my husband's home state of Bengal. It is often served at festive gatherings, and goes magnificently with Loochi (page 204). I learned this recipe from my mother-in-law.

Auyon India's reverence for the coconut is best illustrated through local legend. In Hindu mythology, the creation of the coconut palm is attributed to a sage named Vishwamitra. King Trishanku, a buddy of Vishwamitra, got himself expelled from the gates of heaven on account of various indecencies. To break his companion's fall, Vishwamitra used his sage powers to produce a tree that caught Trishanku in midair. The coconut remains an auspicious fruit within Hindu rituals today.

The Christians of Goa, on the other hand, describe how Joseph, Mary, and baby Jesus once sought shelter in a (curiously Goa-like) countryside. The trio first asked the banana tree for help, but they were refused. They then petitioned the coconut tree, which kindly offered assistance. Mary rewarded the plant with two blessings: to be fruitful throughout the year, and to have every one of its parts—spines, leaves, trunk, and fruit—be useful to humankind. The banana tree, meanwhile, was doomed to die after bearing fruit just once.

---

1 cup (190 g) yellow channa daal, rinsed

1 teaspoon salt, plus more as needed

1½ teaspoons sugar

Tadka
4 cloves

4 green cardamom pods

2 tablespoons unsalted ghee (store-bought or homemade, page 38)

Pinch of heeng (ground asafoetida, see page 274)

One 3-inch (7.5-cm) cinnamon stick

1 teaspoon cumin seeds

¾ cup (65 g) thinly sliced unsweetened coconut, cut into 1-inch (2.5-cm) pieces (see Note, opposite), thawed if frozen

1. Combine the channa daal and salt with 4 cups (960 ml) water in a large bowl. Stir well to combine, then soak for at least 6 hours.

2. Combine the channa daal, soaking liquid, and sugar in a medium, lidded (but uncovered for now) pot (see Pressure Cooker Alternative, opposite). Bring to a rolling boil over high heat.

3. Reduce the heat to low and cook at a gentle boil. Any foam or scum that develops over the first few minutes of cooking should be removed (but no need to get surgical). Keep an eye on the water level during cooking, and add water if it gets lower than the level of the legumes.

4. Once the pot stops threatening to boil over, after about 10 minutes of cooking, cover it completely. Cook, stirring once or twice, until the legumes are totally tender, an additional hour or so. (The actual cooking time depends on the freshness of the beans and can vary a lot. Tenderness, rather than time, should be your focus. Check the pot often, don't hesitate to add water if the level gets low, and trust your senses.)

5. Using a potato masher or the back of a ladle, mash about a quarter of the daal into the liquid to thicken the mixture. The consistency should be akin to that of a thick but pourable porridge, and the liquid should turn opaque as the legumes are mashed. Taste for salt. Remove the pot from the heat.

TADKA

6. To prepare the tadka (see page 31), use a mortar and pestle to coarsely crush the cloves. Add the cardamom pods to the mortar and crack them open so that the seeds are exposed.

7. Heat the ghee in a small pan over medium heat. Once the ghee is good and hot, add the heeng and sizzle, undisturbed, for 10 seconds.

8. Add the cinnamon, cumin, cardamom, and cloves. Cook, giving the pan a shake or two, until the spices darken a couple of shades and become fragrant, about 30 seconds.

9. Add the coconut and cook, stirring constantly, until the coconut is heated through, a minute or two. Pour the tadka over the daal and serve hot.

Serving Tips

→ The cardamom pods and crushed cloves in the final dish are totally edible and we love chewing them, but they can be pushed aside if the flavor is too intense. Advise your guests.

→ This dish may thicken as it cools, especially if left uncovered. If cooking in advance, you may need to add ¼ cup (60 ml) boiling water (or bring the daal to a boil after adding tap water) to get it back to the right consistency.

Note

For the coconut, we recommend using the frozen, unsweetened, sliced (not grated) stuff found at Indian markets—just let it thaw at room temperature for 30 minutes or so before using. Make sure you buy fresh frozen (as opposed to desiccated frozen). You are welcome to slice your own fresh coconut if you would prefer.

PRESSURE COOKER ALTERNATIVE

You can use a pressure cooker or an Instant Pot for the initial cooking of the channa daal if you'd prefer. Combine the channa daal, soaking liquid, and sugar in the pressure cooker. Seal the machine and cook for 5 minutes once the pressure has built up and/or the hissing starts. Turn the heat off and then release the pressure. Check the channa daal for tenderness; if it is still slightly firm, continue cooking on the stovetop at a gentle boil until totally tender. Proceed with the rest of the recipe as written, starting at Step 5.

Lauki Channa Daal

SPLIT and HULLED CHICKPEAS with BOTTLE GOURD

SERVES 4 • **SOAK TIME:** *6 hours*
COOK TIME: *1¾ hours* • **PHOTO:** *page 113*

Jyoti This version of channa daal is from my home state of Punjab. The distinguishing ingredient is lauki, also known as calabash, cucuzza, or bottle gourd. It should be available at any Indian grocery. The vegetable is spongy and light, and is about 12 inches (30 cm) long. It has a mild, zucchini-like flavor and takes beautifully to spices and seasonings. Trim the top and bottom extremities before peeling.

Auyon Lauki is a well-traveled vegetable. It originated in tropical Africa, but prehistoric people are thought to have brought the thick-skinned gourds, which were used as containers, to the Americas around ten thousand years ago. Mentions of lauki in the *Rigveda*, an ancient collection of Sanskrit hymns dating back to the second millennium BCE, demonstrate its long (though not quite as impressive) history in India. The hard, dried shells are still used as water bottles, cups, and musical instruments.

1 cup (190 g) yellow channa daal, rinsed

1¾ teaspoons salt, plus more to taste

1 lauki (1½ pounds // 670 g), peeled, quartered lengthwise, and cut into slightly larger-than-bite-size pieces (if your lauki has hard seeds, scoop them out before cutting)

1 tablespoon ground coriander

½ teaspoon ground turmeric

Tadka

7 teaspoons unsalted ghee (store-bought or homemade, page 38)

1 cup (170 g) chopped yellow onion (¼-inch // 6-mm dice, about 1 small onion)

¾ cup (90 g) chopped tomato (¼-inch // 6-mm dice, about 1 small tomato)

½ teaspoon ground cayenne (optional)

1. Combine the channa daal and salt with 4 cups (960 ml) water in a large bowl. Stir well to combine, then soak for at least 6 hours.

2. Transfer the channa daal and soaking liquid to a large, lidded pot (see Pressure Cooker Alternative, opposite). Add the lauki, coriander, and turmeric. Stir to combine, then bring the mixture to a rolling boil, uncovered, over high heat.

3. Reduce the heat to low and cook at a gentle boil, uncovered. Any foam or scum that develops over the first few minutes of cooking should be removed (but no need to get surgical). Keep an eye on the water level during cooking, and add water if it gets lower than the level of the legumes.

4. Once the pot stops threatening to boil over, after about 10 minutes of cooking, cover it completely. Cook, stirring once or twice, until the legumes are totally tender, an additional hour or so. (The actual cooking time depends on the freshness of the beans and can vary a lot. Tenderness, rather than time, should be your focus. Check the pot often, don't hesitate to add water if the level gets low, and trust your senses.)

5. Taking care to avoid the lauki as best you can, use a potato masher or the back of a ladle to mash about a quarter of the daal into the liquid to thicken the mixture. The consistency should be akin to that of a thick but pourable porridge, and the liquid should turn opaque as the legumes are mashed. Taste for salt. Remove the pot from the heat.

TADKA

6. To prepare the tadka (see page 31), heat the ghee in a medium pan over medium heat. Once the ghee is good and hot, add the onion. Cook, stirring frequently, until the onion is soft and translucent and about half the edges are browned, 8 to 10 minutes.

7. Add the tomato (watery bits and all) and cook, stirring once or twice, until the tomato starts to break down, 3 minutes or so.

8. Remove from the heat and add the cayenne (if using). Swirl to combine, then pour the tadka over the daal. You can leave the tadka floating on top (the more traditional presentation) or stir it in. Serve hot.

Serving Tip

→ This dish may thicken as it cools, especially if left uncovered. If cooking in advance, you may need to add ¼ cup (60 ml) boiling water (or bring the daal to a boil after adding tap water) to get it back to the right consistency.

PRESSURE COOKER ALTERNATIVE

You can use a pressure cooker or an Instant Pot for the initial cooking of the channa daal if you'd prefer. Combine the channa daal, soaking liquid, coriander, and turmeric (but not the lauki) in the pressure cooker. Seal the machine and cook for 5 minutes once the pressure has built up and/or the hissing starts. Turn the heat off and then release the pressure. Add the lauki to the pot and continue cooking on the stovetop at a gentle boil until the lauki and channa daal are both totally tender, 20 minutes or so. Proceed with the rest of the recipe as written, starting at Step 5.

LAUKI

Channa Masala

CHICKPEAS with POMEGRANATE and GINGER

SERVES 6 • **SOAK TIME:** *4 hours*
COOK TIME: *2¾ hours* • **PHOTO:** *page 98*

Jyoti This versatile garbanzo bean dish is equally at home in a tureen at a street food stall as it is as part of an elaborate Punjabi brunch spread. The combination of ground, dried pomegranate and black salt lend its distinctive color. We especially love it with Loochi (page 204).

2 cups (400 g) dried chickpeas, rinsed

1 fresh Indian green chili (optional; see page 271—jalapeño may be substituted), stemmed

¼ cup (30 g) anardana powder (ground dried pomegranate, see page 271)

5 teaspoons grated, peeled fresh ginger

2 teaspoons garam masala (store-bought or homemade, page 53)

2 teaspoons kaala namak (black salt, see Kaala Namak, page 249)

½ teaspoon salt, plus more to taste

Pinch of baking soda

2 tablespoons + ⅓ cup canola oil

1 tablespoon cumin seeds, roasted (lightly!) and ground (see page 43)

⅓ cup (30 g) julienned fresh ginger (cut into short, thin matchsticks, see page 245)

Garnish
2 tablespoons finely chopped fresh cilantro, stems and leaves

Handful (1½ ounces // 45 g) thinly sliced yellow onion (about ¼ small onion)

Handful (1½ ounces // 45 g) thinly sliced tomato (about ½ small tomato)

1. Combine the chickpeas and 6 cups (1.4 L) water in a large bowl. Soak for at least 6 hours.

2. Transfer the chickpeas and soaking liquid to a large, lidded pot (see Pressure Cooker Alternative, opposite). Add the whole green chili (if using), anardana, ginger, garam masala, kaala namak, salt, and baking soda. Stir to combine, then set the mixture aside.

3. Heat 2 tablespoons of the oil in a small pan over medium heat. Once the oil starts to shimmer, reduce the heat to low and add the ground cumin. Swirl to combine and then immediately pour the mixture over the pot with the chickpeas—the ground cumin can easily scorch and should only cook in the oil for a couple of seconds.

4. Place the pot over high heat, uncovered, and bring to a rolling boil. Reduce the heat to low and continue to cook at a gentle boil. Any foam or scum that develops over the first few minutes of cooking should be removed (but no need to get surgical). Keep an eye on the water level during cooking, and add water if it gets lower than the level of the beans.

5. Once the pot stops threatening to boil over, after about 10 minutes of cooking, cover it completely. Cook, stirring a few times, until the chickpeas are meltingly tender but still hold their shape, an additional 90 minutes or so. Remove from the heat. The liquid in the pot should barely be covering the cooked beans. (The actual cooking time depends on the freshness of the beans and can vary a lot. Tenderness, rather than time, should be your focus. Check the pot often, don't hesitate to add water if the level gets low, and trust your senses.)

6. Heat the remaining ⅓ cup (80 ml) oil in a large, lidded (but uncovered for now) pan over medium-high heat. Once the oil starts to shimmer, add the julienned ginger and cook, shaking the pan once or twice, for 2 minutes to allow the ginger to infuse into the oil.

7. Add the beans and cooking liquid to the pan and stir well to combine. Cover the pan. Cook, undisturbed, at a steady boil for about 10 minutes to allow the flavors to meld.

8. Reduce the heat to medium and mash about a quarter of the beans into the liquid with a potato masher or the back of a ladle to thicken the dish.

9. Cook, uncovered and stirring continuously, until most of the remaining liquid in the pan evaporates, 8 to 10 minutes. The final dish should have only a bit of thickened liquid intermixed with the beans. It should be pleasantly moist, but not so wet that when you scrape the bottom of the pan with a spatula, liquid immediately flows into the canal you created. Taste for salt.

GARNISH

10. Garnish with cilantro, sliced (raw) onion, and tomato. Serve hot.

Serving Tip

→ This dish may thicken as it cools, especially if left uncovered. If cooking in advance, you may need to add ¼ cup (60 ml) boiling water (or bring the mixture to a boil after adding tap water) to get it back to the right consistency.

PRESSURE COOKER ALTERNATIVE

You can use a pressure cooker or an Instant Pot to speed up the initial cooking of the beans. Combine the chickpeas, soaking liquid, whole green chili (if using), anardana, ginger, garam masala, kaala namak, salt, and baking soda in the pressure cooker, but don't yet turn it on. Follow Step 3, adding the cumin-oil to the chickpea mixture. Seal the pressure cooker and cook the mixture for 25 minutes once the pressure has built up and/or the machine starts to hiss. Turn the heat off and leave the mixture to cool in the pressure cooker for 20 minutes before releasing the steam. Check the beans for tenderness and continue cooking as necessary, either on the stove or for another few minutes under pressure. Assess and adjust the amount of liquid remaining (the liquid should barely be covering the cooked beans). Proceed with the rest of the recipe as written, starting with Step 6.

Sukha Kaala Channa

DRY BLACK CHICKPEAS with MANGO

SERVES 6 • **SOAK TIME:** *8 hours (ideally overnight)*
COOK TIME: *1¾ hours* • **PHOTO:** *page 116*

Auyon Bengal gram, also known as kaala channa or Desi channa, is the familiar white garbanzo bean's smaller, darker cousin. The British first encountered the bean in Bengal, hence the appellation. Although it is assumed to have originated in Asia Minor, its history in India dates back as far as 2500 BCE. The garbanzo bean, by contrast, was introduced to parts of India as recently as the eighteenth century. You should be able to find kaala channa at any Indian grocery.

Due to its dry consistency, this dish is best served with flatbread and Homemade Yogurt (page 40) or as a stand-alone snack, rather than with rice.

2 cups (390 g) dried kaala channa, rinsed

1½ teaspoons salt, plus more to taste

Pinch of baking soda

Tadka
⅓ cup (80 ml) canola oil

1 tablespoon cumin seeds

2 tablespoons amchoor (ground dried mango, see page 271)

2 tablespoons ground coriander

1 teaspoon ground cumin

¼ teaspoon ground cayenne (optional)

1. Combine the kaala channa and salt with 7 cups (1.7 L) water in a large bowl. Stir well to combine, then soak overnight, or for at least 8 hours.

2. Transfer the kaala channa and soaking liquid to a medium, lidded pot (see Pressure Cooker Alternative, opposite). Add the baking soda and stir to combine. Bring the mixture to a rolling boil over high heat, uncovered, then reduce the heat to low and cook the mixture at a gentle boil for about 20 minutes. Any foam or scum that develops over the first few minutes of cooking should be removed (but no need to get surgical). Keep an eye on the water level during cooking, and add water if it gets lower than the level of the legumes.

3. Cover the pot completely and cook, stirring a few times, until the chickpeas have softened but still hold their shape, an additional hour or so. Note that the thicker skins of kaala channa give them a bit more chew than regular garbanzo beans, even when fully cooked. That said, if they seem too firm, continue cooking for an additional 20 minutes, or until they feel totally tender. (The actual cooking time depends on the freshness of the beans and can vary a lot. Tenderness, rather than time, should be your focus. Check the pot often, don't hesitate to add water if the level gets low, and trust your senses.)

4. Remove the pot from the heat and allow the beans to cool until lukewarm. Drain the beans but reserve the cooking liquid (see Note, opposite).

TADKA

5. Heat the oil in a large pan over medium-high heat. Once the oil starts to shimmer, add the cumin seeds and cook, giving the pan a shake or two, until they darken a couple of shades and become fragrant, about 30 seconds.

6. Reduce the heat to low. Add the amchoor, ground coriander, ground cumin, and cayenne (if using). Swirl to combine and then immediately add the drained beans—the powders can easily scorch and should only cook alone in the oil for a couple of seconds.

7. Stir well to coat the beans in the spices and oil and cover the pan. Cook, stirring once or twice, for about 10 minutes to allow the flavors to meld. The final dish should be dry and not have any gravy. Taste for salt and serve hot.

PRESSURE COOKER ALTERNATIVE

You can use a pressure cooker or an Instant Pot to speed up the initial cooking of the beans. Combine the kaala channa, soaking liquid, and baking soda in the pressure cooker. Seal the machine and cook for 10 minutes once the pressure has built up and/or the hissing starts. Turn the heat off and leave the beans to cool in the pressure cooker for 20 minutes before releasing the steam. Check the beans for tenderness and continue cooking as necessary, either on the stove or for another few minutes under pressure. Drain the beans but reserve the cooking liquid. Proceed with the rest of the recipe as written, starting with Step 5.

Note

The reserved cooking liquid from the beans makes a simple, earthy soup. Dilute the reserved bean broth with as much boiling water as you need, usually about 1 cup (240 ml) to bring the total volume to 3 cups (720 ml). Heat 1 tablespoon ghee in a medium pot and sizzle 1 teaspoon cumin seeds until they darken a shade or two and become fragrant, about 30 seconds. Add the diluted broth to the pot, stir well, and cook to heat through. Garnish with 1 teaspoon lemon juice just before serving. Taste for salt and lemon and serve hot.

• Sundal •

CHICKPEAS with COCONUT and CURRY LEAVES

SERVES 4 • **THAW TIME:** *30 minutes*
COOK TIME: *5 minutes (longer if cooking chickpeas from scratch)* • **PHOTO:** *page 109*

Jyoti Sundal is often served as a prasad, or blessed food, in Hindu temples in South India during the late summer and fall festival season. Prasad, which is always vegetarian, is first offered to the idols of deities that line the altar, after which it is distributed to the temple-goers.

I love making this dish year-round, but most of all when I have some spare cooked or canned chickpeas around. It takes only a couple of minutes to prepare, and it makes for a satisfying and protein-rich snack. The taste is a lovely balance of savory, nutty, spicy (both ginger and chili), and sour—no single flavor or ingredient should overpower the others.

As with all of our recipes, you can always increase or reduce the chili quantity to taste.

2½ cups (430 g) drained Cooked and Seasoned Chickpeas (page 45), or 2½ cups drained, canned chickpeas (from two 15-ounce // 420-g cans)

2 tablespoons grated, peeled fresh ginger

1 tablespoon grated unsweetened coconut (see Frozen Coconut, right), thawed if frozen

1 tablespoon finely chopped fresh cilantro, stems and leaves

Tadka
2 tablespoons canola oil

½ teaspoon black or brown mustard seeds

1 fresh Indian green chili (optional; see page 271—jalapeño may be substituted), minced

1 sprig fresh curry leaves, stripped from the stem (see page 273)

Garnish
4½ teaspoons fresh lemon juice

Salt, to taste

1. Combine the chickpeas, ginger, coconut, and cilantro in a large bowl. Mix well and set aside.

TADKA

2. To prepare the tadka (see page 31), heat the oil in a small pan over medium heat. Once the oil starts to shimmer, add the mustard seeds and cook, undisturbed, until they are popping vigorously, about 30 seconds (watch out for oil splatter—use a splatter screen if you have one).

3. Add the chili (if using) and curry leaves—again, beware of oil splatter. Cook, giving the pan a shake to distribute them evenly, until the leaves crisp up, about 10 seconds. If it's hard to tell visually, you should be able to feel the texture change while stirring them around in the pan. Drizzle the tadka over the chickpeas.

GARNISH

4. Just before serving, add the lemon juice and mix well. Taste for salt and lemon. (We don't prescribe any salt in this recipe because it was tested with seasoned chickpeas, but if you're using unsalted legumes, be sure to season.) Serve chilled or at room temperature.

Frozen Coconut

For the coconut, we recommend using the frozen, unsweetened, pre-grated stuff found at Indian markets—just let it thaw at room temperature for 30 minutes or so before using. Make sure you buy fresh frozen (as opposed to desiccated frozen). You are welcome to grate fresh coconut if you would prefer, but know that it's an investment.

• Kadhi •

CHICKPEA YOGURT CURRY with DUMPLINGS

SERVES *8* • **SOURING TIME:** *2 to 3 days*
COOK TIME: *2½ hours* • **PHOTO:** *page 102*

Jyoti This dish is an investment, but the final result justifies the effort: perfectly soft chickpea dumplings, or pakoras, enveloped in a velvety, turmeric-golden curry. Be warned that you will need to start souring the yogurt a few days in advance. Also, keep in mind that some pakoras will come out smooth, while others will sport bumps, ridges, and tendrils. The consistency of the batter plays a role, but so does the unpredictable way the batter hits the oil. Fear not. All pakora shapes are good pakora shapes.

Since this recipe requires deep-frying, check out the note on deep-frying (page 210) before getting started. For those of you who are deep-frying-disinclined, we don't recommend trying to bake or air fry the pakoras. Deep-frying really is necessary to get the proper texture. You can substitute green beans, snap peas, or carrots for the dumplings, though—any vegetable that will retain a bit of crunch will do. Add them in for the last 15 minutes of cooking, just as the recipe instructs with the pakoras.

Auyon This recipe includes both a technique and an ingredient that may cause some trepidation among cooks new to Indian cuisine. The technique of souring yogurt, which involves leaving it at room temperature for a couple of days, seems to go against everything the FDA has taught us about the perishability of dairy products. Yogurt, though, is fermented and contains active cultures, which guard against spoilage in the short to medium term. By leaving yogurt out of the fridge for a few days, we are waking those cultures back up and encouraging them to consume the remaining milk sugars. The lactic acid they produce is the source of that lovely tang. Trust your eyes and nose—if you see mold or if something smells like rotten milk, toss it. Reviewing the process for how yogurt is made (page 40) may provide some reassurance.

For more on mustard oil, a potentially anxiety-inducing ingredient, see page 171.

recipe continues

ALL GOOD SHAPES

Kadhi
• continued •

Kadhi
2 cups (480 g) whole, unflavored yogurt (store-bought or homemade, page 40)

½ cup (120 ml) mustard oil or canola oil

2 dried red chilies, broken into thirds (see page 271)

2 teaspoons coriander seeds, coarsely crushed

1 teaspoon black or brown mustard seeds

1 teaspoon cumin seeds

1 teaspoon methi (fenugreek) seeds

2 small sprigs fresh curry leaves, stripped from the stems (see page 273)

2 cups (235 g) halved, thinly sliced yellow onion (about 1 medium onion)

4 teaspoons grated, peeled fresh ginger

1 cup (115 g) besan (see Besan, opposite)

1 tablespoon salt, plus more to taste

1 teaspoon ground turmeric

¼ teaspoon ground cayenne (optional)

Pakoras
2 cups (230 g) besan

1 cup (160 g) finely chopped yellow onion (about ⅔ medium onion)

2 tablespoons finely chopped fresh cilantro, stems and leaves

1 fresh Indian green chili (optional; see page 271—jalapeño may be substituted), minced

¾ teaspoon salt

¼ teaspoon ground cayenne (optional)

Pinch of baking soda

2 cups (480 ml) canola oil, plus more as needed

Tadka
1 tablespoon canola oil

½ teaspoon ground cayenne or paprika

Garnish
2 tablespoons finely chopped fresh cilantro, stems and leaves

KADHI

1. Sour the yogurt by keeping it in a warm place for 48 hours (in the summer) to 72 hours (in the winter). There's no strict definition here, but the yogurt should have a pleasantly tart taste and smell. Whey may separate from the yogurt, which is fine. Use all of it.

2. Heat the oil in a large pot over medium heat. Once the oil starts to shimmer, add the dried chilies and cook, giving the pan a shake to distribute them evenly, until they darken a shade or two, about 30 seconds.

3. Add the coriander seeds, mustard seeds, cumin seeds, and methi seeds. Cook, undisturbed, until the mustard seeds are popping vigorously, an additional 30 seconds (watch out for oil splatter—use a splatter screen if you have one).

4. Stir in the curry leaves and again, beware of oil splatter. Cook, giving the pan a shake to distribute them evenly, until the leaves crisp up, about 15 seconds. If it's hard to tell visually, you should be able to feel the texture change while stirring them around in the pan.

5. Add the sliced onion and ginger and stir well to combine. Cook, stirring occasionally, until the onion is translucent and just starting to brown, 7 to 9 minutes.

6. While the onion is cooking, combine the soured yogurt, besan, salt, turmeric, and cayenne (if using) with 3 cups (720 ml) water in a large bowl. Whisk well to fully incorporate, then dilute the mixture with an additional 6 cups (1.4 L) water.

7. Once the onion is cooked, add the besan-yogurt mixture to the pot. Stir well to combine and increase the heat to medium-high. Cook, stirring frequently, until the kadhi comes to a boil, about 10 minutes. The mixture will thicken in consistency from the addition of the besan. Stirring and scraping are crucial, as the yogurt component of the kadhi could otherwise separate.

8. Cover the pot and reduce the heat to low. Cook at a simmer, stirring and scraping once or twice, until the kadhi thickens further, about 30 minutes. The final texture should be silky and smooth, slightly thicker than cream.

PAKORAS

9. While the kadhi thickens, prepare the pakora batter. In a large bowl, combine the besan, chopped onion, cilantro, fresh chili (if using), salt, cayenne (if using), and baking soda. Mix well to combine.

10. Add 1 cup (240 ml) water slowly, stirring in a few tablespoons at a time. The final mixture should be thicker than pancake batter, but still pourable—add a tablespoon or two more water if necessary. Try to move quickly from here on out, as the salt will draw moisture out of the onion and change the consistency of the batter if it rests for too long.

11. Heat the oil in a deep wok or Dutch oven over medium-high heat until it gets up to around 375°F (190°C), 5 to 10 minutes depending on the cooking vessel and stove. The oil should be at least 1 inch (2.5 cm) deep, so add more if necessary. If you don't have a thermometer handy, check the oil by dropping in a bit of batter—if it sizzles vigorously and then comes up to the surface of the oil after a second or two, the oil is hot enough to fry in. If the batter only sizzles a bit or not at all, the oil isn't hot enough, and if the oil starts to smoke, it is too hot. As you wait for the oil to heat up, line a large plate or baking sheet with paper towels and set aside.

12. When the oil is up to temperature, carefully drop a tablespoon-size spoonful of batter into the oil and repeat with a few more spoonfuls. Be sure to space them out a bit so that they don't glom onto one another. Don't otherwise overcrowd the wok—adding too much at once will cool the oil and produce greasy results.

13. Cook the first batch, flipping a couple of times for evenness, until the pakoras turn golden yellow, 4 to 5 minutes. When done, use a slotted spoon or spider to transfer the pakoras to the paper-lined plate.

14. Repeat with the remaining batter, working in batches. Check the temperature and allow the oil to return to temperature between batches as necessary. Once all the batter is fried, remove the oil from the heat to cool. Allow the last batch of pakoras to cool for at least 10 minutes as well before proceeding to the next step.

15. Add the cooled pakoras to the kadhi and stir gently. Simmer for a final 15 minutes to allow the kadhi to penetrate and soften the pakoras. Taste for salt.

TADKA

16. To prepare the tadka (see page 31), heat the oil in a small pan over medium heat. Once the oil is good and hot, remove from the heat and add the cayenne or paprika. Swirl the pan to combine.

17. Pour the tadka over the kadhi. Stir some but not all of it in, so that you can still see some of the red oil floating on top of the kadhi.

GARNISH

18. Garnish with cilantro. Serve hot.

Besan

Besan, or gram flour, is a gluten-free, high-protein flour made from split kaala channa, or Indian black chickpeas. It should be available at any Indian grocery

• Rajma •

RED BEAN CURRY with POTATO and BLACK CARDAMOM

SERVES 8 • **SOAK TIME:** *8 hours (ideally overnight)*
COOK TIME: *2¼ hours* • **PHOTO:** *page 97*

Jyoti Rajma is a quintessential North Indian lunchtime dish, one of my childhood favorites. We love it with rice, Homemade Yogurt (page 40), and a simple vegetable like Kachumbar (page 56) or Kalonji Broccoli (page 95). Potatoes are not traditionally part of the dish, but they are a requisite Mukharji family addition.

Auyon The kidney bean is a variety of the common bean *Phaseolus vulgaris*, native to the Americas. It was first grown in India by French colonizers. The name *rajma* is thought to derive from *rajmasha*, the Sanskrit word for black-eyed peas, a distinct but similar-looking legume.

Beans
2 cups (360 g) dried red kidney beans, rinsed

1½ teaspoons salt

Pinch of baking soda

Masala
⅝ cup (150 ml) canola oil

2 dried red chilies, broken into thirds (see page 271)

2 Indian bay leaves

2 black cardamom pods, cracked open so the seeds are exposed

1½ cups (360 g) blended or grated yellow onion (about 1 large onion, see Onion Blending, page 144)

1 large russet potato (11¼ ounces // 320 g), peeled, halved lengthwise, and cut crosswise into 1-inch- (2.5 cm-) thick slices

1 teaspoon salt, plus more to taste

⅝ cup (160 g) tomato puree, diluted with 5 tablespoons water (see Tomato Puree, opposite)

4 teaspoons grated, peeled fresh ginger

1 teaspoon cumin seeds, roasted (lightly!) and ground (see page 43)

1 teaspoon coriander seeds, roasted and ground with the cumin

½ teaspoon ground turmeric

Garnish
2 tablespoons finely chopped fresh cilantro, stems and leaves

BEANS

1. Combine the kidney beans and salt with 6 cups (1.4 L) water in a large bowl. Stir well to combine, then soak overnight, or for at least 8 hours.

2. Transfer the kidney beans and soaking liquid to a large, lidded pot (see Pressure Cooker Alternative, opposite). Add the baking soda, then bring the mixture to a rolling boil, uncovered, over high heat.

3. Reduce the heat to medium-low and cook at a gentle boil, uncovered. Any foam or scum that develops over the first few minutes of cooking should be removed (but no need to get surgical). Keep an eye on the water level during cooking, and add water if it gets lower than the level of the beans.

4. Once the pot stops threatening to boil over, after about 15 minutes of cooking, partially cover the pot, leaving the lid cracked open ⅛ inch (3 mm). Cook for 25 minutes, stirring occasionally, and then cover the pot completely.

5. Cook, stirring once or twice, with the pot completely covered, until the beans are totally tender and starting to break open, an additional 15 minutes. There should be 1 cup or so of liquid left in the pot. Add water to make up the difference if necessary, and don't worry if there's a little extra—you'll just have a bit more gravy. (The actual cooking time depends on the freshness of the beans and can vary a lot. Tenderness, rather than time, should be your focus. Trust your senses.)

MASALA

6. Heat the oil in a large, nonstick pan over medium-high heat. Once the oil starts to shimmer, add the chilies and cook, giving the pan a shake to distribute them evenly, until they darken a couple of shades, about 30 seconds.

7. Add the bay leaves and cardamom pods and sizzle, undisturbed, for an additional 30 seconds or so.

8. Add the onion, potato, and salt—watch out for oil splatter and use a splatter screen if you have one. Cook, stirring frequently, until the onion is generously speckled with brown flecks and the potato is browning at the edges, 15 to 20 minutes. This browning is crucial to the flavor of the dish, so don't undercook (see page 32). If you notice the onion starting to burn before it gets to the right color, stir more often. You may need to cook for a bit longer if the onion doesn't seem dark enough.

9. Add the diluted tomato puree, ginger, cumin, coriander, and turmeric. Stir well to incorporate. Cook, stirring frequently, until the mixture is heated through and the oil starts to separate out of the masala (see page 162), 3 or so minutes.

10. Add 1½ cups (360 ml) water, then the beans and their cooking liquid. Reduce the heat to medium-low. Cover the pan and cook, stirring once or twice, until the curry thickens and the potato pieces are totally soft but still hold their shape, about 20 minutes. The consistency of the curry should be akin to that of a bean-based chili. Taste for salt.

GARNISH

11. Garnish with cilantro. Serve hot.

Serving Tip

→ This dish may thicken as it cools, especially if left uncovered. If cooking in advance, you may need to add ¼ cup (60 ml) boiling water (or bring the rajma to a boil after adding tap water) to get it back to the right consistency.

PRESSURE COOKER ALTERNATIVE

You can use a pressure cooker or an Instant Pot to speed up the initial cooking of the beans. Combine the kidney beans, soaking liquid, and baking soda in the pressure cooker. Seal the machine and cook for 10 minutes once the pressure has built up and/or the hissing starts. Turn the heat off and leave the beans to cool in the pressure cooker for 20 minutes before releasing the steam. Check the beans for tenderness and continue cooking as necessary, either on the stove or for another few minutes under pressure. Assess and adjust the amount of liquid remaining with the cooked beans; there should be about 1 cup (240 ml). Proceed with the rest of the recipe as written, starting at Step 6.

Tomato Puree

If you can't find canned tomato puree (lightly cooked pureed tomatoes), you can substitute ¾ cup (195 g) canned, diced tomatoes. Blitz the diced tomatoes in a blender, and don't dilute them with any water. (The backstory here is that Jyoti used to use a very specific canned tomato sauce, and she got quite attached to its consistency. Rather than directing you, dear reader, to seek out a single brand, we came up with a dilution solution that works more universally.)

CHAPTER THREE

Vegetables!

Aloo Tamatar

POTATO with TOMATO and FENNEL

SERVES 6 • COOK TIME: *50 minutes* **• PHOTO:** *page 98*

Jyoti This delightfully simple potato and tomato dish is a North Indian classic. Growing up, I knew it as "station wale aloo," one of the dependably delicious wares hawked by railway station vendors in the state of Madhya Pradesh. The ground fennel adds a lovely dimension, but if you don't have any on hand, the dish tastes great without it too.

Auyon Although it is now impossible to imagine contemporary Indian gastronomy without potato or the tomato, neither vegetable is native to the subcontinent. Exact dates are fuzzy, but the earliest conjectured arrivals from the New World date no further back than the sixteenth century (while widespread cultivation and use are sometimes pinned as late as the nineteenth century). Potatoes, which were introduced by the Portuguese and promoted by the British, were first incorporated into the cuisine as a substitute for indigenous tubers. Tomatoes, similarly, replaced souring agents like tamarind and kokum (a fruit in the mangosteen family).

6 tablespoons canola oil

3 dried red chilies, broken into thirds (see page 271)

¾ teaspoon cumin seeds

4 large russet potatoes (2¾ pounds // 1280 g total), cubed into ½-inch (12-mm) chunks

1¼ teaspoons salt, plus more to taste

¾ teaspoon ground turmeric

⅝ cup (160 g) tomato puree, diluted with 5 tablespoons water (for a substitute, see Tomato Puree, page 83)

1½ teaspoons ground fennel seed

Garnish

3 tablespoons finely chopped fresh cilantro, stems and leaves

1. Heat the oil in a large pot over medium-high heat. Once the oil starts to shimmer, add the chilies and cook, giving the pan a shake to distribute them evenly, until they darken a shade or two, about 30 seconds.

2. Add the cumin seeds and sizzle, giving the pan another shake or two, until they darken a bit and become fragrant, another 30 seconds.

3. Add the potato, salt, and turmeric. Stir well to incorporate and cook, stirring a few times, until the potato is just starting to brown, 6 to 8 minutes.

4. Stir in the diluted tomato puree and 2 cups (480 ml) water. Bring the mixture to a boil, then reduce the heat to low and cover. Cook at a gentle boil, gently stirring occasionally, until the potato is totally tender, about 20 minutes.

5. Add the ground fennel and stir to incorporate. Remove the pot from the heat and lightly mash about a quarter of the potatoes into the sauce to thicken it slightly. The final dish should consist of perfectly soft chunks of potato in a thick curry. Taste for salt.

GARNISH

6. Garnish with cilantro. Serve hot.

Serving Tip

→ This dish may thicken as it cools, especially if left uncovered. If cooking in advance, you may need to add ¼ cup (60 ml) boiling water (or bring the mixture to a boil after adding tap water) to get it back to the right consistency.

• Bharva Bhindi •

STUFFED OKRA with MANGO and CORIANDER

SERVES *2* • **COOK TIME:** *50 minutes* • **PHOTO:** *page 102*

Jyoti In my childhood home, breakfast and dinner were always heavier meals, typically eaten as a family, while lunch was a less consequential affair. The current focus on lighter eating makes that schedule sound antiquated and indulgent, but it did leave me with many fond memories of lavish breakfasts and brunches. This stuffed okra dish was often part of a weekend brunch spread, always accompanied by a flatbread like Roti (page 189) or Paratha (page 192) and a dollop of Homemade Yogurt (page 40). For the globe eggplant version of this dish, see page 130.

Auyon Okra's sliminess is intensified by lower temperature cooking methods like boiling and braising. In North Indian cooking, okra is generally cooked in oil, which keeps its mucilaginous qualities at bay. Acidity (provided here by the amchoor) also helps subdue the goo.

1 pound (455 g) okra, stemmed

2½ teaspoons ground coriander

1½ teaspoons amchoor (ground dried mango, see page 271)

1 teaspoon ground cumin

1 teaspoon salt, plus more to taste

½ teaspoon ground turmeric

¼ teaspoon ground cayenne (optional)

⅓ cup (80 ml) canola oil

1. Make a lengthwise slit in each okra pod without cutting through the entire length or depth, such that they remain intact but can be stuffed with spices.

2. Combine the coriander, amchoor, cumin, salt, turmeric, and cayenne (if using) in a small bowl. Amchoor has a tendency to stick together, so stir well to break up any clumps.

Okra Shopping

Look for tender okra pods. A great way to test them is by gently applying pressure to the pointed (non-stem) end of a single pod. If it breaks easily, you've got what you're looking for. If it bends, don't buy it. Avoid packaged (and therefore untestable) pods.

3. Hold one okra pod in your nondominant hand and use the fingernail of the same thumb to widen the slit. Load up a small spoon with about ¼ teaspoon of masala in your other hand and carefully stuff the pod—if you have a spoon that has a bit of a point to it, this is its time to shine. Usually only about half of the masala makes it in, so work over the masala bowl to catch what falls out. Place the stuffed pod on a large plate with the slit facing up, then repeat with the remaining pods (you may have some masala left over).

4. Heat the oil in a large, lidded (but uncovered for now) pan over medium heat. Once the oil starts to shimmer, add the stuffed okra in a single layer. A little overlap is fine, because they will shrink as they lose moisture, but work in batches for this step if necessary. Cook uncovered for a couple of minutes to allow some of the moisture to escape.

5. If working in batches, reintroduce all the cooked okra back into the pan. Sprinkle any leftover masala over the okra (not into the oil, if possible) and then cover the pan. Cook, stirring or shaking only once or twice to get different bits of the okra in contact with the hot pan, until the okra has totally softened, about 15 minutes. The color of the pods should be a mix of olive green and dark brown, with plenty of blackened crispy bits.

6. Taste for salt. Serve hot, and drizzle the spice-darkened oil over the dish when serving.

CAULIFLOWER + BROCCOLI CUTTING GUIDE

1. Flip the cauliflower or broccoli stem-side up. Trim and discard the outermost leaves and the base of the stem.

2. Cut off the internal leaves, if present, and cut them crosswise into 1-inch (2.5-cm) strips (wash these well, as there is often dirt stuck to them).

3. With the cauliflower still stem-side up, cut the largest florets from the stem, then cut the florets in half lengthwise.

4. Cut away the next layer of florets, leaving them whole, and continue until the stem is bare.

5. If the recipe calls for 2-inch (5-cm) florets (for example), cut any intact florets that are longer/wider than 2 inches (5 cm) in half vertically, and leave the rest whole.

6. Cut up the stem pieces as instructed. Since the stem pieces are denser, we usually cut the stem chunks smaller than the florets to ensure even cooking.

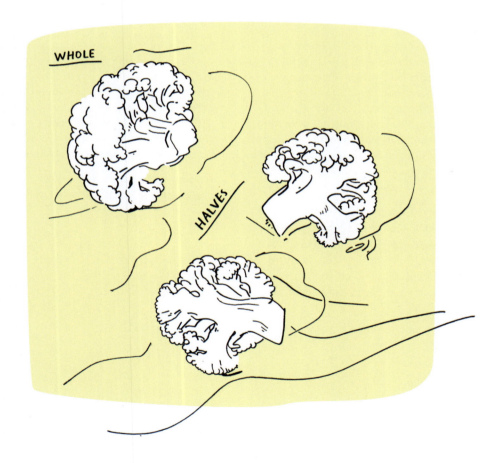

Gobhi Aloo

CAULIFLOWER with GINGER, TURMERIC, and POTATO

SERVES 4 • **COOK TIME:** *80 minutes* • **PHOTO:** *page 107*

Jyoti The texture of the potatoes is key to this restaurant favorite. They should be cooked long enough to be perfectly creamy and soft all the way through, but not so long that they start to disintegrate (see page 49).

Use the largest pan you've got—for reference, we use a 12-inch (30.5-cm) vessel. Otherwise, either cook in batches or halve the recipe.

Auyon Unlike many of its fellow European imports, the cauliflower (native to the Mediterranean and Asia Minor) has a conclusive year of arrival in India: 1822, courtesy of a British botanist. The good people of India have therefore had just over two hundred years to perfect their cauliflower cooking techniques.

⅓ cup (80 ml) canola oil

½ teaspoon cumin seeds

2 medium russet potatoes (14 ounces // 400 g total), peeled, halved lengthwise, and cut crosswise into ¾-inch- (2-cm-) thick slices (see page 82)

1 cup (160 g) finely chopped yellow onion (about ⅔ medium onion)

1 medium head (2 pounds // 910 g) cauliflower, cut into 2-inch (5-cm) florets and ¾-inch (6-mm) stem pieces (see page 90)

2 tablespoons grated, peeled fresh ginger

1 teaspoon salt

½ teaspoon ground turmeric

¼ teaspoon ground cayenne (optional)

Garnish

2 tablespoons finely chopped fresh cilantro, stems and leaves

1. Heat the oil in a large, lidded (but uncovered for now), nonstick pan over medium-high heat. Once the oil starts to shimmer, add the cumin and sizzle, giving the pan a shake or two, until the seeds darken a couple of shades and become fragrant, about 30 seconds.

2. Add the potato and onion and cook, stirring frequently, until the onion is soft, translucent, and browning at the edges, and the potato is starting to brown on a few sides, 6 to 8 minutes.

3. Reduce the heat to medium-low and add the cauliflower, ginger, salt, turmeric, and cayenne (if using). Try to sprinkle the spices evenly over the whole pan to avoid clumping. Stir well to incorporate, then cover the pan. Cook, stirring occasionally, until the potato is totally tender, about 25 minutes. Keep the stirrings brief and gentle (to avoid breaking up the cauliflower and potato as they approach doneness) but thorough. Replace the lid immediately after each stir, as the steam is crucial.

4. Once the potato is totally soft, remove the pan from the heat and let rest, covered, for 15 minutes before serving. Taste for salt.

GARNISH

5. Garnish with cilantro. Serve hot.

MY MOTHER, THE POTATO WIZARD

Auyon I was convinced my mother was a potato wizard because her potatoes always came out perfectly and mine came out either burned, unintentionally mashed, or undercooked. Then I learned about nonstick pans.

The trait that makes regular pans desirable to Western chefs, which is that things will stick to and then release from them to create a crispy, browned crust, becomes an obstacle with my mom's way of cooking Indian-style potatoes and starchy vegetables. It's not impossible to cook these dishes in regular pans, of course—the incorporation of the potato into the Indian diet predates the invention of Teflon by some three hundred years—but it demands more oil, attention, and vigilance while cooking.

If you are caught in a pinch, you could use an enameled (or well-seasoned) cast-iron pot or pan, but you'll need to keep a close eye on it. Get it good and hot, and make sure it is well oiled. Keep the potatoes moving. Add oil (or water, for saucier preparations) as necessary, to prevent a burned crust from forming.

As far as acquiring a nonstick vessel, keep in mind that regardless of the quality, nonstick coatings don't last more than a few years, so getting a cheaper or mid-priced implement is often the right move. A couple of maintenance tips: avoid using nonstick pans over high heat because that degrades the nonstick coating, and be sure to use wooden or plastic cooking implements, rather than metal ones, to avoid scratching the surface.

For more on potato cookery, see A Note on Potatoes on page 49.

Masala Brussels Sprouts

SERVES 4 • COOK TIME: *45 minutes* **• PHOTO:** *page 105*

Jyoti Brussels sprouts were unfamiliar to me until I moved to the United States in the 1970s. When I finally got my hands on some, I had a lot of fun experimenting with different Indian-style preparations. This version emerged as one of my favorites, and it has since become a sought-after recipe among my students as well. The sour tang of the dried mango and the creaminess of the potatoes complement the nutty, spice-darkened sprouts marvelously.

No need to peel the potatoes for this one—as with all of our recipes, potatoes should remain unpeeled unless indicated otherwise.

⅓ cup (80 ml) canola oil

1 tablespoon cumin seeds

1 large russet potato (11¼ ounces // 320 g), cubed into 1-inch (2.5-cm) chunks

2 tablespoons ground coriander

1 tablespoon amchoor (ground dried mango, see page 271)

1 teaspoon ground cumin

1 teaspoon salt, plus more to taste

¼ teaspoon ground cayenne (optional)

1 pound (455 g) Brussels sprouts, trimmed and quartered lengthwise (if some or all of your sprouts are shorter than 1½ inches // 4 cm, halve them lengthwise rather than quartering them)

1. Heat the oil in a large, lidded (but uncovered for now), nonstick pan over medium-high heat. Once the oil starts to shimmer, add the cumin seeds and sizzle, giving the pan a shake or two, until they darken a couple of shades and become fragrant, about 30 seconds.

2. Add the potato and cook, stirring frequently, until the potato is lightly fried all over and starting to brown on all edges, 5 to 7 minutes.

3. Reduce the heat to low and add the coriander, amchoor, ground cumin, salt, and cayenne (if using). Try to sprinkle the spices evenly over the whole pan to avoid clumping. Stir well to combine, and then immediately add the Brussels sprouts. (The ground spices should cook in the hot oil for a second or two before the sprouts join the pan, but they will scorch if you wait too long, so move quickly.)

4. Stir thoroughly again. Increase the heat to medium, cover, and cook, stirring every few minutes to make sure every vegetable piece is eventually coated with ground spices. Keep the pan tightly covered between stirrings to preserve the steam. The dish is done when the potato pieces are totally soft but still keep their shape, 10 to 15 minutes (if the potato takes a bit longer than that to soften, reduce the heat to low and stir often for any additional time to ensure the spices don't burn). The sprouts should be cooked through, but can have a bit of bite, and the spices should darken a few shades but not blacken.

5. Taste for salt and serve hot.

DON'T JUDGE A VEGGIE BY ITS CRISPNESS

Auyon Although some of our preparations involve cooking vegetables no further than the "tender-crisp" stage that is in vogue in contemporary American gastronomy (like Kalonji Broccoli, page 95), the majority of traditional South Asian vegetable dishes, and a great many meat preparations, would be classified as overcooked by Western standards. To judge them so misses the point. The rich and complex spice mixtures that are integral to Indian cooking will not properly infuse a dish unless the ingredients are fully cooked through.

While there is undoubtedly a charm to the snap of raw or lightly cooked produce, it is not the only metric by which to judge a vegetable. A softened, spice-smothered green beats a bland-but-perfectly crisp one any day.

Kalonji Broccoli

SERVES 4 • COOK TIME: *25 minutes* **• PHOTO:** *page 110*

Jyoti This dish is a tribute to the magical flavor of kalonji, or nigella seed, which sits somewhere in the savory intersection of black pepper, thyme, and browned onion. In combination with a bit of chili, salt, and fat, it is one of my favorite ways to elevate any cooked green. I most often serve this preparation as a side dish to round out a simple meal of rice and daal.

Use the largest pan you've got—for reference, we use a 12-inch (30.5-cm) vessel. Otherwise, either cook in batches or halve the recipe.

¼ cup (60 ml) canola oil

2 dried red chilies, broken into thirds (see page 271)

¾ teaspoon kalonji (nigella seeds, see page 274)

2 crowns (1½ pounds // 680 g total) broccoli, cut into 2-inch (5-cm) florets and ½-inch (12-mm) stem pieces (see page 90)

½ teaspoon salt, plus more to taste

1. Heat the oil in a large pan over medium heat. Once the oil starts to shimmer, add the chilies and cook, giving the pan a shake to distribute them evenly, until they darken a shade or two, about 30 seconds.

2. Add the kalonji and sizzle, giving the pan another shake, until the seeds become fragrant, an additional 20 seconds or so.

3. Add the broccoli and salt and stir to combine. Increase the heat to medium-high and allow the broccoli to brown a bit, waiting about 90 seconds before stirring. Repeat the browning-and-stirring process a few times, for a total of about 9 minutes, until the broccoli is vibrant green and lightly mottled with dark brown toasty bits. It should retain a bit of crunch rather than being totally softened.

4. Taste for salt and texture. Serve hot.

Baingan Bharta

SMOKY EGGPLANT with ONION and TOMATO

SERVES 4 • **COOK TIME:** *1½ hours* • **PHOTO:** *page 112*

Jyoti The eggplant is indigenous to India and is an oft-eaten vegetable across the subcontinent. This particular preparation is a Punjabi classic. It was my father's favorite eggplant dish, and I grew up eating it at least twice a week.

Although the ingredient list is small, the finished dish has an enormous depth of flavor. The key to getting it right is really charring the pants off of the eggplant. Blackened, crackly skin is what you are looking for, as that will imbue the flesh with Baingan Bhartha's characteristic warm, smoky flavor. (If you are competent with a grill, try doing Step 1 outside for easier cleanup and, if using charcoal, an enhanced smokiness.)

1 large eggplant (1⅜ pounds // 615 g)

1 teaspoon salt

¼ cup (60 ml) canola oil

1½ cups (235 g) chopped yellow onion (¼-inch // 6-mm dice, about 1 medium onion)

2½ cups (350 g) chopped tomato (¼-inch // 6-mm dice, about 1 large tomato)

1 fresh Indian green chili (optional; see page 271—jalapeño may be substituted), minced

Garnish
1 tablespoon finely chopped fresh cilantro, stems and leaves

1. Put a wire rack over a stovetop burner over medium-low heat. If using an electric range, make sure the rack doesn't come in contact with the burner. For easier cleanup, fit a piece of foil under the wire rack, with a hole cut out for the burner, because the eggplant will leak some juice. Place the eggplant on the rack and cook, turning every few minutes, until the vegetable collapses and is charred black on all sides, at least 30 minutes. Don't skimp on the time here, as proper charring is crucial. Larger eggplants will take longer. Be sure to get the bottom by holding it by the stem with a pair of tongs.

(If you don't have a wire rack, the broiler also works well. Place the eggplant on a rimmed baking sheet a few inches under the broiler for at least 30 minutes, turning occasionally and continuing to cook even after it bursts, until the vegetable has collapsed and is charred black on all sides. Again, don't skimp on the time here, and note that larger eggplants may take as long as 50 minutes.)

2. After cooking, set the eggplant aside to cool for 15 minutes on a plate or pan with a lip, as it will release more liquid.

3. Once cool, carefully separate the burned peel from the eggplant flesh. Use a spoon or the back of a knife to scrape as much flesh as possible off of the peel, and then discard the peel.

4. In a large bowl, mash the roasted eggplant flesh with the salt using a potato masher or fork, taking care to break up the eggplant fibers.

5. Heat the oil in a medium, lidded (but uncovered for now) pan over medium heat. Once the oil starts to shimmer, add the onion and cook, stirring frequently, until soft and translucent, 5 to 7 minutes.

6. Add the tomato and chili (if using) and cook, stirring occasionally, until the tomato starts to break down, another 7 minutes or so.

7. Add the salted eggplant flesh and mix well to incorporate. Cover the pan and cook, stirring a couple of times, until the color of the eggplant darkens and the texture thickens and homogenizes a bit, 15 to 20 minutes. The consistency should be akin to that of a thick porridge—not too dry, but also not soupy. Taste for salt.

GARNISH

8. Garnish with cilantro. Serve hot.

a Rajma (page 82)
b Mutton Aloo Korma (page 159)
c Jeera Mattar (page 138)
d Bharva Baingan (page 130)

a Aloo Tamatar (page 87)
b Loochi (page 204)
c Masala Chai (page 252)
d Channa Masala (page 74)
e Sooji Halwa (page 258)

a Jhaal Mudhi (page 209)
b Aloo Tikki (page 217)
c Chire Bhaja (page 212)
d Ghoogni (page 69)

- **a** Narkol Cholar Daal (page 70)
- **b** Machher Jhol (page 169)
- **c** Tamatar Khajoor Chutney (page 244)
- **d** Ghee Bhaat (page 44)

a Kadhi (page 79)
b Murgh Hariyali (page 146)
c Bharva Bhindi (page 88)

a Imli Chutney (page 243)
b Dhania Pudina Chutney (page 242)
c Gobhi Pakora (page 223)

a Bhutta Chaat (page 139)
b Spiced Watermelon (page 233)

a **Jeera Pulao** (page 177)
b **Murgh Do Pyaaza** (page 144)
c **Masala Brussels Sprouts** (page 93)
d **Arhar Daal with Green Mango** (page 67)

a. **Mattar Paneer** (page 134)
b. **Ghee** (page 38)
c. **Paneer** (page 46)
d. **Gobhi Aloo** (page 91)
e. **Roti** (page 189)
f. **Sukhi Moong Daal** (page 62)

Baghare Baingan (page 132)

a Sundal (page 78)
b Lemon Rice (page 179)
c Dimer Debhil (page 215)

a **Kalonji Broccoli** (page 95)
b **Ghee Bhaat** (page 44)
c **Shorshe Chingri** (page 171)

Rogan Josh (page 164)

a **Paratha** (page 192)
b **Keema Mattar** (page 156)
c **Murgh Rezala** (page 148)
d **Lauki Channa Daal** (page 72)
e **Baingan Bharta** (page 96)
f **Kheera Tamatar Raita** (page 239)

a Bengali Khichudi (page 180)
b Tamatar Khajoor Chutney (page 244)
c Beguni (page 222)

a **Sabudana Khichudi** (page 229)
b **Spiced Liver Toast** (page 232)
c **Sabudana Vada** (page 220)
d **Fruit Chaat** (page 235)

a Boondi Raita (page 241)
b Sukha Kaala Channa (page 76)
c Saag Paneer (page 136)

Samosa (page 225)

Kaathi Roll (page 230)

- a Kachumbar (page 56)
- b Daal Paalak (page 59)
- c Pyaaz Pulao (page 178)
- d Murgh Kaali Mirch (page 142)

a Nimbu Pani (page 249)
b Aam Lassi (page 250)
c Aam Panna (page 254)
d Thandai Old-Fashioned (page 257)
e Aam Panna Punch (page 257)
f Thandai (page 255)

- **a** Adarak Nimbu Achaar (page 245)
- **b** Gobhi Paratha (page 194)
- **c** Homemade Yogurt (page 40)
- **d** Aloo Paratha (page 197)

- a Paapdi Chaat (page 213)
- b Tomato, Red Lentil & Ginger Soup (page 58)
- c Moongphali Aloo Chaat (page 208)

a Goan Machhli (page 168)
b Vindaloo (page 166)

a Mushroom Dum Biryani (page 184)
b Bhuna Gosht (page 162)
c Kacchi Hyderabadi Biryani (page 186)
d Paalak Raita (page 240)

- a Salted Caramel Almond Flan (page 261)
- b Cardamom Rose Kulfi (page 266)
- c Pista Kesar Kulfi (page 266)
- d Aam Kulfi (page 265)
- e Doodh Seviyan (page 260)
- f Mishti Doi (page 259)
- g Sesame Jaggery Brittle (page 267)
- h Fruit Cream (page 263)

a Daal Makhani (page 63)
b Aloo Baingan (page 129)
c Murgh Makhani (page 151)
d Lachhedaar Paratha (page 200)

Aloo Baingan

EGGPLANT with TOMATO and POTATO

SERVES 6 • **COOK TIME:** *1 hour* • **PHOTO:** *page 129*

Jyoti This recipe is another common North Indian homestyle dish. Alongside a daal and a bowl of raita or Homemade Yogurt (page 40), it is a complete lunch or dinner. The amchoor, or dried mango powder, is my own addition—I love the layered acidity that results from the combination of amchoor and cooked-down tomatoes. Note that the tomatoes will release plenty of liquid as they cook. This is the liquid you're watching for in Step 4.

⅔ cup (160 ml) canola oil

2 medium russet potatoes (14 ounces // 400 g total), halved lengthwise and then cut crosswise into ¾-inch- (2-cm-) thick slices (see page 82)

1 cup (160 g) finely chopped yellow onion (about ⅔ medium onion)

1 large eggplant (1⅜ pounds // 615 g), stemmed, halved lengthwise, and cubed into 1¼-inch (3.2-cm) chunks

1½ cups (205 g) chopped tomato (¼-inch // 6-mm dice, about 1½ medium tomatoes)

⅝ cup (160 g) tomato puree, diluted with 5 tablespoons water (for a substitute, see Tomato Puree, page 83)

2 tablespoons grated, peeled fresh ginger

4½ teaspoons ground coriander

2 teaspoons amchoor (ground dried mango, see page 271)

1 teaspoon salt, plus more to taste

¼ teaspoon ground cayenne (optional)

Garnish
2 tablespoons finely chopped fresh cilantro, stems and leaves

1. Heat the oil in a large, lidded (but uncovered for now), nonstick pan over medium-high heat. Once the oil starts to shimmer, add the potato and onion and cook, stirring frequently, until both the potato and the onion pieces are browning at the edges, 8 to 10 minutes.

2. Add the eggplant and cook, stirring frequently, until the eggplant starts to brown at the edges and has soaked up all the oil, about 4 minutes.

3. Reduce the heat to medium. Add the chopped tomato, diluted tomato puree, ginger, coriander, amchoor, salt, and cayenne (if using). Stir well to incorporate.

4. Cover the pan and cook, stirring once or twice, until the potato pieces have totally softened (but still keep their shape) and most of the liquid has been absorbed or evaporated, 20 to 25 minutes. Taste for salt.

GARNISH

5. Garnish with cilantro. Serve hot.

Bharva Baingan

STUFFED EGGPLANT with MANGO and CORIANDER

SERVES 6 • COOK TIME: *50 minutes (longer if cooking in batches)* • PHOTO: *page 97*

Jyoti This dish is the eggplant-cousin of Bharva Bhindi (page 88). Indian eggplants, or globe eggplants, are small (roughly 3 inches // 7.5 cm long) and almost spherical. They should be available at any Indian grocery.

12 Indian, or small globe, eggplants (1½ pounds // 720 g total)

5 teaspoons ground coriander

1 tablespoon amchoor (ground dried mango, see page 271)

2 teaspoons ground cumin

2 teaspoons salt, plus more to taste

1 teaspoon ground turmeric

½ teaspoon ground cayenne (optional)

½ cup (120 ml) canola oil

1. Make two perpendicular lengthwise cuts from the base of each eggplant three-quarters of the way to the stem, such that each eggplant is almost split into quarters but remains intact **a**. Leave the stems attached.

2. Combine the coriander, amchoor, cumin, salt, turmeric, and cayenne (if using) in a small bowl. Amchoor has a tendency to stick together, so stir well to break up any clumps.

3. Stuff about 1 teaspoon of the masala into the cross-shaped cavity of each eggplant. Not all of the masala will stay in, so work over the masala bowl to catch what falls out. Reserve the remaining masala and set aside.

4. Heat the oil in a large, lidded (but uncovered for now) pan over medium heat. Once the oil starts to shimmer, add the stuffed eggplants flat in a single layer **b**. Each eggplant should touch the base of the pan, so work in batches for this step if necessary. Cook, undisturbed, until the skin in contact with the pan turns an iridescent brown-black, about 10 minutes.

5. Flip the eggplants and repeat on a second side, another 10 minutes.

6. If working in batches, reintroduce all of the cooked eggplant back into the pan and give the contents a good stir so the eggplants are browned on all sides. Sprinkle any leftover masala over the eggplants (not into the oil, if possible) and reduce the heat to medium-low. Cover the pan. Cook, undisturbed, until the eggplants are cooked through and totally soft, about 10 minutes.

7. Uncover and flip the eggplants once more. Cook for a couple of minutes to ensure the masala that was sprinkled on top gets fried.

8. Remove from the heat and taste for salt. Serve hot, and drizzle the spice-darkened oil over the dish when serving.

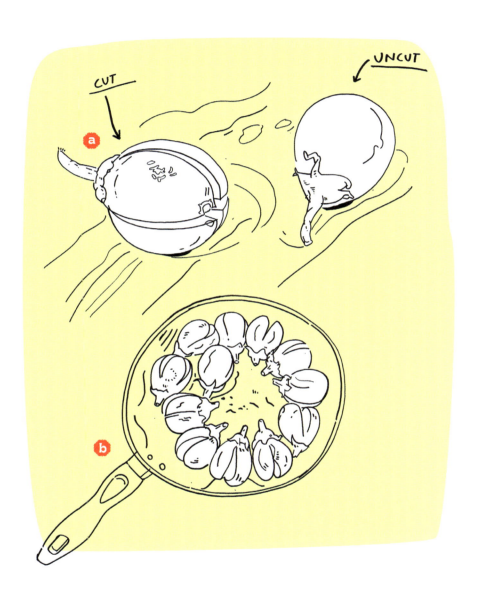

Baghare Baingan

EGGPLANT with COCONUT, SESAME, and TAMARIND

SERVES 6 • **THAW TIME:** *30 minutes*
COOK TIME: *1¾ hours* • **PHOTO:** *page 108*

Jyoti Baghare Baingan is the Cadillac of Indian eggplant preparations. It is both ingredient-intensive and involved, but the final product is truly exceptional. The combination of sesame seeds, peanuts, and coconut makes a rich, creamy base for the tangy, sweet-sour trifecta of fried spices, tamarind, and jaggery. Since it takes a bit of time to get everything together, I usually reserve this dish for special occasions and big get-togethers, but it can easily be made a day or two in advance and then rewarmed just before serving.

As with all of our recipes, we recommend you read through all the instructions first to get a sense of how things fit together. Since this dish involves so many interlocking parts, it wasn't possible to split it into separate sections (as we did with our other more-complicated recipes), so a careful pre-read is especially important.

Auyon Gastronomy has long been linked with the southeastern city of Hyderabad, where this dish originated. The city's royal flag once even featured a flatbread! The culinary association is due in part to a succession of opulent, wealthy rulers known as the Nizam dynasty, who ruled from 1724 until 1948. Gourmet one-upmanship among the royal family and noblemen was par for the course during their reign, with a curious focus on dishes that were made to look like other dishes—i.e. "rice and lentils" that were actually almonds and pistachios painstakingly sliced and carved to look like rice and green lentils, respectively. Before you get started on the following dish, we invite you to consider how long it might have taken to produce a whole platter's worth of fake rice and lentils, just to keep things in perspective.

½ cup (120 ml) + ¼ cup (60 ml) canola oil

2½ cups (360 g) chopped yellow onion (¼-inch // 6-mm dice, about 1 large onion)

12 Indian, or small globe, eggplants (1½ pounds // 720 g total)

½ teaspoon + 1 teaspoon salt, plus more to taste

¼ cup (35 g) raw, shelled peanuts

¼ cup (35 g) white sesame seeds

¼ cup (25 g) grated unsweetened coconut (see Frozen Coconut, page 78), thawed if frozen

1 tablespoon coriander seeds

1 tablespoon cumin seeds

1 ounce (30 g) peeled fresh ginger (equivalent to about 4 teaspoons grated fresh ginger)

5 cloves garlic

1 fresh Indian green chili (optional; see page 271—jalapeño may be substituted), finely chopped

4½ teaspoons tamarind paste (see page 277)

1 teaspoon jaggery (see Jaggery, opposite)

½ teaspoon ground turmeric

¼ teaspoon ground cayenne (optional)

1 teaspoon black or brown mustard seeds

1 teaspoon kalonji (nigella seeds, see page 274)

½ teaspoon methi (fenugreek) seeds

1 sprig fresh curry leaves, stripped from the stem (see page 273)

1. Heat ½ cup (120 ml) of the oil in a large, lidded (but uncovered for now) pan over medium-high heat. Once the oil starts to shimmer, add the onion and cook, stirring occasionally, until the onion is golden brown, deeper than oatmeal, with plenty of darker caramelized edges, about 15 minutes (see page 32).

2. Transfer the browned onion to a plate with a slotted spoon and set aside. Remove the pan from the heat but don't discard the oil.

3. Make two perpendicular lengthwise cuts from the base of each eggplant three-quarters of the way to the stem, such that each eggplant is almost split into quarters but remains in one piece (see page 131). Leave the stems intact.

4. Place ½ teaspoon of the salt into a small bowl and rub a pinch or two of it into the cut flesh of each eggplant.

5. Heat the oiled pan used for the onion over medium-high heat until the oil starts to shimmer. Add the eggplants. Make sure that each eggplant is touching the pan (and cook them in batches if your pan isn't large enough to accommodate them all). Cook, undisturbed, until the skin in contact with the pan has darkened to an iridescent brown-black, about 8 minutes.

6. Flip the eggplants and cook the other side to the same degree, an additional 8 minutes. Remove the pan from the heat but leave the eggplants in the pan, covered.

7. Heat a medium pan over medium heat. Once good and hot, add the peanuts, sesame, coconut, coriander, and cumin. Cook, stirring constantly, until the spices and nuts start to brown and emit a toasty aroma, about 5 minutes.

8. Transfer the peanut-sesame mixture to a plate or bowl to cool. Remove the pan from the heat, but don't wash it.

9. Using a blender or a food processor (or an impressive proficiency with a large mortar and pestle), combine the ginger, garlic, fresh chili (if using), and 1¼ cups (300 ml) water with the browned onion and cooled peanut mixture. Grind to a smooth paste. Add a tablespoon or two more water if necessary. (If using a blender, make sure to scrape down the sides of the machine a few times between blend attempts—a silicone spatula is handy here—to get any renegade seeds and spices properly incorporated.)

10. Add the tamarind, jaggery, turmeric, cayenne (if using), and remaining 1 teaspoon salt to the mixture. Grind or blend to combine.

11. In the same medium pan in which you roasted the nuts and spices, heat the remaining ¼ cup (60 ml) oil over medium heat. Once the oil starts to shimmer, add the mustard seeds and cook, undisturbed, until they are popping vigorously, about 30 seconds (watch out for oil splatter—use a splatter screen if you have one).

12. Add the kalonji and methi seeds. Sizzle, giving the pan a shake or two, until the methi seeds darken and redden a couple of shades, another 20 seconds.

13. Stir in the curry leaves and watch out for oil splatter—use a splatter screen if you have one. Cook, giving the pan a shake to evenly distribute them, until the leaves crisp up, about 10 seconds. If it's hard to tell visually, you should be able to feel the texture change while stirring them around in the pan.

14. Finally, add the onion-coconut paste and stir to incorporate into the oil. Cook, stirring frequently, until heated through, about 3 minutes. Add 1½ cups (360 ml) water to the mixture and stir thoroughly to incorporate.

15. On a separate burner, place the large pan with the eggplants over medium-high heat. Pour the onion-coconut-spice masala over the eggplants. Using a butter knife or spatula, carefully widen the slits in each eggplant, one by one, to allow the masala to better penetrate. Once the mixture comes to a gentle boil, reduce the heat to medium, cover, and cook until the eggplant is totally tender, 10 to 12 minutes.

16. Remove from the heat and let rest for 15 minutes, covered, for the flavors to meld before serving. Taste for salt and serve hot, making sure to drizzle a bit of the masala into the cavity of each eggplant.

Jaggery

Jaggery, or gur, is unrefined cane or palm sugar, produced by boiling down sugarcane juice or palm sap. It is available at all Indian markets either in block form or broken up into pieces. Dark brown sugar is an acceptable substitute.

Mattar Paneer

FRESH CHEESE with PEAS and TOMATO

SERVES 4 • COOK TIME: *1 hour* • PHOTO: *page 106*

Jyoti This dish, another Punjabi favorite, is a celebration of fresh cheese disguised as a pea-and-tomato preparation. We encourage you to make your own Paneer (page 46), but store-bought is totally fine. If you have neither access to paneer nor the time to make it, the veggies can of course work without it, but we recommend holding off on this dish until you have some paneer handy. For the dairy-averse, baked extra-firm tofu is a decent substitute.

The frying process in the first step of this recipe (and that of Saag Paneer, page 136) is admittedly painstaking, but it goes relatively quickly. In addition to being delicious, the resultant crisped crust helps keep homemade paneer pieces intact. A true nonstick pan really helps. If you don't have one available, use a few more tablespoons of oil, and wait to flip each piece until the fried edge releases easily from the pan. Even with extra fat and patience, know that some pieces may still fuse to the pan.

The frying is optional for store-bought paneer, which is more heavily compacted and does not need to be fried to maintain its integrity.

4 to 5 tablespoons canola oil, as needed

12 ounces (340 g) paneer (store-bought or homemade, page 46), cubed into bite-size pieces (about 2 cups)

2 Indian bay leaves

One 3-inch (7.5-cm) cinnamon stick

1 black cardamom pod, cracked open so the seeds are exposed

1 cup (235 g) blended or grated yellow onion (about 1 medium onion, see Onion Blending, page 144)

⅝ cup (160 g) tomato puree, diluted with 5 tablespoons water (for a substitute, see Tomato Puree, page 83)

4 teaspoons grated, peeled fresh ginger

1 teaspoon cumin seeds, roasted (lightly!) and ground (see page 43)

1 teaspoon coriander seeds, roasted and ground with the cumin

1 teaspoon salt

½ teaspoon ground turmeric

3 cups (455 g) frozen peas, no need to thaw

Garnish

2 tablespoons finely chopped fresh cilantro, stems and leaves

¼ teaspoon garam masala (store-bought or homemade, page 53)

1. If using homemade paneer, heat 1 tablespoon of oil in a large, lidded (but uncovered for now), nonstick pan over medium-low heat. (If using store-bought, skip to Step 4.) Once the oil starts to shimmer, add a single layer of paneer pieces, lying flat.

2. After about 75 seconds, gently flip one piece with a spoon or butter knife. Don't scratch your pan! If the paneer piece is cooked (it should have a crispy, orange-brown crust with a marbling of white paneer peeking through), quickly remove the pan from the heat and carefully flip the rest of the pieces, one at a time.

3. Place the pan back on the stove and cook the other side of the paneer pieces for another 75 seconds or so. Remove from the heat and transfer the pieces to a plate to cool. Repeat with the remaining paneer until all the pieces are fried on the two broad sides.

4. Add 4 tablespoons of oil to the same large pan (no need to wash it once the paneer is removed) over medium heat. Once the oil starts to shimmer, add the bay leaves, cinnamon stick, and cardamom pod. Sizzle, giving the pan a shake or two, until the spices darken a couple of shades and become fragrant, about 30 seconds.

5. Add the onion and watch out for oil splatter—use a splatter screen if you have one. Cook, stirring frequently, until the onion is well browned, darker than golden, with plenty of even darker caramelized flecks, 12 to 15 minutes. This browning is crucial to the flavor of the dish, so don't undercook (see page 32). If you notice the onion starting to burn before it gets to the right color, stir more often. You may need to cook for a bit longer if the onion doesn't seem dark enough.

6. Add the diluted tomato puree, ginger, ground cumin and ground coriander, salt, and turmeric. Cook, stirring frequently, until the oil starts to separate out of the masala (see page 162), about 3 minutes.

7. Add the peas and stir well for a minute to combine thoroughly.

8. Add 1½ cups (360 ml) water and stir to combine, then gently fold in the paneer. Cover the pan and bring the mixture to a boil. Cook at a rolling boil for 2 minutes.

9. Remove the pan from the heat and let rest, covered, for 10 minutes before serving. This is not a dry dish—the paneer and peas should be partially submerged in gravy. Taste for salt.

GARNISH
10. Garnish with cilantro and garam masala. Serve hot.

Serving Tips

→ The bay leaves, cinnamon stick, and cardamom pod in the final dish are not meant to be eaten and should be moved to the side of the plate—warn your guests.

→ This dish may thicken as it cools, especially if left uncovered. If cooking in advance, you may need to add ¼ cup (60 ml) boiling water (or bring the mixture to a boil after adding tap water) to get it back to the right consistency.

PROPERLY FRIED PANEER

Saag Paneer

FRESH CHEESE with CREAMY GREENS and GINGER

SERVES 4 • **COOK TIME:** *1 hour, plus time to cool if using a ventless stand blender* • **PHOTO:** *page 116*

Jyoti Although the Hindustani word *saag* is often simply translated to "spinach" on restaurant menus, "greens" is a more accurate translation. Most recipes call for a mix of at least a few different greens. This preparation is one of our favorite versions—it includes mustard greens, fenugreek leaves, and a bit of broccoli in addition to the spinach, striking just the right balance of earthy bitterness and subtle sweetness.

We recommend making your own Paneer (page 46), but store-bought is totally fine. If you have neither access to paneer nor the time to make it, you can substitute cooked and seasoned chickpeas, boiled and seasoned potatoes, baked extra-firm tofu, or cooked meat or poultry. Saag is also great unadorned, especially when served alongside a hot flatbread and a dollop of Homemade Yogurt (page 40).

See page 134 for some tips on Step 1 of this recipe (frying the paneer).

- 4 to 5 tablespoons canola oil, as needed
- 12 ounces (340 g) paneer (store-bought or homemade, page 46), cubed into bite-size pieces (about 2 cups)
- 1½ cups (235 g) chopped yellow onion (¼-inch // 6-mm dice, about 1 medium onion)
- 4 cloves garlic, finely chopped
- ⅝ cup (160 g) tomato puree, diluted with 5 tablespoons water (for a substitute, see Tomato Puree, page 83)
- 10 ounces (285 g) frozen spinach (about 3 cups when roughly broken up)
- 3 ounces (85 g) frozen mustard greens (about 1 cup when roughly broken up)
- 1 cup (75 g) roughly chopped broccoli florets, fresh or frozen
- 1 tablespoon coarsely ground Kasuri methi (dried fenugreek leaves, see page 275; 3 tablespoons finely chopped fresh methi or 1 tablespoon frozen methi may be substituted)
- 1 teaspoon salt, plus more to taste
- ¼ teaspoon ground cayenne (optional)
- ⅔ cup (160 ml) whole milk
- 2 tablespoons unsalted butter
- 1 tablespoon julienned fresh ginger (cut into short, thin matchsticks, see page 245)

1. If using homemade paneer, heat 1 tablespoon of oil in a large, nonstick pan over medium-low heat. (If using store-bought, skip to Step 4.) Once the oil starts to shimmer, add a single layer of paneer pieces, lying flat.

2. After about 75 seconds, gently flip one piece with a spoon or butter knife. Don't scratch your pan! If it is cooked (it should have a crispy, orange-brown crust with a marbling of white paneer peeking through), quickly remove the pan from the heat and carefully flip the rest of the pieces, one at a time.

3. Place the pan back on the stove and cook the other side of the paneer pieces for another 75 seconds or so. Remove from the heat and transfer the pieces to a plate to cool. Repeat with the remaining paneer until all the pieces are fried on the two broad sides.

4. Add 4 tablespoons of oil to the same large pan (no need to wash it once the paneer is removed) over medium heat. Once the oil starts to shimmer, add the onion and cook, stirring occasionally, until the onion is soft, translucent, and just starting to brown at the edges, 8 to 10 minutes.

5. Add the garlic and stir to incorporate. Add the diluted tomato puree and cook to heat through, another minute or two.

6. Add the spinach, mustard greens, broccoli, and methi to the pan and cover. Cook, stirring occasionally, until the broccoli has totally softened and the greens have darkened and dulled to a deep olive green, 12 to 15 minutes.

7. Remove from the heat and let rest, covered, for 15 minutes.

8. Add the salt and cayenne (if using) and stir to incorporate. Cool to lukewarm, uncovered. (Feel free to skip the cooling and move on to the next step if using a Vitamix or similar fancy blender with a steam vent—just be sure the steam vent is open.)

9. Transfer the cooled broccoli-spinach mixture to a blender. Add the milk and grind, with the blender lid cracked ever so slightly away from you, until smooth (a slightly chunky texture is fine too). Set aside.

10. In the same pan that the greens were cooked in (no need to wash it), heat the butter over medium heat. As soon as the butter has melted completely, add the ginger and sizzle, stirring to coat, for a minute (or for a few minutes more if you want to crisp it up).

11. Add the blended greens and cook to heat through, another minute or two. The consistency should be akin to that of a thick porridge.

12. Fold in the paneer. Taste for salt and serve hot.

Serving Tip

→ If prepared in advance, the saag may thicken a bit. Add some boiled milk (or bring the whole dish to a gentle boil after adding the milk) to get the texture right.

Jeera Mattar

PEAS with CUMIN, GINGER, and GREEN CHILI

SERVES 4 • COOK TIME: *25 minutes* • PHOTO: *page 97*

Jyoti Some of my fondest childhood memories are of returning home from school with my older brother Deepak, racing into the house in eager anticipation of whatever snack my mother had prepared for us that afternoon. These gingery peas, usually accompanied by two tall glasses of milk, were a favored feature in the colder months.

¼ cup (60 ml) canola oil

1½ teaspoons cumin seeds

4 teaspoons grated, peeled fresh ginger

1 fresh Indian green chili (optional; see page 271—jalapeño may be substituted), minced

3 cups (455 g) frozen peas, no need to thaw

½ teaspoon salt, plus more to taste

Garnish

1 tablespoon fresh lemon juice, plus more to taste

2 tablespoons finely chopped fresh cilantro, stems and leaves

1. Heat the oil in a large pan over medium-high heat. Once the oil starts to shimmer, add the cumin seeds and sizzle, giving the pan a shake or two, until they darken a couple of shades and become fragrant, about 30 seconds.

2. Add the ginger and chili (if using) and cook for an additional 20 seconds, stirring constantly to prevent the mixture from scorching.

3. Add the peas and salt. Cook, stirring occasionally, until the peas are cooked through, about 7 minutes. Don't overcook the peas to dullness—they should retain their bright green hue. Most of the liquid released by the peas should evaporate, but a bit of moisture should remain.

GARNISH

4. Just before serving, stir in the lemon juice. Taste for salt and lemon. Garnish with cilantro. Serve hot or at room temperature.

Bhutta Chaat

CORN with GINGER, LEMON, and CILANTRO

SERVES 4 • **COOK TIME:** *30 minutes* • **PHOTO:** *page 104*

Jyoti This recipe features both a short ingredient list and a simple process, but the trade-off is that it leans heavily on the freshness and quality of the starring vegetable. We therefore recommend saving it for summertime, when sweet corn is at its peak. Like Jeera Mattar (opposite), this preparation works well as both a vegetable side dish and an afternoon snack.

- 4 ears fresh corn (1¾ pounds // 780 g total)
- 2 teaspoons canola oil
- ½ fresh Indian green chili (optional; see page 271—jalapeño may be substituted), minced
- 1 tablespoon fresh lemon juice, plus more to taste
- 1 tablespoon finely chopped fresh cilantro, stems and leaves
- 1 teaspoon grated, peeled fresh ginger
- ½ teaspoon salt, plus more to taste
- A few generous grinds of black pepper

1. Over a large bowl, scrape the kernels off of the corn cobs using a sharp knife. Discard the stripped cobs. (If you're so inclined, the stripped cobs can be saved and used to make a quick corn stock for soup.)

2. Heat the oil in a medium pan over medium-high heat. Once the oil starts to shimmer, add the corn kernels and cook, stirring frequently, until the kernels are speckled with plenty of toasty brown flecks, 8 to 10 minutes.

3. Remove from the heat and stir in the green chili (if using), lemon juice, cilantro, ginger, salt, and black pepper. Taste for salt and lemon. Serve hot.

CHAPTER FOUR

Poultry, Meat, and Fish

Murgh Kaali Mirch

DRY CHICKEN CURRY with GARLIC and BLACK PEPPER

SERVES 6 • **COOK TIME:** *1½ hours* • **PHOTO:** *page 119*

Jyoti Don't be put off by what looks like an enormous amount of garlic and black pepper in the ingredient list. Their combined sharpness is tempered by the cooking process, resulting in a flavor that is enticingly piquant and surprisingly balanced. As with Bhuna Gosht (page 162), the word *dry* in the English title refers to the dish's low moisture content—the tender chunks of meat and potato will be surrounded by a thick, concentrated mixture of oil and ground spices. A nonstick pan is crucial to getting the texture just right. We recommend serving this dish with flatbread rather than with rice.

Auyon The chicken traces its lineage back to the red junglefowl *Gallus gallus*, indigenous to Southeast Asia. The meat is favored across India, especially in the northern region of Punjab. The bird is always skinned before cooking for hygienic reasons (the skin is thought to be unclean) and for superior flavor penetration.

- 20 cloves garlic (2¼ ounces // 120 g, about 2 heads)
- ⅔ cup (160 ml) canola oil
- 1½ cups (360 g) blended or grated yellow onion (about 1 large onion, see Onion Blending, page 144)
- 2 tablespoons grated, peeled fresh ginger
- 2 pounds (910 g) skinless, fat-trimmed chicken thighs (see Bone-In, below), cut into 1½-inch (4-cm) chunks
- 2 medium russet potatoes (14 ounces // 400 g total), peeled, halved lengthwise, and then cut crosswise into 1-inch- (2.5-cm-) thick slices
- 1½ teaspoons salt, plus more to taste
- ¼ cup (35 g) whole black peppercorns, coarsely crushed
- Boiling water (optional), as needed

Garnish
- 2 tablespoons finely chopped fresh cilantro, stems and leaves
- 1 tablespoon cumin seeds, roasted (lightly!) and ground (see page 43)

Bone-In

If possible, include a few bone-in chicken thighs as part of the 2 pounds (910 g) of meat, as they will improve the flavor. Cut each bone-in thigh in half through the bone with a sturdy pair of kitchen shears to expose the marrow, then cut each half into three pieces for a total of six chunks per thigh (or fewer if the thighs are small).

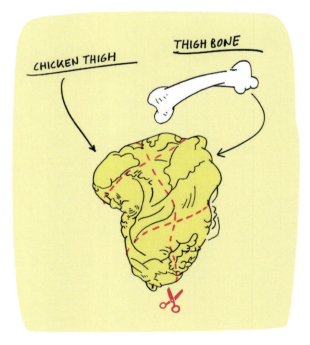

1. Grind the garlic to a smooth paste using a blender, small food processor, or mortar and pestle. You can add a tablespoon or two of water to keep things moving, but the paste should remain quite thick. Set aside.

2. Heat the oil in a large, lidded (but uncovered for now), nonstick pan over medium-high heat. Once the oil starts to shimmer, add the onion and watch out for oil splatter—use a splatter screen if you have one. Cook, stirring occasionally, until the onion is soft and cooked through but not yet starting to brown, about 8 minutes.

3. Stir in the garlic paste and ginger. Cook, stirring constantly, for a couple of minutes to heat through.

4. Add the chicken, potatoes, and salt. Keep the heat at medium-high. Cook, stirring frequently, until the chicken is totally opaque, the potato is slightly translucent, and everything is starting to brown a bit (especially the onions), 15 to 20 minutes.

5. Cover the pan and reduce the heat to medium. Cook for about 10 minutes, stirring once or twice, but making sure to replace the lid quickly to preserve steam. The chicken and potato should both start to develop a brown crust.

6. Add the black pepper and stir well to combine. Cover the pan and cook, undisturbed, until the potato pieces have totally softened but still keep their shape, another 5 to 7 minutes. The final dish should have a dark brown onion-and-spice masala that clings to the chicken and potatoes, with a small amount of oil at the bottom of the pan. Add a bit of boiling water (or bring the mixture to a boil after adding tap water) to correct the consistency, or if you want the dish to be saucier.

7. Turn the heat off and keep the dish covered. Let rest, undisturbed, for at least 15 minutes before serving. Taste for salt.

GARNISH

8. Garnish with cilantro and roasted cumin powder. Serve hot.

Serving Tip

→ This dish may thicken as it cools, especially if left uncovered. If cooking in advance, you may need to add ¼ cup (60 ml) boiling water (or bring the mixture to a boil after adding tap water) to get it back to the right consistency.

Murgh Do Pyaaza

DOUBLE ONION CHICKEN CURRY

SERVES 4 • **COOK TIME:** 1¾ hours • **PHOTO:** page 105

Auyon Alliums like onion and garlic are now beloved ingredients across the subcontinent (with a few notable exceptions—see Heeng, page 274), but it was not always so. Ancient Sanskrit texts only mention onions dismissively, as a food of the contemptible non-Aryan natives.

The prejudice persisted: a Tan Dynasty Buddhist monk named Yijing who toured India in the eighth century CE reported that onions were forbidden because they "caused pain, spoiled the eyesight, and weakened the body." Hogwash. We like to think of this recipe, which doubles down on the alliums by including both onions and shallots, as a good way to make up for lost time.

Jyoti As with all our recipes, remember that the physical and sensory cues are just as important as the estimated times we've given. Trust your eyes and nose as much as the clock. Relatedly, we recommend setting out, measuring, and chopping all ingredients before turning the stove on, so that you can focus all your attention on the cooking once it starts.

- 4 cloves
- 6 black peppercorns
- 2 black cardamom pods
- ⅔ cup (160 ml) canola oil
- One 3-inch (7.5-cm) cinnamon stick
- ¼ teaspoon cumin seeds
- 2 pounds (910 g) skinless, fat-trimmed chicken thighs (see Bone-In, page 142), cut into 1½-inch (4-cm) chunks
- 1½ cups (360 g) blended or grated yellow onion (about 1 large onion, see Onion Blending, below)
- ⅝ cup (160 g) tomato puree, diluted with 5 tablespoons water (for a substitute, see Tomato Puree, page 83)
- 6 cloves garlic, finely chopped
- 4 teaspoons grated, peeled fresh ginger
- 1 teaspoon ground Kashmiri chili (see page 271)
- 1 teaspoon salt, plus more to taste
- ½ teaspoon ground cinnamon
- ½ teaspoon ground turmeric
- ¼ teaspoon ground cayenne (optional)
- 12 whole, peeled shallots (15½ ounces // 440 g total) with the root ends trimmed
- Boiling water (optional), as needed

Garnish
- 1 teaspoon garam masala (store-bought or homemade, page 53)

Onion Blending

Blending the onion will likely require a food processor or grinder. We recommend against adding any water to speed things along, and most stand blenders aren't quite up to the task. Also, we recommend grinding the onion just before using it—if the blended mixture sits for more than a couple of minutes, the liquid will separate from the solids and spit violently when it hits the oil.

1. Use a mortar and pestle to coarsely crush the cloves and black peppercorns. Add the cardamom pods to the mortar and crack them open so that the seeds are exposed.

2. Heat the oil in a large, lidded (but uncovered for now) pan over medium-high heat. Once the oil starts to shimmer, add the cloves, black peppercorns, cardamom pods, cinnamon stick, and cumin seeds. Cook, giving the pan a shake or two, until the lighter spices darken a couple of shades and all the spices become fragrant, about 30 seconds.

3. Add the chicken and cook, stirring frequently, until the chicken is totally opaque and just starting to brown, 6 to 8 minutes. Work in batches if your pan isn't big enough to comfortably accommodate the meat. It doesn't necessarily need to all fit in one layer, but if the chicken looks like it's boiling or steaming rather than browning (due to the liquid it releases), it's too tightly packed.

4. Remove the chicken from the pan using tongs or a slotted spoon, cover, and set aside.

5. Immediately add the onion to the hot pan—watch out for oil splatter, and use a splatter screen if you have one. Cook, stirring frequently, until the onion is golden brown, deeper than oatmeal, with plenty of darker, caramelized flecks, 10 to 15 minutes. This browning is crucial to the flavor of the dish, so don't undercook (see page 32). If you notice the onion starting to burn before it gets to the right color, stir more often and lower the heat to medium. You may need to cook for a bit longer if the onion doesn't seem dark enough.

6. Reduce the heat to medium. Add the diluted tomato puree, garlic, ginger, Kashmiri chili, salt, ground cinnamon, turmeric, and cayenne (if using). Cook, stirring frequently, until the mixture thickens and the oil starts to separate out of the masala (see page 162), about 4 minutes.

7. Add the cooked chicken, and any released juices, back into the pan. Stir well to coat, then add ½ cup (120 ml) water. Cover the pan and cook, undisturbed, at a steady boil for about 10 minutes. Meanwhile, make a deep incision into the root end of each peeled shallot, about two-thirds of the way to the tip.

8. Give the meat a stir, add the shallots, then cover the pan. Keep the heat at medium. Cook, stirring once or twice, until the shallots, which should open up like two-petaled flowers, have largely softened, 8 to 10 minutes. The final dish should have a thick masala that clings to the chicken pieces. Add a bit of boiling water (or bring the mixture to a boil after adding tap water) to correct the consistency, or if you want the dish to be saucier.

GARNISH

9. Turn the heat off and keep the dish covered. Let rest, undisturbed, for at least 15 minutes before serving. Garnish with garam masala. Taste for salt and serve hot.

Serving Tips

→ The black cardamom pods and the cinnamon stick in the final dish are not meant to be eaten and should be moved to the side of the plate—warn your guests. The crushed cloves are totally edible and we love them, but they can be pushed aside as well if the flavor is too intense.

→ This dish may thicken as it cools, especially if left uncovered. If cooking in advance, you may need to add ¼ cup (60 ml) boiling water (or bring the mixture to a boil after adding tap water) to get it back to the right consistency.

Murgh Hariyali

GREEN CURRY CHICKEN

SERVES 6 • **MARINATION TIME:** *4½ hours*
COOK TIME: *75 minutes* • **PHOTO:** *page 102*

Jyoti This fresh, green curry gets its color from cilantro, broccoli, spinach, and fenugreek. The generous mix of greens precludes the need for an additional vegetable side, making it a complete meal alongside rice (or flatbread) and a bowl of Homemade Yogurt (page 40).

Auyon According to historian Colleen Taylor Sen, the prevalence of slow-cooked curries in Indian cuisine may be linked to the institution of the joint family, wherein an extended family lives together under one roof. In contrast to stir-frying and other cooking methods that benefit from prompt dining, long-simmering is more forgiving—an attractive feature when catering to multiple people who might be eating on slightly different schedules.

Marinade

2½ cups (115 g) roughly chopped, lightly packed fresh cilantro stems and leaves (2 generous bunches should be enough for both this and the cilantro needed for the masala)

½ cup (120 ml) canola oil

6 cloves garlic

1 fresh Indian green chili (optional; see page 271—jalapeño may be substituted), chopped

1 tablespoon fresh lemon juice

½ ounce (15 g) peeled fresh ginger (equivalent to about 2 teaspoons grated fresh ginger)

1½ teaspoons coarsely ground Kasuri methi (dried fenugreek leaves, see page 275; 4½ teaspoons finely chopped fresh methi or 1½ teaspoons frozen methi may be substituted)

1 teaspoon salt

¼ teaspoon ground cayenne (optional)

2 pounds (910 g) skinless, fat-trimmed chicken thighs (see Bone-In, page 142), cut into 1½-inch (4-cm) chunks

1 large russet potato (11¼ ounces // 320 g), halved lengthwise and then cut crosswise into 1-inch- (2.5-cm-) thick slices (see page 82)

Masala

½ cup (120 ml) canola oil

1 cup (235 g) blended or grated yellow onion (about 1 medium onion, see Onion Blending, page 144)

5 ounces (140 g) frozen spinach (about 1½ cups when roughly broken up)

½ cup (50 g) chopped broccoli florets (¼-inch // 6-mm dice), fresh or frozen and thawed

1 cup (45 g) roughly chopped, lightly packed fresh cilantro stems and leaves

Boiling water (optional), as needed

Salt, to taste

MARINADE

1. Grind the cilantro, oil, garlic, fresh chili (if using), lemon juice, ginger, methi, salt, and cayenne (if using) to a smooth paste using a blender, food processor, or mortar and pestle. (If using a blender, note that it may take scraping down the sides of the blender and stirring between attempts—a silicone spatula is handy here—to get everything properly incorporated. Resist the temptation to add any additional liquid.)

2. Place the chicken and potato in a large bowl. Transfer the blended marinade to the bowl and massage the paste into each piece of meat and potato with your hands. Cover the mixture and marinate in the fridge for at least 4 hours (and up to 8).

MASALA

3. Heat the oil in a large, lidded (but uncovered for now), nonstick pan over medium-high heat. Once the oil starts to shimmer, add the onion and marinated potato (but not the chicken)—watch out for oil splatter, and use a splatter screen if you have one. Cook, stirring frequently, until the potato pieces are lightly fried on most sides and are starting to brown, and plenty of caramelized flecks are visible in the onion puree, 12 to 15 minutes. The onion browning will be subtle due to the green color introduced by the marinated potato, but it is crucial to the flavor of the dish, so don't undercook (see page 32). If you notice the onion starting to burn before it gets to the right color, stir more often. You may need to cook for a bit longer if the onion doesn't seem dark enough.

4. Add any marinated bone-in chicken pieces (if using) to the pan and cook, stirring frequently, until the bone-in pieces turn opaque on all sides, about 5 minutes.

5. Reduce the heat to medium. Add the spinach, broccoli, remaining marinated chicken pieces, and any excess marinade to the pan. Cook, stirring frequently, until all of the chicken pieces are opaque on all sides, another 5 minutes.

6. Stir well and reduce the heat to medium-low. Cover the pan and cook until the potato pieces have softened completely but still hold their shape, 20 to 25 minutes. Stir gently every few minutes to make sure nothing sticks to the pan. The chicken and greens will release plenty of liquid as they cook.

7. While the potato and chicken are cooking, combine the cilantro with ¼ cup (60 ml) water and grind to a smooth puree using a blender, food processor, or mortar and pestle. (Again, if using a blender, it may take scraping down the sides and stirring between attempts to get everything properly incorporated.)

8. When the chicken and potato are done cooking, stir the cilantro puree into the pan. Bring the mixture to a gentle boil. The final dish should have a thick, porridge-like curry surrounding the meat and potatoes. Add a bit of boiling water (or bring the mixture to a boil after adding tap water) to correct the consistency, or if you want the dish to be saucier.

9. Turn the heat off and keep the dish covered. Let rest, undisturbed, for at least 15 minutes before serving. Taste for salt and serve hot.

Serving Tip

→ This dish may thicken as it cools, especially if left uncovered. If cooking in advance, you may need to add ¼ cup (60 ml) boiling water (or bring the mixture to a boil after adding tap water) to get it back to the right consistency.

Murgh Rezala

CHICKEN CURRY with WATER LILY SEEDS and CASHEWS

SERVES 4 • **MARINATION TIME:** *2½ hours*
COOK TIME: *1¾ hours* • **PHOTO:** *page 113*

Auyon The roots of this dish trace back to the elaborate Indo-Persian cuisine of the Mughal empire, which began in 1526 with the arrival of the Central Asian ruler Babur and persisted until 1858, when the empire was formally dissolved by the British Raj. Today, Murgh Rezala is a Kolkata Muslim specialty, said to have arrived in Bengal in the mid-nineteenth century along with one of the nawabs, or local rulers, deposed by the British. Wajid Ali Shah, the eleventh and final nawab of Awadh, landed in Bengal along with a large retinue of musicians, dancers, cooks, advisors, and of course, recipes.

The opulence here is apparent. A garnish of two different hydrosols (rose water and kewra water) lend it a beguiling, perfumed quality. The poppy-thickened curry (a suspected Bengali modification) and the delightful chew of phool makhana, or puffed water lily seeds, are also hallmarks.

Marinade

- ½ cup (120 ml) warm water
- 14 raw unsalted cashews
- 2 teaspoons white poppy seeds
- 2 pounds (910 g) skinless, fat-trimmed chicken thighs (see Bone-In, page 142), cut into 1½-inch (4-cm) chunks
- 1 large yellow onion (14½ ounces // 410 g), cut into rough chunks
- 8 cloves garlic
- 1 fresh Indian green chili (optional; see page 271—jalapeño may be substituted), finely chopped
- ½ cup (120 g) whole, unflavored yogurt (store-bought or homemade, page 40), stirred
- 2 teaspoons black peppercorns, coarsely crushed
- 1 teaspoon salt

Masala

- 2 cups (30 g) phool makhana (see Note, page 150)
- 5 cloves
- 8 black peppercorns
- 3 green cardamom pods
- 1 black cardamom pod
- 3 tablespoons canola oil
- 3 tablespoons unsalted ghee (store-bought or homemade, page 38)
- 3 Indian bay leaves
- 2 dried red chilies, broken into thirds (see page 271)
- One 3-inch (7.5-cm) cinnamon stick
- 3 blades mace (see page 275)
- ½ teaspoon salt
- Boiling water (optional), as needed

Garnish

- 1 teaspoon rose water (see page 276)
- 1 teaspoon kewra water (see page 275)
- ½ teaspoon garam masala (store-bought or homemade, page 53)
- Salt, to taste

Poppy Seeds

Arab traders introduced opium (dried latex from the seedpods of the opium poppy) to India in the eleventh and twelfth centuries. The seeds themselves, which have no narcotic effect, were merely a by-product of opium production for a few hundred years. By the fifteenth or sixteenth century, the seeds had found their way into the Islamic Indian kitchen, where they were often employed as a thickening agent for meat preparations.

MARINADE

1. Combine the warm water, cashews, and poppy seeds in a small bowl. Set aside to soak at room temperature while the meat marinates.

2. Place the chicken in a large container or bowl. Grind the onion, garlic, and fresh chili (if using) to a smooth puree using a blender, food processor, or mortar and pestle.

3. Pour the puree over the chicken, then add the yogurt, crushed black pepper, and salt—do not blend the yogurt, as doing so could compromise the texture. Mix well by hand, and make sure to massage the marinade into each piece of meat. Cover the mixture and marinate in the fridge for at least 2 hours (and up to 4).

MASALA

4. Heat a medium pan over medium heat. Once good and hot, add the phool makhana and cook, stirring constantly, until they take on a light brown, toasted marshmallow color, about 5 minutes. The coloring will be uneven, but be sure to keep the seeds moving to avoid blackened hot spots. Remove from the heat and immediately transfer to a plate to cool.

5. Use a mortar and pestle to coarsely crush the cloves and black peppercorns. Add both the green and black cardamom pods to the mortar and crack them open so that the seeds are exposed. Set aside.

6. Heat the oil and ghee in a large, lidded (but uncovered for now) pan over medium-high heat. Once the oil starts to shimmer, add the bay leaves, dried chilies, and cinnamon. Cook, giving the pan a shake or two, until the spices darken a couple of shades and become fragrant, about 30 seconds.

7. Add the crushed spices (cloves, black peppercorns, green cardamom, and black cardamom) and mace, and cook, giving the pan another shake, until the second round of spices darken a bit and become fragrant, another 45 seconds.

8. Moving quickly, transfer half of the chicken to the pan, but try to remove and reserve as much of the onion marinade as possible from each piece before adding. All of the chicken pieces should fit in a single layer, but if the pan looks crowded, work in smaller batches. Keep the heat at medium-high and cook, undisturbed, until the chicken is beginning to brown at the edges on the bottom, 3 to 5 minutes. Flip and cook the other side to the same point, another 5 minutes or so.

9. Using tongs or a slotted spoon, remove the chicken pieces from the pan once the edges are lightly browned on both sides. Some of the pieces may need an extra minute or two if they were put in later, and it is okay if a few of the spices come out with the chicken.

10. Repeat with the remaining chicken pieces. Since the chicken releases water as it cooks, the second batch may not brown as evenly as the first (and some pieces might not brown much at all, which is fine).

11. Once the last batch of the chicken has been cooked, add all of the meat back into the pan along with the reserved onion marinade and the salt. Cook, stirring frequently, until the masala darkens to a golden beige and the smell of raw onion is no longer perceptible, 15 to 20 minutes.

12. Reduce the heat to medium and cover the pan. Cook, undisturbed, for about 6 minutes. The chicken should release a bit more liquid and the masala should darken a shade or two. In the meantime, grind the poppy seeds and cashews into their soaking liquid using a blender.

13. Add the toasted phool makhana, cashew-poppy puree, and 3 tablespoons water. Stir to combine. Reduce the heat to low, cover the pan, and cook for a final 5 minutes to allow the flavors to meld.

recipe continues

Murgh Rezala
· continued ·

14. Turn the heat off. The final consistency of the masala should be thick but still fluid, and it should cling to the chicken pieces and water lily seeds. Add a bit of boiling water (or bring the mixture to a boil after adding tap water) to correct the consistency, or if you want the dish to be saucier.

GARNISH

15. Garnish with rose water, kewra water, and garam masala. Stir to incorporate.

16. Cover the pan. Let rest, undisturbed, for at least 15 minutes before serving. Taste for salt and serve hot.

Serving Tips

→ The black cardamom pods, bay leaves, dried chilies, cinnamon stick, and mace in the final dish are not meant to be eaten and should be moved to the side of the plate—warn your guests. The crushed cloves and green cardamom pods are totally edible and we love them, but they can be pushed aside as well if the flavor is too intense.

→ This dish may thicken as it cools, especially if left uncovered. If cooking in advance, you may need to add ¼ cup (60 ml) boiling water (or bring the mixture to a boil after adding tap water) to get it back to the right consistency.

Note

Phool makhana, also known as fox nuts, are made from the starchy, white seeds of the prickly water lily or Gorgon plant (*Euryale ferox*). The dried seeds are roasted and popped much like popcorn. Phool makhana should be available at any Indian grocery.

Murgh Makhani

BUTTER CHICKEN

SERVES 4 • **MARINATION TIME:** *4½ hours*
COOK TIME: *1 hour* • **PHOTO:** *page 128*

Jyoti This recipe is really two dishes in one. The first is chicken tikka, a marinated skewer traditionally cooked in tandoor (see below). The second recipe, butter masala, is what brings the extravagance: butter, tomato, spices, and oil combine to create the dish's rich, signature sauce.

A few logistical notes: The oven portion of this recipe can be done on a grill, too. Just make sure the internal temperature of the chicken gets up to at least 165°F (74°C). Skewers will be necessary either way, whether you choose the oven or the grill. If using wooden skewers, be sure to soak them for at least half an hour before using. Lastly, the chicken tikka may be cooked in advance, but make the masala just before serving.

Auyon Before the magic of central heating, ovens served to both cook food and heat the home. Such a dual-function cooking apparatus never made much sense in the subtropical climate of India, which explains why traditional recipes rarely call for roasting or the use of an oven.

The notable exception to India's ovenlessness is the tandoor, a cylindrical clay oven from the northern transnational region of Punjab, which comprises both the Indian state and a Pakistani province. For more on how the tandoor became symbolic of Indian cuisine worldwide thanks to a pair of identically monikered entrepreneurs in the mid-twentieth century, see page 155.

Marinade + Tikka

2 pounds (910 g) chicken tenders, cubed into 1½-inch (4-cm) chunks (see Notes, page 153)

½ cup (30 g) finely chopped, lightly packed fresh cilantro, stems and leaves

1 fresh Indian green chili (optional; see page 271—jalapeño may be substituted), finely chopped

6 cloves garlic

3 tablespoons canola oil

2 tablespoons fresh lemon juice (from about ½ lemon)

¾ ounce (22 g) peeled fresh ginger (equivalent to about 1 tablespoon grated fresh ginger)

½ teaspoon salt

½ teaspoon paprika

¼ teaspoon ground cayenne (optional)

¼ teaspoon ground turmeric

2 tablespoons hung curd (page 41)

Skewers (soaked for at least 30 minutes if wooden)

Masala

¼ cup (60 ml) canola oil

2 cups (235 g) halved, thinly sliced yellow onion (about 1 medium onion)

1 cup tomato puree (see Notes, page 153)

½ teaspoon ground turmeric

½ teaspoon coarsely ground Kasuri methi (dried fenugreek leaves, see page 275; 1½ teaspoons finely chopped fresh methi or ½ teaspoon frozen methi may be substituted)

½ teaspoon garam masala (store-bought or homemade, page 53)

½ teaspoon sugar

½ teaspoon salt, plus more to taste

¼ teaspoon ground cayenne (optional)

¾ cup (180 ml) whole milk

¼ cup (55 g) butter

Boiling water (optional), as needed

recipe continues

Poultry, Meat, and Fish

Murgh Makhani
· continued ·

MARINADE + TIKKA

1. Place the chicken in a large bowl. Grind the cilantro, fresh chili (if using), garlic, oil, lemon juice, ginger, salt, paprika, cayenne (if using), and turmeric to a smooth paste using a blender, food processor, or mortar and pestle.

2. Add the hung curd to the blended mixture and stir it in by hand (we typically just stir it directly into the blender cup). Do not operate the blender or food processor to incorporate the curd, as that could compromise the texture. Transfer the marinade to the bowl with the chicken and thoroughly massage it into each piece of meat with your hands. Cover the mixture and marinate in the fridge for at least 4 hours (and up to 8).

3. Position a rack in the middle of the oven and preheat the oven to 375°F (190°C). Thread the chicken pieces, or tikkas, onto skewers. Suspend the skewers over a baking pan or casserole dish so that only the ends of the skewers (and none of the chicken bits!) are touching the pan. (For reference, we use a 12 x 17 x 1½-inch // 30.5 x 43 x 4-cm roasting pan and 15-inch // 38-cm skewers.) Collect any marinade that is still in the bowl and apply it to the chicken.

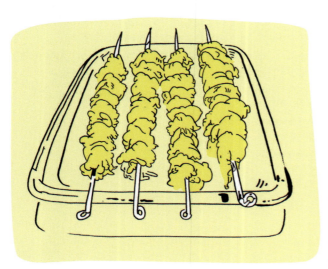

4. Once the oven is up to temperature, place the skewers and pan into the middle of the oven. Cook until the internal temperature of the chicken reaches 165°F (74°C), about 25 minutes.

5. Remove the tikkas from the oven, unskewer, and transfer to a plate. (Reserve the drippings if possible and set them aside to be added to the sauce later.) Cover the plate with foil and set aside.

MASALA

6. Heat the oil in a large pan or wok over medium-high heat. Once the oil starts to shimmer, add the onion. Cook, stirring frequently, until the slices are golden brown, deeper than oatmeal, with well-browned edges, 10 to 12 minutes (see page 32).

7. Reduce the heat to low. Add the tomato puree, turmeric, methi, garam masala, sugar, salt, cayenne (if using), and any reserved drippings. Stir well and cook for about 4 minutes, stirring once or twice, to ensure the spices and tomato cook through. Remove from the heat and let cool to room temperature.

8. Combine the milk with the cooled mixture. Grind to a smooth paste using an immersion blender (our preference), stand blender, or food processor. (If using a stand blender, note that it may take scraping down the sides of the blender and stirring between attempts—a silicone spatula is handy here—to get everything properly incorporated. Resist the temptation to add any additional liquid.)

9. In the same pan, heat the butter over low heat. Watch carefully, as overcooking the butter will render it grainy and ruin the texture of the dish. As soon as the butter melts, add the chicken tikkas and the blended masala.

10. Increase the heat to medium and cook, stirring constantly, until the mixture comes to a gentle boil. The final dish should have a creamy masala that clings to the chicken pieces. Add a bit of boiling water (or bring the mixture to a boil after adding tap water) to correct the consistency, or if you want the dish to be saucier.

11. Remove from the heat and cover the pan. Let rest, undisturbed, for at least 15 minutes before serving. Taste for salt—the sauce should be a pleasant balance of savory and slightly sweet—and serve hot.

Serving Tip

→ This dish may thicken as it cools, especially if left uncovered. If cooking in advance, you may need to add ¼ cup (50 ml) boiling water (or bring the mixture to a boil after adding tap water) to get it back to the right consistency.

Notes

Chicken tenders are strips of white meat from the pectoralis minor muscle. They can be found at the raw meat counter of most any grocery store (and are not to be confused with the breaded, precooked variety found in the freezer section).

This is a recipe in which tomato puree (lightly cooked, pureed tomatoes) is a crucial ingredient. If you're in a bind, you can substitute 1¼ cups (325 g) canned, diced tomatoes, but it won't have quite the right flavor. Puree the diced tomatoes in a blender and then increase the cooking time in Step 7 by a few minutes to boil off the excess water.

JAGGI

GUJRAL

KUNDAN LAL

ALSO KUNDAN LAL

THERE IS NO TEAM IN TANDOOR

Auyon Murgh Makhani (page 151), Daal Makhani (page 63), and tandoori chicken are now three of the most globally recognizable preparations of Indian cookery, but prior to the mid-twentieth century, most Indians would not have recognized them as anything more than a set of obscure regional specialties.

Their story starts with Partition, the unspeakably bloody cleaving of the subcontinent (into India and East and West Pakistan) that followed the hasty and chaotic departure of the British in 1947. By 1948, fifteen million people had been displaced and more than a million were dead. Among the uprooted was a team of restaurateurs, two of whom were named Kundan Lal, from the tandoor-laden city of Peshawar in what is now Pakistan.

The Kundan Lals and company headed southeast to New Delhi, where they founded a restaurant called Moti Mahal. Kundan Lal Gujral was the flashy, mustachioed face of the restaurant while Kundan Lal Jaggi was a co-owner (and may have worked in the kitchen). Although the original Delhi restaurant went on to achieve global renown, its legacy has grown complicated in recent decades. Today, the Jaggis and the Gujrals run competing restaurant chains, and each claim that their ancestor was the sole inventor of the now-iconic dishes. The rival dynasties have gone so far as to remove all acknowledgment of the unrelated Kundal Lal from their respective marketing and propaganda. The art of the alternative fact is, like butter chicken, a global phenomenon.

Keema Mattar

GROUND TURKEY with PEAS, CLOVE, and CARDAMOM

SERVES 6 • **COOK TIME:** *1½ hours* • **PHOTO:** *page 113*

Jyoti Keema Mattar was one of the great comfort foods of my childhood, and a staple of my family's Sunday brunches. It is marvelously versatile—in addition to serving it as is, my mother used it as a filling for stuffed vegetables and flatbreads, and as the base for her shepherd's pie. Leftovers were transformed into breaded cutlets, or croquettes, and enjoyed with tea the following day. Keema pizza and keema tacos are also excellent ideas.

The traditional version is made with ground mutton, but I like to swap in turkey (or use a mix of 3:1 turkey to mutton/pork) for a lighter preparation. Feel free to experiment!

Auyon The term *turkey* was originally given to African guineafowl by Europeans, who apparently named the birds after the Turkish traders who ferried them over from Africa. When colonizers came across a similar-looking North American bird, a distant relative of the guineafowl, they got confused and deemed the new bird a "turkey" as well. Meanwhile the Turks, who were well aware that the North American impostor had no relation to their country, opted to call the newfound bird a "Hindi," under the mistaken assumption that such exotic fare must have come from India.

- ¾ cup (180 ml) canola oil
- 2 dried red chilies, broken into thirds (see page 271)
- 2 Indian bay leaves
- 4 cloves
- 4 green cardamom pods, cracked open so that the seeds are exposed
- 1½ cups (360 g) blended or grated yellow onion (about 1 large onion, see Onion Blending, page 144)
- 2 pounds (910 g) ground turkey
- ⅝ cup (160 g) tomato puree, diluted with 5 tablespoons water (for a substitute, see Tomato Puree, page 83)
- 4 cloves garlic, finely chopped
- 4 teaspoons grated, peeled fresh ginger
- 1½ teaspoons salt, plus more to taste
- ¼ teaspoon ground cayenne (optional)
- 2¼ cups (340 g) frozen peas, no need to thaw
- 1 teaspoon cumin seeds, roasted (lightly!) and ground (see page 43)
- 1 teaspoon coriander seeds, roasted and ground with the cumin

Garnish
- 3 tablespoons finely chopped fresh cilantro, stems and leaves
- ¾ teaspoon garam masala (store-bought or homemade, page 53)

1. Heat the oil in a large, lidded (but uncovered for now) pan over medium-high heat. Once the oil starts to shimmer, add the chilies and cook, giving the pan a shake to distribute them evenly, until they darken a shade or two, about 30 seconds.

2. Add the bay leaves, cloves, and cardamom pods. Sizzle, giving the pan another shake, until the spices become fragrant, an additional 30 seconds.

3. Add the onion and watch out for oil splatter—use a splatter screen if you have one. Cook, stirring frequently, until the onion is golden brown, deeper than oatmeal, with plenty of darker caramelized flecks, 10 to 15 minutes. This browning is crucial to the flavor of the dish, so don't undercook (see page 32). If you notice the onion starting to burn before it gets to the right color, stir more often. You may need to cook for a bit longer if the onion doesn't seem dark enough.

4. While the onion is cooking, combine the ground turkey and diluted tomato puree in a large bowl and massage to incorporate. Use your hands and be thorough, as this step is crucial to getting a good, lump-free texture in the final dish.

5. Add the garlic, ginger, salt, cayenne (if using), and turkey-tomato mixture to the onion. Stir constantly for the first few minutes to break up the meat and fully incorporate the spices, then continue to stir frequently. The meat will release juices into the pan, which must evaporate before the meat can properly brown in the fat and oil. The meat is done when all the juices have boiled off and the meat itself has darkened and reddened, 20 to 25 minutes.

6. Add the peas, ground cumin, and ground coriander. Stir well to combine. Reduce the heat to medium, cover the pan, and cook until the peas are cooked through and the flavors have melded, 5 to 7 minutes. The final dish should have plenty of moisture but no visible gravy. The texture should be akin to that of ground meat you would use for American-style hard tacos.

8. Remove from the heat. Let rest, undisturbed, for at least 15 minutes before serving. Taste for salt.

GARNISH

9. Garnish with cilantro and garam masala. Serve hot.

Serving Tip

→ The dried chilies and bay leaves in the final dish are not meant to be eaten and should be moved to the side of the plate—warn your guests. The cardamom pods and cloves are totally edible and we love them, but they can be pushed aside as well if the flavor is too intense.

A NOTE ON BEEF

Auyon Although the strict prohibition of beef consumption is now one of the most conspicuous trappings of Hinduism, it is a relatively recent development in the history of the religion. Cow veneration was first introduced by the semi-nomadic, dairy-loving Indo-Aryan elite, who arrived in India around the second millennium BCE and measured their wealth in cattle. Dairy products like milk, ghee, and yogurt became intertwined with religious ceremony. The cows themselves, while celebrated as divine symbols, were also ritually sacrificed.

By around 1000 CE, the Hindu reverence for cattle had evolved into a universal taboo against beef eating. The modern "cow protection movement," however, which claims the safeguarding of all cattle as a key component of the faith, dates back no further than the nineteenth century.

Today, the fanatical protection of cows in India has become a weaponized emblem of the Hindu political right. By promoting and exporting the falsehood that cattle consumption in India is limited to, as journalist Sharanya Deepak puts it, "foreigners, invaders, and miscreants," the government alienates the millions upon millions of Indians who eat beef, most of whom are Muslims, low-caste Hindus, or otherwise disenfranchised minorities. Stories of property destruction, torture, and lynchings of suspected beef-eaters by self-described cow vigilantes abound. The myth of majority vegetarianism within India is no less bankrupt—nonvegetarians make up more than 60 percent of the population.

This is all to say that the devout Hindu's lamentable abstention from beef is completely unrelated to how delicious the animals are. Our Keema Mattar recipe (page 156) also works well with ground beef.

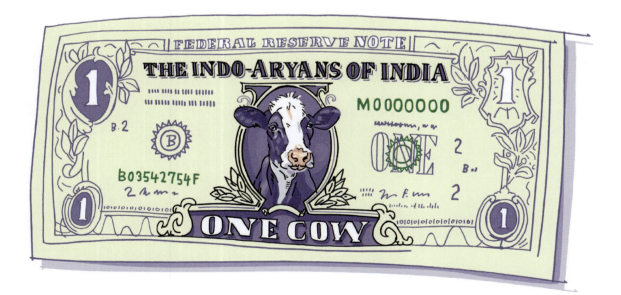

Mutton Aloo Korma

GOAT CURRY with POTATO

SERVES 6 • **COOK TIME:** *3 hours, plus time to rest the meat after cooking* • **PHOTO:** *page 97*

Jyoti Goat is not a familiar meat to most Americans, but it is a much-loved ingredient in South Asian cooking. You can think of it as a less gamey version of lamb, but with its own distinctive, earthy flavor. The texture of goat meat is also singular—when cooked to tenderness, it almost flakes apart. We absolutely love it, and we hope you will too. While you can certainly substitute other red meats for the goat in this recipe, we recommend holding off until you get your hands on some good-quality goat meat, ideally at a halal butcher shop. (Ask for the hind leg of a kid, or young goat, as the meat of older animals is tougher and takes longer to cook.)

This dish has developed something of a cult following among my students. Although the goat meat itself is wonderful, the true stars of the recipe might be the unassuming potatoes, which get impossibly soft while soaking up all of the delicious goat flavor. They should hold their shape when served, but just barely, such that they nearly dissolve when you bite into them (see page 49).

The cook time of this recipe might seem intimidating, but at least an hour is largely (but not completely) hands-off, leaving some time to prep other dishes. Note that this dish is ideally cooked early in the day—or better yet, the day before serving—so that there is plenty of time for the flavors to meld after cooking.

Auyon Although contemporary Indian restaurants often pigeonhole kormas as rich, creamy dishes studded with nuts and raisins, the classical definition of a korma is simply a braised meat or vegetable dish. The term itself, which derives from the Hindustani word for "braise," is usually traced back to the Indo-Persian cuisine of the Mughals.

According to esteemed cookbook author Julie Sahni, the most notable difference between korma-style braising and similar Western techniques is viscosity. Kormas usually employ yogurt, cream, fruit purees, and nut butters, which produce thicker, more velvety sauces than the wine and stocks typical of Western braises.

10 black peppercorns

6 green cardamom pods

1 cup (240 ml) canola oil

3 Indian bay leaves

6 cloves

One 3-inch (7.5-cm) cinnamon stick

3 cups (720 g) blended or grated yellow onion (about 2 large onions, see Onion Blending, page 144)

⅝ cup (160 g) tomato puree, diluted with 5 tablespoons water (for a substitute, see Tomato Puree, page 83)

8 cloves garlic

1½ ounces (45 g) peeled fresh ginger (equivalent to about 2 tablespoons grated fresh ginger)

½ teaspoon ground turmeric

2 pounds (910 g) bone-in goat meat (see Note, page 161), cubed into 1-inch (2.5-cm) chunks (have the butcher do this for you, if possible)

2 teaspoons salt, plus more to taste

½ teaspoon ground cayenne (optional)

3 large russet potatoes (2 pounds // 910 g total), halved lengthwise and then cut crosswise into 1¼-inch- (3.2-cm-) thick slices (see page 82)

¾ cup (180 g) whole, unflavored yogurt (store-bought or homemade, page 40), stirred to a smooth consistency and at room temperature

Boiling water (optional), as needed

Garnish

½ teaspoon garam masala (store-bought or homemade, page 53)

recipe continues

Mutton Aloo Korma

• continued •

1. Use a mortar and pestle to coarsely crush the black peppercorns. Add the cardamom pods to the mortar and crack them open so that the seeds are exposed.

2. Heat the oil in a large, lidded (but uncovered for now), nonstick pot over medium-high heat. Once the oil starts to shimmer, add the crushed black pepper, cardamom pods, bay leaves, cloves, and cinnamon. Sizzle, giving the pan a shake or two, until the spices darken a couple of shades and become fragrant, about 45 seconds.

3. Add the onion and watch out for oil splatter—use a splatter screen if you have one. Cook, stirring frequently, until the onion is golden brown, deeper than oatmeal, with plenty of darker, caramelized flecks, 25 to 30 minutes. This browning is crucial to the flavor of the dish, so don't undercook (see page 32). If you notice the onion starting to burn before it gets to the right color, stir more often. You may need to cook for a bit longer if the onion doesn't seem dark enough.

4. While the onion is cooking, grind the diluted tomato puree, garlic, ginger, and turmeric to a smooth paste using a blender, food processor, or mortar and pestle. Once the onion is properly browned, add the blended tomato mixture to the pot and cook, stirring a couple of times, until the oil starts to separate out of the masala (see page 162), about 3 minutes.

5. Add the goat, salt, and cayenne (if using) to the pot. Cook, stirring and scraping frequently to make sure nothing sticks, until the meat is lightly browned all over, about 15 minutes.

6. Add the potato and continue to stir frequently until the liquid released by the meat has largely evaporated and the oil starts to separate out of the masala (see page 162), 5 to 10 minutes. The slightly thickened masala should be sticking to the chunks of potato and meat (as opposed to the meat and potato pieces swimming in a saucy liquid).

7. Add 1 cup (240 ml) water to the mixture, stir well, and cover the pot. Cook, stirring every 10 minutes or so, until the goat is totally tender, about an hour (see Troubleshooting, opposite). The meat should release plenty of liquid as it cooks. Halfway through, add another 1 cup (240 ml) water to ensure the mixture doesn't dry out. Scrape the bottom of the pot (using a wooden or plastic utensil) every time you stir to make sure nothing is sticking. Do so gently, because the potato will become quite tender (and potentially breakable) toward the end of the hour.

8. Once the meat and potatoes are both done (and the potatoes have been reintroduced to the pot, if you had to take them out), add the yogurt. Stir gently, reduce the heat to low, and cover. Cook for an additional 10 minutes to incorporate. The final dish should have a thick curry that clings to the meat and potatoes, and there should be a good bit of oil floating on top. Add a bit of boiling water (or bring the mixture to a boil after adding tap water) to correct the consistency, or if you want the dish to be saucier.

9. Remove from the heat and let rest, covered, for at least 15 minutes (but ideally for an hour or two) to allow the flavors to meld. Reheat gently if necessary and taste for salt.

GARNISH

10. Garnish with garam masala and serve hot.

Serving Tips

→ The bay leaves and cinnamon stick in the final dish are not meant to be eaten and should be moved to the side of the plate—warn your guests. The cloves and cardamom pods are totally edible and we love chewing them, but they can be pushed aside if the flavor is too intense.

→ This dish may thicken as it cools, especially if left uncovered. If cooking in advance, you may need to add ¼ cup (60 ml) boiling water (or bring the mixture to a boil after adding tap water) to get it back to the right consistency.

Note

Bone marrow vastly improves the flavor of the dish, so make sure to use some bone-in bits. In the same vein, trim some of the fat from the meat if you wish, but don't remove all of it.

Troubleshooting

→ If, while waiting for the meat to soften, the potato pieces become so soft that they start to break down (which might happen if the meat came from an older animal), transfer them to a large plate. Cover the plate with foil and don't reintroduce them until the meat is done.

→ If the meat or potato pieces start to burn at the bottom of the pot, add a bit more water to the pot and stir to keep things moving. If you see a significant burned crust starting to form (which usually only happens if you accidentally forget to stir for a while), don't stir it in. Transfer the mixture to a new pot to continue cooking, leaving the burned bit in the old pot so that it doesn't ruin the dish.

→ The meat, when done, should be perfectly tender and not chewy. In some cases, depending on the age of the butchered animal, getting to this point is difficult without a few minutes in a pressure cooker. Not to worry if you don't own one—the meat will still be delicious with a bit of chew. If you do happen to have a pressure cooker, though, and you find that the meat has not softened to your liking by the end of the hour of covered cooking, transfer the meat and masala (but not the potatoes!) to a pressure cooker, along with 1 cup (240 ml) water. Seal the machine and cook for 5 minutes once the pressure has built up and/or the hissing starts. Check for tenderness and repeat if necessary. (Alternatively, if you have the time, you can transfer the meat and masala to a covered, oven-safe dish and pop it into a 300°F // 150°C oven for a couple of hours, checking every hour and adding water if it starts to look dry.)

Bhuna Gosht

DRY LAMB CURRY with BLACK CARDAMOM

SERVES 4 • COOK TIME: *2 hours* • PHOTO: *page 125*

Jyoti This recipe is defined by the Indian cooking technique of bhunaoing, for which there is no direct Western analog. The basic idea is to simmer meat in a mixture of spices and aromatics until the moisture released by the meat and vegetables evaporates. Once enough water has left the pan that the contents start to stick and brown a bit in the fat, a small amount of liquid is added to the pan to keep things moving. The mixture is then stirred again until the liquid evaporates, and the cycle is repeated a few times.

The final outcome is tender, flavorful chunks of meat in a thick, concentrated blend of oil and ground spices. (The word *dry* in this recipe's English translation refers to the low moisture content of the dish.) The flavor afforded by the repeated process of reducing, browning, and deglazing is crucial to many South Asian preparations, and is impossible to approximate with other methods.

Sometimes it can be hard to tell whether the meat is sticking to the pan. If you're having trouble determining the stickiness of the meat, you can also watch for the oil separating from the sauce. Once all the water in the pan has vaporized, if you scrape some of the thickened mixture, or masala, away from the edge of the pan, you should be able to see oil seeping back out of the masala. (If there is still water in the pan when you try scraping it, the masala will spread more homogeneously, without any leakage of oil.)

Another trick is to distinguish the more viscous oil from the water. Watch and listen closely—while there is still water in the pan, you'll hear a fizzing sound and see larger bubbles. Once the water has vaporized and most of the remaining fluid is hot fat, you will hear more of a snapping and crackling sound, and the bubbles will be smaller. (You will also see the vegetables and meat starting to brown, which is what you want.) In the end, what you are looking for is a sufficient evaporation of moisture so that the contents of the pan are frying in oil rather than boiling in water.

Only once the water has evaporated should you add more liquid. Don't do so too soon, because the dry-cooking (or frying, or meat-sticking) portions of bhunaoing are necessary for the coated meat and vegetables to brown in the fat between each liquid addition.

Bhunaoing is admittedly an attention-intensive process, and it might take a few tries to get right. That said, even a little bhunaoing goes a long way in contributing to the ultimate flavor and texture of the dish. Have fun, and keep stirring!

Lastly, although the cooking time might seem intimidating, about an hour of it only requires you to stir occasionally, leaving plenty of time to prep other dishes.

---

8 cloves

16 black peppercorns

4 black cardamom pods

¾ cup (180 ml) canola oil

4 Indian bay leaves

Two 3-inch (7.5-cm) cinnamon sticks

1½ cups (360 g) blended or grated yellow onion (about 1 large onion, see Onion Blending, page 144)

⅝ cup (160 g) tomato puree, diluted with 5 tablespoons water (for a substitute, see Tomato Puree, page 83)

1½ ounces (40 g) peeled fresh ginger (equivalent to about 2 tablespoons grated, peeled fresh ginger)

8 cloves garlic

2 fresh Indian green chilies (optional; see page 271—jalapeños may be substituted), finely chopped

2 teaspoons ground coriander

1½ teaspoons salt, plus more to taste

1 teaspoon ground turmeric

2½ pounds (1.2 kg) boneless leg of lamb (our favorite meat is from New Zealand), mostly trimmed of fat, cubed into 1-inch (2.5-cm) chunks (have the butcher do this, if possible)

¾ cup (180 g) whole, unflavored yogurt (store-bought or homemade, page 40), stirred to a smooth consistency and at room temperature

Garnish

2 tablespoons finely chopped fresh cilantro, stems and leaves

¾ teaspoon garam masala (store-bought or homemade, page 53)

1. Use a mortar and pestle to coarsely crush the cloves and black peppercorns. Add the cardamom pods to the mortar and crack them open so that the seeds are exposed.

2. Heat the oil in a large, lidded (but uncovered for now) pot over medium-high heat. Once the oil starts to shimmer, add the cloves, black pepper, cardamom pods, bay leaves, and cinnamon. Sizzle, giving the pan a shake or two, until the spices darken a couple of shades and become fragrant, about 45 seconds.

3. Add the onion and watch out for oil splatter—use a splatter screen if you have one. Cook, stirring frequently, until the onion is golden brown, deeper than oatmeal, with plenty of darker caramelized flecks, 10 to 15 minutes. This browning is crucial to the flavor of the dish, so don't undercook (see page 32). If you notice the onion starting to burn before it gets to the right color, stir more often. You may need to cook for a bit longer if the onion doesn't seem dark enough.

4. While the onion is cooking, grind the diluted tomato puree, ginger, garlic, and chilies (if using) to a smooth paste using a blender, food processor, or mortar and pestle. Once the onion is properly browned, add the blended ginger-garlic paste, coriander, salt, and turmeric to the pot, followed by the lamb. Reduce the heat to medium-low and stir well to incorporate.

5. The lamb will release juices as it cooks. As the water evaporates, the meat will darken. Stir occasionally until the water in the pot has mostly evaporated, 35 to 40 minutes. The pot should remain uncovered for the entirety of the cooking process to facilitate evaporation. Stir more frequently toward the end of this period to make sure nothing burns. By the end, you should notice the masala, or sauce, starting to stick to the pan, and that most of the liquid in the pot is oil rather than water or lamb juices.

(The meat will be tough but completely cooked through by this point—the rest of the recipe is necessary to soften and tenderize the lamb. We recommend trying a bit of meat at the end of each successive step to get a sense of what is happening.)

6. Add 6 tablespoons water and stir to incorporate. Cook, stirring frequently, until the water has boiled off (so that most of the liquid in the pot is oil rather than water or lamb juices) and the masala begins to stick again, 5 to 7 minutes.

7. Add another 6 tablespoons water and repeat the process, another 5 to 7 minutes.

8. Add the yogurt, reduce the heat to low, and cover the pan. Cook, undisturbed, until the meat is totally tender and the oil has separated from the rest of the liquid, about 15 minutes.

9. Remove from the heat and let rest, undisturbed, for at least 15 minutes before serving. Taste for salt.

GARNISH

10. Garnish with cilantro and garam masala. Serve hot.

Serving Tips

→ The black cardamom pods, bay leaves, and cinnamon sticks in the final dish are not meant to be eaten and should be moved to the side of the plate—warn your guests. The crushed cloves are totally edible and we love them, but they can be pushed aside as well if the flavor is too intense.

→ While not traditional, you can add a bit of boiling water after cooking (or bring the mixture to a boil after adding tap water) if you want the dish to be saucier.

Rogan Josh

LAMB CURRY with KASHMIRI CHILI, FENNEL, and MACE

SERVES 4 • **COOK TIME:** *75 minutes* • **PHOTO:** *page 111*

Jyoti Kashmir is a lush, transnational territory in the picturesque but politically unstable north of the subcontinent. The region's cuisine, famed for its sumptuous meat dishes, is split along religious lines into two schools (Muslim and Hindu), each with its own spice palette.

Rogan Josh is a Kashmiri lamb preparation known for its characteristic crimson color. Our recipe follows the Hindu, or Pandit, tradition, which favors the use of yogurt and eschews onion and garlic (for more on the Hindu avoidance of alliums, see Heeng, page 274). Some factors that distinguish this dish from the Mutton Aloo Korma and Bhuna Gosht on the preceding pages are the lack of tomato, the inclusion of both black and green cardamom, the use of fennel and mace, and the generous dose of Kashmiri chili, a brightly hued pepper distinctive to the region.

This recipe makes for a pleasantly spicy preparation. Reduce or omit the chili if cooking for the heat-averse.

Finally, as with all our recipes, remember that the physical and sensory cues are just as important as the estimated times we've given. Trust your eyes and nose as much as the clock. Relatedly, we recommend setting out, measuring, and chopping all ingredients before turning the stove on, so that you can focus all your attention on the cooking once it starts.

- 1 cup (240 g) whole, unflavored yogurt (store-bought or homemade, page 40), stirred to a smooth consistency
- 1 tablespoon ground Kashmiri chili (see page 271)
- ⅓ cup (80 ml) canola oil
- 5 cloves
- 2 black cardamom pods, cracked open so the seeds are exposed
- 5 green cardamom pods, cracked open so the seeds are exposed
- 3 Indian bay leaves
- 2 blades mace (see page 275)
- 1 teaspoon cumin seeds
- 2 pounds (910 g) boneless leg of lamb (our favorite meat is from New Zealand), mostly trimmed of fat, cubed into 1½-inch (4-cm) chunks (have the butcher do this, if possible)
- 1 teaspoon salt
- 1½ teaspoons ground coriander
- 1½ teaspoons ground fennel seed
- 1½ teaspoons ground dried ginger
- 1 teaspoon ground cumin
- Boiling water (optional), as needed

Garnish
Pinch of ground Kashmiri chili

1. Combine the yogurt and Kashmiri chili in a small bowl and whisk or stir well to incorporate. Set aside at room temperature.

2. Heat the oil in a large, lidded (but uncovered for now) pot over medium heat. Once the oil starts to shimmer, add the cloves, black cardamom pods, green cardamom pods, bay leaves, mace, and cumin seeds. Sizzle, giving the pan a shake or two, until the spices darken a couple of shades and become fragrant, about 45 seconds.

3. Add the lamb and salt to the pot and stir frequently. The lamb will release plenty of liquid, which will boil off. Cook until the total amount of liquid in the pot starts to subside, 8 to 10 minutes. The majority of the remaining liquid should be fat, which is more viscous than the lamb liquid and will sizzle with small bubbles rather than boil with big ones.

4. Add the coriander, fennel, ginger, and ground cumin to the pot. Stir frequently to allow the lamb to brown in the spice-infused fat. Cook until the lamb darkens a few shades, 5 to 6 minutes. The oil will begin to look more transparent as the lamb juices evaporate and the spices begin sticking to the meat. If the spices start sticking to the bottom of the pot, add a little bit of water and scrape to release (see the bhunao technique description on page 162).

5. Add the chili-yogurt mixture and stir well to incorporate thoroughly. Reduce the heat to medium-low, so that the mixture settles to a gentle boil.

6. Cover the pot and cook, stirring occasionally, until the meat is meltingly tender, about 20 minutes. Again, if anything starts to stick, add a little bit of water to the pot and scrape to release. The finished meat should be partially submerged in a thin, oily gravy. Add a bit of boiling water (or bring the mixture to a boil after adding tap water) to correct the consistency, or if you want the dish to be saucier.

8. Remove from the heat and let rest, undisturbed, for at least 15 minutes before serving. Taste for salt.

GARNISH

9. Garnish with the Kashmiri chili. Serve hot.

Serving Tips

→ The black cardamom pods, bay leaves, and mace in the final dish are not meant to be eaten and should be moved to the side of the plate—warn your guests. The cloves and green cardamom pods are totally edible and we love them, but they can be pushed aside as well if the flavor is too intense.

→ This dish may thicken as it cools, especially if left uncovered. If cooking in advance, you may need to add ¼ cup (60 ml) boiling water (or bring the mixture to a boil after adding tap water) to get it back to the right consistency.

KASHMIRI CHILI POWDER

Vindaloo

VINEGAR PORK CURRY with GARLIC

SERVES 4 • MARINATION TIME: *2½ hours*
COOK TIME: *1½ hours* • PHOTO: *page 124*

Jyoti Vindaloo comes from the state of Goa, which is situated on the Konkan Coast in the west of India. Its namesake is the Portuguese *carne de vinha d'alhos* or "meat with wine vinegar and garlic." The wine vinegar was swapped out for palm wine vinegar during the Indian evolution of the dish, but our recipe calls for white vinegar to keep things a bit simpler.

This dish is traditionally extremely hot. Our version, which features seeded dried chilies, is milder than the original while still retaining a pleasant kick (capsaicin, the compound that makes peppers spicy, is most concentrated in the white pith that surrounds the seeds). For a more authentic—and mouth-numbingly hot—preparation, leave the seeds in. Regardless of which version you choose, we recommend serving this dish with generous amounts of rice and Homemade Yogurt (page 40) to balance out the heat.

Auyon The Portuguese established Europe's first base on the subcontinent in 1510, when they captured Goa from the sultan of Bijapur. In contrast to the British, who in spite of their rapacious imperial exploitation demonstrated little ambition to affect local culture, the Portuguese brought the Inquisition to India. Historian Minakshie Das Gupta recounts the colonial maxim: "[W]hen the Portuguese settled down in a new place, their first priority was a church; for the Dutch, it was a fort, and for the English, a tavern."

The Goa Inquisition was violent and terrifying. Within seven years of its inception, almost all of the Hindu temples in the Portuguese colonial territory had been destroyed. The Inquisitors converted local populations and persecuted individuals for such infractions as wearing traditional garments and refusing to eat meat.

Goa is now famous for its nonvegetarian cuisine.

Marinade
- 12 whole, dried Kashmiri chilies (see Note, opposite)
- ⅓ cup (80 ml) white (distilled) vinegar
- 10 cloves garlic
- 10 cloves
- 6 green cardamom pods, cracked open so the seeds are exposed
- One 1½-inch (4-cm) cinnamon stick, broken in half
- 1 ounce (30 g) peeled fresh ginger (equivalent to about 4 teaspoons grated fresh ginger)
- 1½ teaspoons sugar
- 1 teaspoon cumin seeds
- 1 teaspoon black or brown mustard seeds
- 1 teaspoon salt
- 2 pounds (910 g) pork shoulder, cubed into 1¼-inch (4-cm) chunks (do not substitute leaner cuts of pork, as they will dry out during cooking!)

Masala
- ¾ cup (160 ml) canola oil
- 2¼ cups (540 g) blended or grated yellow onion (about 1½ large onions, see Onion Blending, page 144)
- 2 small sprigs fresh curry leaves, stripped from the stems (see page 273)
- ¾ teaspoon salt, plus more to taste
- Boiling water (optional), as needed

MARINADE

1. Seed the dried chilies by breaking them into thirds and then shaking the seeds out of each section. A small, sharp knife can be helpful in teasing out the more recalcitrant seeds that are stuck close to the stem end, where the seeds are most concentrated. The process can be a bit painstaking, but it is worth the work. Discard the seeds and reserve the dried skins.

2. Combine the chili skins, vinegar, garlic, cloves, cardamom, cinnamon, ginger, sugar, cumin, mustard, and salt in a small bowl. Stir well to incorporate, then soak for 30 minutes.

3. Grind the soaked mixture to a smooth paste using a blender, food processor, or mortar and pestle.

4. Transfer the blended marinade to a large bowl. Add the pork and massage the marinade evenly into the meat with your hands (feel free to wear gloves if you are chili-sensitive, or if you chose not to seed the chilis in Step 1). Cover and marinate in the fridge for 1½ to 2 hours. Do not leave it any longer—acidic marinades will break down meat and produce an undesirable texture if left for too long.

MASALA

5. Heat the oil in a large pan over medium-high heat. Once the oil starts to shimmer, add the onion and watch out for oil splatter—use a splatter screen if you have one.

6. Cook, stirring occasionally, until the onion is slightly darker than golden brown with plenty of darker caramelized flecks, around 15 minutes. This browning is crucial to the flavor of the dish, so don't undercook (see page 32). If you notice the onion starting to burn before it gets to the right color, stir more often. You may need to cook for a bit longer if the onion doesn't seem dark enough.

7. Add the marinated meat. Cook, stirring frequently, until the meat is cooked on all sides and starting to brown, about 10 minutes.

8. Add the curry leaves and stir well for a minute before adding 1 cup (240 ml) water and the salt. (Unlike most of our other recipes that call for curry leaves, the leaves should not be fried before getting added to the mix.) Stir well again, reduce the heat to medium-low, and cover.

9. Cook, stirring once or twice, until the meat is completely tender and partially submerged in a thick, oily curry, 25 to 30 minutes. Add a bit of boiling water (or bring the mixture to a boil after adding tap water) if the dish seems too dry, or if you want it to be saucier.

10. Remove from the heat and let rest, covered, for at least 15 minutes before serving. Taste for salt and serve hot.

Serving Tips

→ The cinnamon stick in the final dish is not meant to be eaten and should be moved to the side of the plate—warn your guests. The cloves and cardamom pods are totally edible and we love them, but they can be pushed aside as well if the flavor is too intense.

→ This dish may thicken as it cools, especially if left uncovered. If cooking in advance, you may need to add ¼ cup (60 ml) boiling water (or bring the mixture to a boil after adding tap water) to get it back to the right consistency.

Note

Dried Kashmiri chilies are different from other dried red chilies and are worth seeking out online or at a local Indian grocer. They are crucial to both the proper flavor and the color of the dish.

Goan Machhli

FISH CURRY with OKRA, TAMARIND, and COCONUT

SERVES 4 • **COOK TIME:** *1 hour* • **PHOTO:** *page 124*

Jyoti Another dish from Goa, and a favorite fish preparation of mine. I learned this recipe from a Goan cook who worked at my husband's home when we were first married. The dish is light and tangy, and the texture of the fish is delightfully delicate.

Make sure your okra pods are fresh and tender. Otherwise, they will be fibrous and tough to chew, even when fully cooked (see Okra Shopping, page 88).

1 cup (170 g) chopped yellow onion (¼-inch // 6-mm dice, about 1 small onion)

1 cup (135 g) chopped tomato (¼-inch // 6-mm dice, about 1 medium tomato)

¼ cup (25 g) grated unsweetened coconut (see Frozen Coconut, page 78), thawed if frozen

½ ounce (15 g) peeled fresh ginger (equivalent to about 2 teaspoons grated fresh ginger)

2 cloves garlic

1 teaspoon tamarind paste (see page 277)

1¼ teaspoons salt, plus more to taste

¾ teaspoon whole cumin seeds

¾ teaspoon whole coriander seeds

¾ teaspoon ground Kashmiri chili (see page 271)

½ teaspoon ground turmeric

½ cup (120 ml) canola oil

½ teaspoon methi (fenugreek) seeds

Four 8-ounce (225-g) white fish fillets (basa, cod, sole, etc.), cut crosswise into 2-inch (5-cm) pieces

14 small and tender okra pods (5¼ ounces // 150 g total), stems removed

Boiling water (optional), as needed

1. Grind the onion, tomato, coconut, ginger, garlic, tamarind, salt, cumin, coriander, chili, and turmeric to a smooth paste using a blender, food processor, or mortar and pestle. (If using a blender, note that it may take scraping down the sides of the blender and stirring between attempts—a silicone spatula is handy here—to get everything properly incorporated. Resist the temptation to add any liquid.)

2. Heat the oil in a large, lidded (but uncovered for now) pan over medium-high heat. Once the oil starts to shimmer, add the methi seeds and cook, giving the pan a shake or two, until they darken and redden a couple of shades, about 20 seconds.

3. Add the onion-spice paste, or masala, and cook, stirring frequently, until the mixture darkens, most of the moisture evaporates, and the oil starts to separate out of the masala (see page 162), 10 to 12 minutes.

4. Add ⅓ cup (80 ml) water and stir well. Add the fish, cover, and give the pan a gentle shake to prevent the fish pieces from sticking to one another. Cook undisturbed until the top layer of fish (or any fish you can see poking out of the masala) is opaque, about 5 minutes.

5. Lay the okra over the top of the fish, cover, and cook undisturbed until the okra is cooked through, about 10 minutes. The fish and okra in the finished dish should be totally tender and largely submerged in a thin curry. Add a bit of boiling water (or bring the mixture to a boil after adding tap water) to correct the consistency, or if you want the dish to be saucier.

6. Remove from the heat and let rest, covered, for 15 minutes before serving. Taste for salt and serve hot.

• Machher Jhol •

FISH CURRY with TOMATO and NIGELLA

SERVES 4 • MARINATION TIME: 30 minutes
COOK TIME: 45 minutes • PHOTO: page 101

Jyoti There are likely as many versions of this Bengali mainstay as there are households in Bengal, a fish-loving region that comprises the Indian state of West Bengal and the neighboring nation of Bangladesh. I learned this iteration from a friend several years ago, and it has since become one of the most popular fish preparations in my classes. The smoky kalonji and earthy, freshly ground cumin are delightful with the simple, tomato-based curry.

Auyon Bengal's fish fanaticism is difficult to overstate. While Hindu priests and gurus in most other regions abstain from any and all animal flesh, their Bengali counterparts make a conspicuous exception for fish, the "fruit of the ocean," which they consume with relish. Fish are also considered auspicious symbols, so wedding invitations are often decorated with piscine motifs. A regional marriage tradition involves the groom's family giving the bride's family a large carp decorated with flowers and makeup (and sometimes wearing a sari).

Four 8-ounce (225-g) white fish fillets (basa, cod, sole, etc.), cut crosswise into 2-inch (5-cm) pieces

2 teaspoons ground turmeric

1 teaspoon salt, plus more to taste

¼ cup (60 ml) canola oil

2 dried red chilies, broken into thirds (see page 271)

½ teaspoon kalonji (nigella seeds, see page 274)

1 tablespoon ground cumin

⅝ cup (160 g) tomato puree, diluted with 5 tablespoons water (for a substitute, see Tomato Puree, page 83)

Boiling water (optional), as needed

Garnish
2 tablespoons finely chopped fresh cilantro, stems and leaves

1 fresh Indian green chili (optional; see page 271—jalapeño may be substituted), halved crosswise and then halved lengthwise

recipe continues

LIPSTICK

169
Poultry, Meat, and Fish

Machher Johl
• *continued* •

1. Combine the sliced fillets, turmeric, and salt in a large bowl. Gently mix with your hands to incorporate. (Beware of the spectacular dyeing power of turmeric. Use a pair of rubber gloves here if you'd prefer to keep your skin and nails unstained.) Cover the mixture and place it in the fridge to marinate for 30 minutes.

2. Heat the oil in a large, lidded (but uncovered for now) pan over medium-high heat. Once the oil starts to shimmer, add the dried chilies and cook, giving the pan a shake to distribute them evenly, until they darken a shade or two, about 30 seconds.

3. Add the kalonji, give the pan another shake, and sizzle until the seeds become fragrant, another 20 seconds or so.

4. Reduce the heat to low and add the ground cumin. Swirl to combine and then immediately add the diluted tomato puree—the cumin can easily scorch and should only cook alone in the oil for a couple of seconds.

5. Stir for a minute to incorporate, then carefully place the fish pieces into the pan, ideally in a single layer. If your pan is not big enough to accommodate the fish in one layer, a second layer is fine as long as you swirl the pan liquid such that it gets between the fish layers (otherwise they may stick together).

6. Increase the heat to medium and cover the pan. Cook, giving the covered pan a gentle shake once or twice to prevent the fish pieces from sticking, until the fish is opaque in the center, 10 to 15 minutes. The fish should be totally tender and largely submerged in a smooth, thin curry. Add a bit of boiling water (or bring the mixture to a boil after adding tap water) to correct the consistency, or if you want the dish to be saucier.

7. Remove from the heat and let rest, covered, for 15 minutes before serving. Taste for salt.

GARNISH

8. Garnish with cilantro and sliced chili (if using) and serve hot.

Shorshe Chingri

SHRIMP CURRY with POTATO, MUSTARD, and COCONUT

SERVES 6 • SOAK + MARINATION TIME: *3 hours*
COOK TIME: *1½ hours* • **PHOTO:** *page 110*

Jyoti The combination of seafood and mustard in this dish, which I learned from my mother-in-law, is quintessentially Bengali. The recipe calls for mustard oil, the preferred cooking fat of Bengal and a common pickling medium across India. The spicy uncooked oil surrenders its pungency when heated to its smoke point, but this preparation keeps the oil cool enough that it retains plenty of kick. All to say, this is not a dish to serve to the mustard-shy. To offset the spiciness, it is traditionally eaten with copious amounts of white rice.

Note that this shrimp is traditionally cooked to a firmness that might feel overdone to those who are used to very lightly steamed shrimp (see page 94).

Auyon You should be able to find mustard oil at any Indian grocery, but be warned that the bottles will likely declare themselves "for external use only." Mustard oil, which is pressed from the seeds of mustard plants in the *Brassica* genus, cannot be legally sold for consumption in the United States (or the European Union or Canada) due to its high erucic acid content. It is instead imported as a massage oil, but stocked in quantities that suggest customers are not buying it solely for cosmetic purposes. If the prospect of cooking with an FDA-disapproved cooking fat horrifies you, please skip this recipe.

Poppy Seeds + Potatoes

½ cup (120 ml) warm water

1 tablespoon white poppy seeds

¼ cup (60 ml) canola oil

2 medium russet potatoes (14 ounces // 400 g total), halved crosswise and then cut into ⅛ x ¼-inch (4 x 6-mm) flat batons

Marinade

¾ cup (75 g) grated unsweetened coconut (see Frozen Coconut, page 78), thawed if frozen

3 tablespoons mustard oil

3 tablespoons canola oil

3 tablespoons yellow mustard powder (we like Colman's, but any yellow mustard powder will do; see Note, page 173)

1 fresh Indian green chili (optional; see page 271—jalapeño may be substituted), finely chopped

1 teaspoon ground turmeric

2 tablespoons all-purpose flour

2 tablespoons whole, unflavored yogurt (store-bought or homemade, page 40), stirred to a smooth consistency

1½ teaspoons salt, plus more to taste

1½ pounds (680 g) 13/15 shrimp, peeled and deveined with tails left on

Boiling water (optional), as needed

Garnish

2 tablespoons finely chopped fresh cilantro, stems and leaves

recipe continues

Shorshe Chingri
• *continued* •

POPPY SEEDS + POTATOES

1. Place the warm water and poppy seeds in a small bowl. Soak for an hour.

2. Heat the oil in a large, nonstick pan over medium-low heat. Once the oil starts to shimmer, add only as many potato pieces as will fit in a single layer (for reference, we usually cook them in two batches). Cook, flipping once or twice, until the first batch of potatoes is translucent, about 4 minutes.

3. Remove the first batch from the pan and repeat with the remaining potatoes, in as many batches as necessary. You shouldn't need to add any more oil for successive batches. Once the last batch is cooked, set aside to cool to lukewarm (at least 10 minutes) while assembling the marinade.

MARINADE

4. Drain the poppy seeds using a fine-mesh strainer or cheesecloth.

5. Grind the drained seeds, coconut, mustard oil, canola oil, mustard powder, chili (if using), and turmeric with ¼ cup (60 ml) water to a smooth paste with a small blender or wet spice grinder (or an impressive proficiency with a mortar and pestle) until the poppy seeds are crushed and fully incorporated. (If using a blender, note that it may take scraping down the sides of the blender and stirring between attempts—a silicone spatula is handy here—to get everything properly incorporated. Resist the temptation to add any liquid.)

6. Add the flour, yogurt, and salt to the mixture and stir thoroughly by hand to combine—don't use the blender for this part, because it could compromise the texture of the yogurt.

7. Place the shrimp and parcooked potato pieces in a large, lidded, oven-safe baking dish and add the oil-coconut-yogurt marinade. Massage the marinade thoroughly into each piece of shrimp and potato with your hands. (Use rubber gloves to avoid inadvertently dyeing your hands yellow.)

8. Tightly cover the dish with foil and then place an oven-safe lid over the foil. (If you don't have an oven-safe lid for the shrimp and potato container, just double up on the foil and crimp it tightly to seal.) Marinate in the fridge for at least 2 hours, and up to 4 hours.

COOKING

9. Half an hour before you are ready to cook the shrimp, remove the sealed dish from the fridge to take the chill off. Prepare a water bath by filling a roasting pan (large enough that the dish with the shrimp can comfortably sit in it) with ½ inch (12 mm) of water and placing it in the oven. Preheat the oven to 350°F (180°C).

10. Once the oven is up to temperature, carefully place the sealed dish into the water bath and cook for 45 minutes. ⓑ

11. Turn the oven off and let the dish sit undisturbed in the unopened oven for a final 30 minutes before serving. When you unwrap the foil (careful of the steam!), give the shrimp and potato pieces a quick stir. They should be partially submerged in a spiced gravy that's roughly the thickness of tomato sauce. Add a bit of boiling water to correct the consistency, if necessary. Taste for salt and potato texture, which should be totally tender. (If the potatoes are somehow still undercooked, remove them from the dish as best you can, add them to a pot along with ½ cup // 60 ml water, and cook until tender, adding water as necessary.)

GARNISH

12. Garnish with cilantro. Serve hot.

> *Note*
>
> For a bolder mustard flavor, you can replace the 3 tablespoons of yellow mustard powder with 2 tablespoons of black or brown mustard seeds, 1 tablespoon of yellow mustard powder, and ½ teaspoon of salt ground together in a coffee grinder reserved for spices (or using a mortar and pestle.)

CHAPTER FIVE

Rice and Bread

Pulaos

JYOTI The following preparations demonstrate a couple of different ways to gussy up a basic rice recipe. They are wonderfully flexible—served with a dollop of Homemade Yogurt (page 40) and a bit of Adarak Nimbu Achaar (page 245), they make for a lovely light lunch, but they can also be used as a replacement for plain rice to accompany heartier fare on special occasions.

These recipes are a great jumping-off point for further experimentation. Making a mixed vegetable pulao by adding peas or a chopped vegetable in with the water, for example, is an easy way to incorporate some roughage. Both pulao recipes can easily be halved or doubled, also.

AUYON Pulao is an etymological cousin of the more familiar pilaf. The geographic origin of the two terms is debated. One theory traces them back to the Dravidian language family of South India, while another suggests Persian ancestry.

Jeera Pulao

CUMIN RICE

SERVES 4 • COOK TIME: *35 minutes* **• PHOTO:** *page 105*

3 tablespoons canola oil

2 Indian bay leaves

1 teaspoon cumin seeds

2 cups (390 g) white basmati rice, rinsed (see page 44)

1¾ teaspoons salt, plus more to taste

1. Heat the oil in a medium, lidded (but uncovered for now) pot over medium-high heat. Once the oil starts to shimmer, add the bay leaves and cumin seeds. Sizzle, giving the pan a shake or two, until the spices darken a couple of shades and become fragrant, about 30 seconds.

2. Reduce the heat to medium and add the rice. Cook for a minute or two, stirring constantly, until roughly half of the rice grains have whitened.

3. Add the salt and 4 cups (960 ml) water. Increase the heat to medium-high and bring the mixture to a rolling boil.

4. Reduce the heat to medium, half-cover the pot and cook until the level of the water is just at or below the surface of the rice, about 5 minutes. It should look like there are soap bubbles coming out of the rice.

5. Reduce the heat to low, cover the pot completely, and cook undisturbed for 10 minutes.

6. Without cracking the lid open, remove the pot from the heat and let sit, covered, for an additional 10 minutes before fluffing the rice gently with a fork. Taste for salt and serve hot.

Serving Tip

→ The bay leaves in the final dish are not meant to be eaten and should be moved to the side of the plate—warn your guests.

Pyaaz Pulao

ONION RICE

SERVES 4 • COOK TIME: *50 minutes* **• PHOTO:** *page 119*

- 6 black peppercorns
- 4 green cardamom pods
- ¼ cup (50 g) unsalted ghee (store-bought or homemade, page 38)
- 2 Indian bay leaves
- One 3-inch (7.5-cm) cinnamon stick
- 4 whole cloves
- 3 cups (360 g) halved, thinly sliced yellow onion (about 1 large onion)
- ½ teaspoon + ½ teaspoon salt, plus more to taste
- 2 cups (390 g) white basmati rice, rinsed (see page 44)

1. Use a mortar and pestle to coarsely crush the black peppercorns. Add the cardamom pods to the mortar and crack them open so that the seeds are exposed.

2. Heat the ghee in a medium pot over medium heat (see Note, page 39). Once the ghee is good and hot, add the crushed black pepper, cardamom, bay leaves, cinnamon, and cloves. Sizzle, giving the pan a shake or two, until the spices darken a couple of shades and become fragrant, about 45 seconds.

3. Add the onion and ½ teaspoon of the salt. Cook, stirring frequently, until the onion is golden brown, deeper than oatmeal, with well-browned edges, 12 to 15 minutes (see page 32).

4. Stir in the rice and cook for a minute or two, stirring constantly, until roughly half of the rice grains have whitened.

5. Add the remaining ½ teaspoon salt and 3¾ cups (840 ml) water. Increase the heat to medium-high and bring the mixture to a rolling boil.

6. Half-cover the pot and reduce the heat to low. Cook until the level of the water is just at or below the surface of the rice, 3 to 5 minutes. It should look like there are soap bubbles coming out of the rice.

7. Cover the pot completely and cook undisturbed for 10 minutes.

8. Without cracking the lid open, remove the pot from the heat and let sit, covered, for an additional 10 minutes before fluffing the rice gently with a fork. Taste for salt and serve hot.

Serving Tip

→ The bay leaves and cinnamon stick in the final dish are not meant to be eaten and should be moved to the side of the plate—warn your guests. The cloves and cardamom pods are totally edible and we love chewing them, but they can be pushed aside if the flavor is too intense.

Lemon Rice

SERVES 4 • **COOK TIME:** *20 minutes (plus time to cook and chill rice)* • **PHOTO:** *page 109*

Jyoti Perhaps the simplest way to spruce up plain rice is to incorporate flavorings into already cooked grains, as with this simple, colorful preparation from the South Indian state of Karnataka. It is a wonderful way to use up leftover rice (and a favorite snack of my youngest son, Aroop.)

¾ cup (105 g) raw, shelled peanuts (raw cashews may be substituted)

3 tablespoons canola oil

2 dried red chilies, broken into thirds (see page 271)

1 teaspoon black or brown mustard seeds

3 small sprigs fresh curry leaves, stripped from the stems (see page 273)

¾ teaspoon ground turmeric

4 cups (600 g) cooked and seasoned white basmati rice (see Notes, right), chilled in the fridge overnight

2 tablespoons fresh lemon juice (from about ½ lemon), plus more to taste

Salt, to taste (see Notes, right)

1. Heat a large pan over medium-low heat. Once good and hot, add the peanuts and cook, stirring constantly, until they darken slightly and become fragrant, 7 to 9 minutes. Be vigilant about keeping them moving to avoid blackened hot spots. Remove from the heat and immediately transfer to a plate to cool. Do not wash the pan.

2. Heat the oil in the same pan you just used for the peanuts over medium heat. Once the oil starts to shimmer, add the chilies and cook, giving the pan a shake to distribute them evenly, until they darken a shade or two, about 30 seconds.

3. Add the mustard seeds and cook, undisturbed, until they are popping vigorously, another 20 seconds or so (watch out for oil splatter—use a splatter screen if you have one).

4. Add the curry leaves and again, watch out for oil splatter. Cook, giving the pan another shake to distribute them evenly, until the leaves crisp up, about 15 seconds. If it's hard to tell visually, you should be able to feel the texture change while stirring them around in the pan.

5. Remove the pan from the heat and immediately add the turmeric and roasted nuts. Stir to coat in the hot oil, making sure to keep the mixture moving to prevent the turmeric from scorching.

6. Add the rice and place the pan back on the stove over low heat. Mix well to yellow the grains evenly.

7. Stir in the lemon juice and continue cooking, stirring once or twice, until the rice is heated through, a couple of minutes. Taste for lemon and salt and serve warm.

Notes

To prepare the rice, use the Ghee Bhaat recipe on page 44—but omit the ghee, because you'll be adding plenty of oil in this recipe. Steamed takeout rice is also fine. Either way, the rice should be well chilled to ensure the grains don't clump up as you cook them.

If the rice you are using is unseasoned, add ¾ teaspoon salt with the lemon juice.

Bengali Khichudi

SPICED RICE with DAAL and GINGER

SERVES 6 • **COOK TIME:** *1½ hours* • **PHOTO:** *page 114*

Jyoti Khichudi is the consummate comfort food—it is warming, simple to make, and delicious. Different versions can be found in most every region of India. While they all generally consist of rice and daal cooked together (a notable exception being Sabudana Khichudi, page 229), the variations differ markedly in spicing and consistency. Some are served dry and solid, while others are more porridge-like.

The recipe here is for the richly spiced Bengali version that my husband grew up with. It is traditionally served with a heap of crispy Beguni (page 222) and Tamatar Khajoor Chutney (page 244) on the side. (Freshly fried shoestring potatoes are a great alternative garnish.)

Note that you'll need a large pot, as the volume expansion is significant. We like using a 6- to 8-quart (5.7- to 7.5-L) enameled cast-iron Dutch oven.

Auyon On the Mughal emperor Jahangir's regular days of abstinence from meat, his preferred vegetarian dish was an extravagant Gujarati incarnation of khichudi.

Khichudi
⅓ cup (80 ml) canola oil

1 dried red chili, broken into thirds (see page 271)

6 cloves

6 green cardamom pods, cracked open so the seeds are exposed

2 Indian bay leaves

One 3-inch (7.5-cm) cinnamon stick

¾ teaspoon cumin seeds

1½ cups (325 g) yellow moong daal, rinsed

1 cup (195 g) white basmati rice, rinsed (see page 44)

¾ teaspoon ground turmeric

2 tablespoons grated, peeled fresh ginger

1¾ teaspoons salt, plus more to taste

Cauliflower leaves (from the head used for the garnish), roughly chopped into ½-inch (12-mm) pieces

1 cup (140 g) frozen peas, no need to thaw

Garnish
½ cup (120 ml) canola oil

½ medium head (1 pound // 455 g) cauliflower, cut into 1-inch (2.5-cm) florets and ½-inch (12-mm) stem pieces (see page 90)

¼ teaspoon salt

2 tablespoons unsalted ghee (store-bought or homemade, page 38), melted

KHICHUDI

1. Heat the oil in a large, lidded (but uncovered for now) pot over medium-high heat. Once the oil starts to shimmer, add the chili and cook, giving the pan a shake to distribute the chili pieces evenly, until they darken a shade or two, about 30 seconds.

2. Add the cloves, cardamom, bay leaves, cinnamon, and cumin. Sizzle, giving the pan another shake, until the second round of spices darkens and becomes fragrant, about 45 seconds.

3. Add the daal, rice, and turmeric. Cook for a minute or two, stirring constantly, until roughly half the rice grains have whitened and the turmeric is fully incorporated.

4. Add the ginger, salt, and 8 cups (2 L) water. Increase the heat to high, partially cover, and bring the mixture to a rolling boil. Any foam or scum that develops over the first few minutes of cooking should be removed (but no need to get surgical).

5. Reduce the heat to medium-low and cook, stirring once or twice, until the pot stops threatening to boil over, about 5 minutes.

6. Give the pot a final stir before covering it completely. Cook until the rice and daal are cooked through but the rice grains are still distinct, about 15 minutes.

7. Add the cauliflower leaves and 2 cups (480 ml) water. Stir well to combine. Cook, covered, until the daal and rice are meltingly tender and indistinguishable from one another, about 15 minutes.

8. Add the peas and stir for a minute, making sure to scrape anything that is sticking to the bottom of the pot.

9. Remove from the heat. Let rest, covered, for at least 10 minutes. The texture should be akin to that of a thick porridge. Taste for salt.

GARNISH

10. Heat the oil in a medium pan over medium-high heat. Once the oil starts to shimmer, add the cauliflower and salt. Give the pan a good stir, then let the cauliflower brown for about 4 minutes before giving it another stir.

11. Repeat the process, waiting a couple of minutes to stir each time, until the cauliflower is cooked through and roughly half of the surface of the florets and stems are browned, 10 to 12 minutes total.

12. Use a slotted spoon or spider to transfer the cauliflower to a plate or a bowl. (The oil can be strained and reused for future cooking or frying.)

13. Just before serving, lay the cauliflower over the khichudi. To keep the presentation traditional, don't stir it in.

14. Drizzle the ghee over the top of the khichudi and cauliflower. Serve hot.

Serving Tips

→ The bay leaves and cinnamon stick in the final dish are not meant to be eaten and should be moved to the side of the plate—warn your guests. The cloves and cardamom pods are totally edible and we love them, but they can be pushed aside as well if the flavor is too intense.

→ If made in advance, the khichudi will thicken and solidify as it sits. Reheat gently over low heat, and add 1 cup (240 ml) or so of water to thin it out to the proper consistency before garnishing with the cauliflower.

THE CURIOUS CASE OF KEDGEREE

Auyon Of the great many atrocities committed by the British in India, their corruption of a humble comfort food ranks neither among the most barbaric nor the most economically devastating. It is, however, a contender for the most distasteful.

As noted on the previous page, khichudi in its most basic form consists of rice and daal cooked together. Some misguided colonizers decided to replace the daal with flaked fish and boiled eggs. They christened their creation *kedgeree*, and this defilement can now be found on breakfast menus across the United Kingdom. Modern versions sometimes feature a sprinkling of golden raisins atop the mess.

We are, of course, all in favor of experimentation when it comes to cooking. That said, it is important to recognize that not all substitutions are deserving of celebration. Kedgeree is an excellent case in point.

Biryanis

AUYON Biryanis are festive mixed rice preparations. They are most closely associated with the Muslim communities of South Asia, but the immense popularity of the dish is universal. Chicken biryani was the most searched Indian food on the internet in 2019 according to one study, and biryani has been the most ordered dish on Swiggy, one of India's largest delivery platforms, for 8 years running.

At banquets and special occasions, biryanis often serve as the lavishly decorated centerpiece of the meal, replete with silver leaf, saffron, dried fruit, nuts, and the like. The specific cooking process varies depending on the biryani type. In some productions, like the Mushroom Dum Biryani that follows, the flavoring inclusion is cooked, or partially cooked, before layering with the rice. In others, like our Kacchi Hyderabadi Biryani (page 186), the meat addition is only cooked as part of the layered dish (*kacchi* means "raw" in Hindi).

JYOTI Don't expect the rice in these dishes to have the same texture as the other rice recipes in this book—biryani rice often feels more delicate than its boiled counterpart due to the hybrid cooking method.

Mushroom Dum Biryani

LAYERED RICE with MUSHROOMS, CARDAMOM, and HERBS

SERVES 6 • **COOK TIME:** *2¼ hours* • **PHOTO:** *page 125*

Auyon The *dum* designation is a reference to the Mughlai dum pukht style of cooking, which is usually translated as "to breathe and to cook" or "cooking over a slow fire." The vessel is sealed and its contents cooked for a long time, allowing the flavors and aromas to better penetrate all of the ingredients. Dough is traditionally used to seal the container, but we keep things simple by using a combination of lids and foil.

When incorporating this dish into a menu, think of it as a starch rather than a vegetable dish. The mushrooms are a flavoring agent, not the main component.

Rice
- 4 cloves
- 2 green cardamom pods
- 2 black cardamom pods
- 1 Indian bay leaf
- One 3-inch (7.5-cm) cinnamon stick
- 1 blade mace (see page 275)
- 2 tablespoons canola oil
- 2 teaspoons salt
- 3 cups (585 g) white basmati rice, rinsed (see page 44)

Mushrooms + Assembly
- 1 tablespoon + ¼ cup (60 ml) canola oil
- ¼ cup (50 g) unsalted ghee (store-bought or homemade, page 38)
- 4 cups (470 g) halved, thinly sliced yellow onion (about 2 medium onions)
- 3 cloves garlic, finely chopped
- 2 teaspoons grated, peeled fresh ginger
- 12 black peppercorns, coarsely crushed
- 1 teaspoon cumin seeds, roasted (lightly!) and ground (see page 43)
- 1 teaspoon coriander seeds, roasted and ground with the cumin
- ½ teaspoon ground turmeric
- ¼ teaspoon ground cayenne (optional)
- ⅝ cup (160 g) tomato puree, diluted with 5 tablespoons water (for a substitute, see Tomato Puree, page 83)
- 1 pound (455 g) shiitake, baby portobello, or button mushrooms, cut into ½-inch- (12-mm-) thick slices (about 5 cups)
- ½ cup (120 g) whole, unflavored yogurt (store-bought or homemade, page 40), stirred to a smooth consistency and at room temperature
- 2 tablespoons finely chopped fresh cilantro, stems and leaves
- 1½ teaspoons finely chopped fresh mint leaves
- 1¼ teaspoons salt, plus more to taste
- ½ teaspoon garam masala (store-bought or homemade, page 53)

Garnish
- ¾ teaspoon kewra water (see page 275)
- 2 tablespoons finely chopped fresh cilantro, stems and leaves
- 1½ teaspoons finely chopped fresh mint leaves

RICE

1. Use a mortar and pestle to coarsely crush the cloves. Add both the green and black cardamom pods to the mortar and crack them open so that the seeds are exposed.

2. Combine the crushed cloves, green cardamom, and black cardamom with the bay leaf, cinnamon, mace, oil, salt, and 10 cups (2.4 L) water in a large pot. Bring the mixture to a rolling boil over high heat.

3. Add the rice and cook for about 10 minutes, uncovered, until the rice has softened but still retains a delicate crunch—it should feel just barely undercooked.

4. Transfer the rice to a colander and gently rinse with cold water for a few seconds to halt the cooking. Drain thoroughly and set aside. (Proper draining is crucial—you don't want to end up with a wet biryani.)

MUSHROOMS

5. Prepare a water bath by filling a roasting tray or rimmed baking sheet with ½ inch (12 mm) of water and placing it at the bottom of the oven. Position a rack in the center and preheat the oven to 325°F (165°C).

6. Grease the bottom of a large, ovenproof, lidded dish with 1 tablespoon of the canola oil and set aside.

7. Heat the remaining ¼ cup (60 ml) canola oil with the ghee in a large pan over medium-high heat. Once the fats start to shimmer, add the onion and cook, stirring frequently, until soft, translucent, and starting to brown at the edges, 10 to 12 minutes.

8. Add the garlic, ginger, crushed peppercorns, ground cumin and coriander, turmeric, and cayenne (if using). Stir for a couple of minutes to fully incorporate.

9. Add the diluted tomato puree and cook, stirring frequently, until the mixture thickens slightly, about 3 minutes.

10. Add the mushrooms, yogurt, cilantro, mint, salt, and garam masala. Stir well for a couple of minutes to combine and then remove from the heat.

11. Taste for salt—the mushrooms should be a touch salty because they will serve to further season the rice.

ASSEMBLY

12. Evenly spread half of the drained rice in the prepared baking dish. Layer all of the tomato-mushroom mixture over it, and then top evenly with the remaining rice. While adding the rice, remove the cinnamon stick, cardamom pods, bay leaf, and any other large spices you happen to catch (no need to get too fussy).

13. Seal the cooking vessel with aluminum foil and place the lid on top. (If you don't have an oven-safe dish with a lid, just double up on the foil and crimp it tightly to seal.) Cook, in the center of the oven, for 45 minutes.

14. Turn the oven off and let the dish sit undisturbed in the unopened oven for a final 15 minutes. Unseal with care (watch out for steam!) and taste for salt.

GARNISH

15. Garnish with the kewra water, cilantro, and mint. Serve hot.

Serving Tip

→ The black cardamom pods, bay leaf, cinnamon stick, and mace in the final dish are not meant to be eaten and should be moved to the side of the plate—warn your guests. The crushed cloves and green cardamom pods are totally edible and we love them, but they can be pushed aside as well if the flavor is too intense.

Kacchi Hyderabadi Biryani

LAYERED RICE with CHICKEN and BROWNED ONION

SERVES 6 • **MARINATION TIME:** *5 hours*
COOK TIME: *1¾ hours* • **PHOTO:** *page 125*

Jyoti This recipe involves several hours of marination time, but the potent aroma of saffron, onion, and spice (released in one fell swoop when you uncover the dish after removing it from the oven) makes all the prep feel worthwhile. Frying the onions the day before can be helpful, because you can then quickly assemble the marinade the following morning and have everything ready in time for dinner.

Do not skimp on the oil. The amount we prescribe is necessary, because you will need it to both cook the onions and have some onion-flavored oil left over to season the rice afterward.

Marinade
12 cloves

12 green cardamom pods

1 cup (240 ml) canola oil

7½ cups (900 g) halved, thinly sliced yellow onion (about 2½ large onions)

½ teaspoon + 1¼ teaspoons salt

¾ cup (190 g) hung curd (page 41)

6 cloves garlic, finely chopped

4 teaspoons grated, peeled fresh ginger

1 teaspoon garam masala (store-bought or homemade, page 53)

½ teaspoon ground cinnamon

½ teaspoon ground turmeric

¼ teaspoon ground nutmeg

¼ teaspoon ground cayenne (optional)

2 pounds (910 g) skinless, bone-in chicken thighs, each thigh cut in half through the bone to expose the marrow (have your butcher do this for you, or use a pair of heavy-duty kitchen shears; drumsticks cut in half may be substituted for the thighs)

Rice
½ teaspoon lightly packed saffron threads

2 tablespoons canola oil

1¼ teaspoons salt, plus more to taste

2½ cups (490 g) white basmati rice, rinsed (see page 44)

¾ cup (45 g) finely chopped, lightly packed fresh cilantro, stems and leaves (1 generous bunch should be enough for both this and the garnish)

½ cup (20 g) finely chopped, lightly packed fresh mint leaves (1 generous bunch should be enough for both this and the garnish)

Garnish
¾ cup (45 g) finely chopped, lightly packed fresh cilantro, stems and leaves

½ cup (20 g) finely chopped, lightly packed fresh mint leaves

MARINADE

1. Use a mortar and pestle to coarsely crush the cloves. Add the cardamom pods to the mortar and crack them open so that the seeds are exposed.

2. Divide the crushed spices in half, and reserve one half to be used with the marinade and the other to be used with the rice.

3. Heat the oil in a large pan over medium-high heat. Once the oil starts to shimmer, add the onion and ½ teaspoon of the salt. Stir well to coat. Cook, stirring occasionally, until the onion is darker than golden brown, with a healthy proportion of well-browned (but not quite blackened!) bits, 35 to 40 minutes (see page 32).

4. Drain the onion and reserve the oil for use with the rice later. Let the cooked onion cool to room temperature, then divide it into three equal parts.

5. Store two parts (two-thirds of the total) in the fridge to be used later. Place the remaining third in a large, oven-safe, lidded dish to prepare the marinade. (The dish you use for this recipe should ideally be big enough to hold the chicken in a single layer, sitting flat, with no overlap. We use a large Dutch oven.)

6. Add the remaining 1¼ teaspoons salt, half of the crushed cloves and cardamom, the hung curd, garlic, ginger, garam masala, cinnamon, turmeric, nutmeg, and cayenne (if using) to the marinade onions in the baking dish. Mix well to combine.

7. To absorb any excess moisture on the chicken, quickly dab or wrap each piece with a paper towel, working with one piece at a time and replacing the paper towel as necessary. Add the chicken to the onion-spice mixture and massage the marinade into each piece using your hands.

8. Spread the chicken out into a relatively even layer, with as little overlap as possible, at the bottom of the dish. Cover the mixture and marinate in the fridge for 4 to 8 hours.

RICE

9. Position a rack in the middle of the oven and preheat the oven to 425°F (220°C).

10. Warm 2 tablespoons water and combine it with the saffron threads in a small bowl. Soak for at least 15 minutes.

11. In the meantime, combine the remaining half of the crushed cloves and cardamom, canola oil, salt, and 10 cups (2.4 L) water in a large pot. Bring the mixture to a rolling boil over high heat.

12. Add the rice and cook, uncovered, until the rice has softened but still retains a delicate crunch, about 6 minutes—it should feel just barely undercooked. Stir a couple of times to prevent clumping.

13. Transfer the rice to a colander and gently rinse with cold water for a few seconds to halt the cooking. Drain thoroughly. (Proper draining is crucial—you don't want to end up with a wet biryani.)

14. Combine the drained rice, half of the remaining cooked onion (one-third of the total), cilantro, and mint in a large bowl. Mix well to combine.

15. Remove the marinated chicken from the fridge. Layer the rice-herb mixture evenly over the chicken in the baking dish. Drizzle the reserved onion-flavored oil over the top of the rice.

16. Using a spoon, make five or six shallow (1-inch- // 2.5-cm-deep) depressions in the top of the rice. Sprinkle a bit of the saffron water and threads into each depression.

17. Add a few tablespoons of the partially cooked, herbed rice to the saffron-water soaking bowl and stir it around to get any remaining saffron water out. Use the colored rice to even out the depressions in the biryani dish (without getting too fussy).

18. Seal the cooking vessel with aluminum foil and place the lid on top. (If you don't have an oven-safe dish with a lid, just double up on the foil and crimp it tightly to seal.) Cook, in the center of the oven, for 20 minutes.

19. Lower the oven temperature to 350°F (180°C) and cook for an additional 40 minutes.

20. While the biryani cooks, remove the remaining fried onion from the fridge and set aside to warm up to room temperature.

21. When the biryani is done cooking, turn the oven off and let the dish sit undisturbed in the unopened oven for a final 15 minutes. Unseal with care (watch out for steam!) and stir well. Taste for salt.

GARNISH

22. Garnish with cilantro, mint, and the remaining fried onion. Serve hot.

Serving Tip

→ The cardamom pods and crushed cloves in the final dish are totally edible and we love chewing them, but they can be pushed aside if the flavor is too intense. Advise your guests.

THE SEVENTY-YEAR-OLD ROTI QUESADILLA

Auyon In the early 20th century, several thousand Punjabi men arrived in the US to work as migrant laborers, farming and logging their way across the American West. The influx continued through 1917, when Congress passed the Asiatic Barred Zone Act, a sweeping piece of legislation that largely limited immigration from Asia.

California's miscegenation laws made it illegal to marry outside of one's race. Few Punjabi women arrived in the U.S. before the border closed, largely due to pre-existing anti-Asian immigration policy. As a result, many of the Punjabi men ended up marrying local Mexican women (who belonged, as far as county officials were concerned, to the same race: "brown"). These cross-cultural marriages eventually produced a web of Punjabi-Mexican communities that spanned the southwest, from El Paso, Texas all the way up to Yuba City, California.

Children born of these cross-cultural marriages were typically raised Catholic and spoke Spanish at home, but the household cooking was often demonstrably bicultural. The Punjabi men taught their Mexican wives how to make the Indian dishes of their homeland, and the Mexican wives in turn adjusted and amended the dishes to reflect local ingredients. The mixed-heritage cuisine was served at restaurants as well—El Ranchero, later rechristened Rasul's El Ranchero, opened in 1954 in Yuba City and served both Mexican and Indian fare. The Punjabi and Mexican elements remained distinct from one another on the menu, with the exception of a single crossover dish: the restaurant's roti quesadilla, which featured onions, shredded beef, and melted cheese stuffed inside a paratha (page 192).

A relaxation of immigration laws in the 1960s changed the landscape dramatically. Today, Yuba City is home to the largest concentration of Punjabi Sikhs in the country. Although none of the aforementioned restaurants remain open, small but distinct Punjabi-Mexican enclaves persist across the southwest, unplanned legacies of early twentieth-century nativist legislation.

We encourage you to celebrate this curious bit of American history by hosting a Mexican-Indian dinner some evening. If you're feeling adventurous, maybe even try your hand at a roti quesadilla.

• Roti •

SIMPLE FLATBREAD

MAKES 24 • **COOK TIME:** 3 hours • **PHOTO:** page 106

Jyoti Anyone can make a roti! It is the simplest bread—no yeasting or baking involved—and requires only a handful of ingredients. Although it takes practice to turn out consistent, perfectly puffed rotis, the oddballs you will inevitably produce as you go will be no less delicious. Misshapen or not, rotis freeze and defrost well, so we wrote the recipe for a large batch to allow for plenty of repetitions. That said, if you're new to flatbreads, you can always start with just a half batch.

The only special equipment you will need are a rolling pin and a thin tea towel, but an empty wine bottle and an old (clean!) T-shirt will work just as well. As with all of our recipes, we recommend you read the recipe all the way through before getting started.

Auyon The traditional way to eat rotis is to tear off a bit and use it as a scoop in lieu of a spoon or fork, but they also work well filled taco style with paneer or chickpeas. I love eating them rolled up with an omelet for breakfast, too.

Dough
3¾ cups (490 g) roti or chapati flour (see Roti Flour, below)

¼ teaspoon salt

¼ teaspoon ground cayenne (optional)

Shaping
1 cup (130 g) roti or chapati flour

Ghee or canola oil, as needed

DOUGH

1. Combine the roti flour, salt, and cayenne (if using) in a large bowl and mix well by hand.

2. Add 2 cups (480 ml) water slowly, a couple of tablespoons at a time, incorporating the liquid into the flour mixture with each addition until you have a slightly tacky, claylike dough that holds together. Use only as much water as you need to get all of the dry flour incorporated. There will usually be a few tablespoons of water left over (save it), and it may take up to 10 minutes of slowly adding and mixing.

3. Dip your fingertips into the leftover water and make several shallow indentations in the dough (think bowling ball holes) to help hydrate the dough as it rests. Cover with an airtight lid and let rest at room temperature for at least 45 minutes. If you don't have an appropriate lid, cover the dough with a damp towel to prevent it from drying out. (The dough can also be made a day ahead, sealed with foil, and refrigerated. Remove from the fridge at least an hour before shaping to allow it to warm up.)

SHAPING

4. Place the flour in a pie pan or large plate and set aside.

5. Briskly knead the rested dough on a clean, dry work surface until it feels noticeably more tacky and pliable, just a couple of minutes or so. Do not knead for much longer than that, as you don't want the dough to get too sticky. If the dough is sticking to your hands too much, grease your hands with a bit of ghee or oil.

6. Divide the dough into 24 equal portions—if you don't have a kitchen scale, an easy way to do this is to divide it in half three times to yield eighths, and then divide each eighth into thirds.

recipe continues

Roti Flour

Roti flour, also known as chapati flour or atta, is a stone-milled, finely ground wheat flour that should be available at any Indian grocery. We haven't found any decent substitutions, so we recommend ordering it online if you can't find it locally. Avoid anything labeled "multigrain."

ROLLING TECHNIQUE

Rolling back and forth at different angles will work to flatten the roti, but try making a long oval shape with the rolling pin as you roll instead of going straight back and forth. With the right rhythm and an amply floured roti, rolling back and forth like this should spin the roti as you go so that you don't have to pick it up and spin it by hand to get it evenly rolled out. Don't get discouraged if it doesn't work the first several times—it takes a lot of practice.

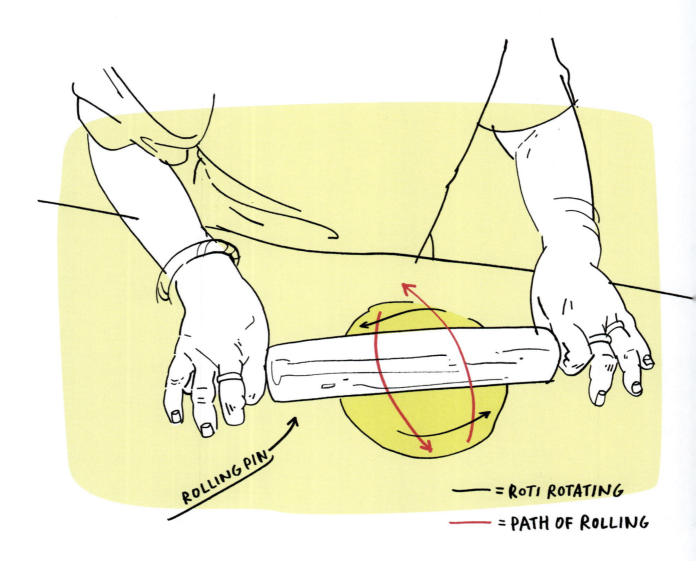

Roti
• continued •

7. Shape each portion into a smooth ball by rolling it between your palms. Place the dough balls back in the large bowl and cover with a damp cloth. Take them out one at a time, keeping the rest covered so that the last few don't dry out by the time you get to them.

8. Take one ball and flatten it into a 3-inch- (7.5-cm-) diameter patty between your palms. Press both sides of the patty into the dry flour on the flour plate, then roll it out on the clean, dry work surface with a rolling pin. Roll from edge to edge, until the roti is roughly 6 inches (15 cm) in diameter. Don't roll it too much more than that. If it's too thin, it won't puff up properly. Re-flour the roti in the flour plate as necessary while rolling.

9. Set the rolled roti aside and place a piece of wax paper or foil over it. Repeat the process with the remaining 23 dough balls. Stack each uncooked, rolled roti over the first, with a piece of wax paper or foil between each one.

COOKING

10. Heat a large pan or griddle over medium-high heat. Once the pan is hot enough to make a drop of water sizzle, place the first roti in the pan. Cook until you see bubbles start to form inside the dough (as long as 60 seconds when you start cooking, and as quick as 45 seconds once the griddle has heated up).

11. Flip the roti. You should see a light speckling of brown spots on the cooked side. Cook for another 30 to 45 seconds, until new bubbles start to form.

12. Flip the roti again. Moving quickly, and with a thin towel or cloth protecting your fingers, carefully rotate the roti on the griddle in a steady constant motion. It should start to balloon a bit. Push around the air bubble to distribute it evenly within the roti. Use gentle pressure to make the air go as close to the edges as possible (if you press too hard, you could get a hot air burn, so be careful). A fully inflated roti is a fully cooked roti. The edges can be stubborn, so make sure to push them down into the griddle to ensure they cook, even if they don't fill with air. After 45 to 60 seconds of cooking, flip and cook for another 20 to 30 seconds, continuing to move the air around inside the roti. If things seem like they are moving too quickly or too slowly, feel free to lower or increase the heat.

13. In total, the cooking should take 2½ to 3½ minutes, and the cooked flatbread should be golden beige with brown speckles on both sides. Repeat with the remaining rotis, and brush off any excess flour that builds up with a tea towel or cloth in between.

Serving Tips

→ Rotis are best consumed hot off the stove, but if you're making them in advance, best practice is to store them in a lidded glass or plastic container (or a tortilla warmer) that is large enough that the rotis can sit flat. Line the container with a clean dishcloth, layer a piece of parchment paper over the cloth, and then place the rotis on top of the parchment. (The fabric will help absorb the steam that is released as the flatbreads cool—otherwise, the moisture may compromise the texture of the bottom few.) Keep the container covered. After all of the rotis are cooked, place a paper towel over the top roti, and then cover the paper towel with foil before placing the lid on the container. Store at room temperature and consume within 24 hours (or keep them in the fridge for a couple of days).

→ When served alongside vegetarian dishes, a small amount (¼ teaspoon) of ghee or butter is traditionally applied to each roti just after it is taken off the heat. The fat helps to keep the flatbreads from drying out. When serving with meat dishes, the flatbreads are typically served unadorned.

→ To reheat, wrap them in foil and place them in a preheated 300°F (150°C) oven for 10 minutes. Alternatively, you can reheat them one by one on a griddle over medium heat, cooking each side for up to a minute.

Paratha

LAYERED FLATBREAD

MAKES 8 • COOK TIME: *2 hours* • PHOTO: *page 112*

Jyoti Parathas are the decadent, griddle-fried cousins of rotis (page 189). They are often layered and sometimes stuffed. Traditional techniques for folding and filling vary widely, and the next four recipes showcase a few different options.

If you'd like to get some prep out of the way the day before, you can make the dough (Steps 1 through 3) ahead and seal it with foil or plastic wrap before storing it in the fridge. Take the dough out an hour before shaping to allow it to come back to room temperature. Parathas keep well in the freezer once cooked.

Dough
3¾ cups (490 g) roti or chapati flour (see Roti Flour, page 189)

½ teaspoon salt

¼ teaspoon ground cayenne (optional)

Shaping + Cooking
1 cup (130 g) roti or chapati flour

⅓ cup (67 g) unsalted ghee (store-bought or homemade, page 38), warmed

DOUGH

1. Combine the flour, salt, and cayenne (if using) in a large bowl and mix well by hand.

2. Add 2 cups (480 ml) water slowly, a couple of tablespoons at a time, incorporating the liquid into the flour mixture with each addition until you have a slightly tacky, claylike dough that holds together. Use only as much water as you need to get all of the dry flour incorporated. There will usually be a few tablespoons of water left over (save it).

3. Dip your fingertips into the leftover water and make several shallow indentations in the dough (think bowling ball holes) to help hydrate the dough as it rests. Cover with an airtight lid and let rest at room temperature for at least 45 minutes. If you don't have an airtight lid, cover the dough with a damp towel to prevent it from drying out.

SHAPING

4. Place the dry flour into a pie pan or a large plate and set aside.

5. Briskly knead the rested dough on a clean, dry work surface until it feels noticeably more tacky and pliable, just a couple minutes or so. Don't knead for much longer than that, as you don't want the dough to get too sticky. If the dough is sticking to your hands too much, grease your hands with a bit of oil.

6. Divide the dough into 8 equal portions. Shape each into a smooth ball by rolling it between your palms. Place the dough balls back in the large bowl and cover with a damp cloth. Take them out one at a time, keeping the rest covered so that the last few don't dry out by the time you get to them.

7. Take one ball and flatten it into a 4-inch- (10-cm-) diameter patty between your palms. Press both sides of the patty into the dry flour on the flour plate, and then roll it out on the clean, dry work surface with a rolling pin until the disk is roughly 8 inches (20 cm) in diameter (see Rolling Technique, page 190).

8. Use your fingers to apply a thin layer of ghee, about ½ teaspoon, to the surface of the disk. Fold the top and bottom of the disk in toward the center so that they overlap to form a long strip **(a)**. Apply ¼ teaspoon ghee to the top surface of the strip, then fold the ends of the strip over the center to form a thick square **(b)**. Press both sides of the square into the flour plate, then roll it out with a rolling pin, re-flouring as necessary, until the square is roughly 9¼ x 9¼ inches (24 x 24 cm) **(c)**.

9. Set the paratha aside and place a piece of wax paper or foil over it. Repeat the process (flattening, greasing, folding, and re-flattening) with the remaining 7 dough balls. Stack each uncooked paratha over the first, with a piece of wax paper or foil between each one.

COOKING

10. Heat a large pan or griddle over medium-high heat. Once the pan is hot enough to make a drop of water sizzle, brush any excess flour off the first paratha and place it in the pan. Cook until the raw dough darkens slightly and the bottom layer of the paratha starts to bubble, about 45 seconds.

11. Flip the paratha. You should see a few small, brown spots starting to form on the cooked side. Use the back of a spoon to apply a thin layer of ghee, about ½ teaspoon, to the cooked side. The whole flatbread may start to puff up, in which case the ghee application will feel a bit like greasing an inflating balloon. As you spread the ghee, press the edges and corners of the paratha down into the griddle to ensure it cooks evenly. Cook the second side for about 40 seconds before flipping again.

12. Apply another ½ teaspoon ghee to the freshly cooked side. Let cook for about 20 seconds or so before flipping once more and cooking for a final 20 seconds. (The basic idea is to cook each side both without ghee and with ghee, requiring a total of three flips and around 2 minutes on the griddle total.) The final cooked paratha should be golden beige with a generous speckling of brown.

13. Repeat with the remaining 7 parathas. Serve hot.

Serving Tips

→ Parathas are best consumed hot off the stove, but if you're making them in advance, best practice is to store them in a lidded glass or plastic container (or a tortilla warmer) that is large enough that the parathas can sit flat. Line the container with a clean dishcloth, layer a piece of parchment paper over the cloth, and then place the parathas on top of the parchment. (The fabric will help absorb the steam that is released as the flatbreads cool—otherwise, the moisture may compromise the texture of the bottom few.) Keep the container covered. After all of the parathas are cooked, place a paper towel over the top paratha, and then cover the paper towel with foil before placing the lid on the container. Store at room temperature and consume within 24 hours (or keep them in the fridge for a couple of days).

→ To reheat, wrap with foil and place them in a preheated 300°F (150°C) oven for 10 minutes. Alternatively, you can reheat them one by one on a griddle over medium heat, cooking each side for up to a minute. We prefer the griddle.

Gobhi Paratha

CAULIFLOWER-STUFFED FLATBREAD

MAKES 12 • **COOK TIME:** 2½ hours • **PHOTO:** *page 122*

Jyoti This paratha iteration, which features a layer of spiced cauliflower sandwiched between two layers of dough, is a classic Punjabi winter dish. Served with a side of Homemade Yogurt (page 40) and a spoonful of Adarak Nimbu Achaar (page 245), it makes for a delicious and substantial brunch.

Once you've gotten the hang of the stuffing process, we encourage you to try substituting other fillings. Just make sure that whatever you choose is relatively dry, because too much moisture risks compromising the texture of the flatbread. Crumbled, seasoned Paneer (page 46) and Keema Mattar (page 156) with most of the liquid boiled off are two great places to start.

If you'd like to get some prep out of the way the day before, you can make the dough (Steps 1 through 3) ahead and seal it with foil or plastic wrap before storing it in the fridge. Take the dough out an hour before shaping to allow it to come back to room temperature. Parathas keep well in the freezer once cooked.

For the grated or riced cauliflower, we either buy packaged riced cauliflower or use a food processor. You can also use the largest holes on a box grater, but be warned that it can get messy.

Dough
3¼ cups (490 g) roti or chapati flour (see Roti Flour, page 189)

½ teaspoon salt

¼ teaspoon ground cayenne (optional)

Stuffing + Assembly
3¼ cups (680 g) grated or riced cauliflower (about 1 small head cauliflower, stem included; see headnote)

½ fresh Indian green chili (optional; see page 271—jalapeño may be substituted), minced

2 tablespoons finely chopped fresh cilantro, stems and leaves

4 teaspoons grated, peeled fresh ginger

½ teaspoon garam masala (store-bought or homemade, page 53)

¼ teaspoon ground cayenne (optional)

1 cup (130 g) roti or chapati flour

2 teaspoons salt

Cooking
½ cup (100 g) unsalted ghee (store-bought or homemade, page 38), warmed

DOUGH

1. Combine the flour, salt, and cayenne (if using) in a large bowl. Mix well by hand.

2. Add 2 cups (480 ml) water slowly, a couple of tablespoons at a time, incorporating the liquid into the flour mixture with each addition until you have a slightly tacky, claylike dough that holds together. Use only as much water as you need to get all of the dry flour incorporated. There will usually be a few tablespoons of water left over (save it).

3. Dip your fingertips into the leftover water and make several shallow indentations in the dough (think bowling ball holes) to help hydrate the dough as it rests. Cover with an airtight lid and let rest at room temperature for at least 45 minutes. If you don't have an airtight lid, cover the dough with a damp towel to prevent it from drying out.

STUFFING + ASSEMBLY

4. While the dough rests, combine the cauliflower, fresh chili (if using), cilantro, ginger, garam masala, and cayenne (if using) in a large bowl. Stir well to fully incorporate. Don't add any salt yet—doing so prematurely will draw moisture out of the cauliflower and ruin the texture of the stuffing. Set aside.

5. Place the dry flour in a pie pan or a large plate and set aside.

6. Briskly knead the rested dough on a clean, dry work surface until it feels noticeably more tacky and pliable, just a couple of minutes or so. Don't knead for much longer than that, as you don't want the dough to get too sticky. If the dough is sticking to your hands too much, grease your hands with a bit of oil.

7. Divide the dough into 24 equal portions—if you don't have a kitchen scale, an easy way to do this is to divide it in half three times to yield eighths, and then divide each eighth into thirds.

8. Shape each portion into a smooth ball by rolling it between your palms. Place the dough balls back in the large bowl and cover with a damp cloth. Take them out two at a time (each paratha will be composed of two parts), keeping the rest covered so that the last few don't dry out by the time you get to them.

9. Take two balls and flatten them out, one at a time, into 3-inch- (7.5-cm-) diameter patties between your palms. Press both sides of one patty into the dry flour on the flour plate, then repeat with the second patty. Roll the patties out with a rolling pin, one at a time, on the clean, dry work surface until each disk is roughly 6 inches (15 cm) in diameter (see Rolling Technique, page 190). Re-flour the disks in the flour plate as necessary.

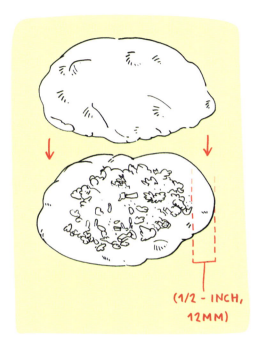

(1/2 - INCH, 12MM)

10. In a small bowl, place ¼ cup (35 g) of the cauliflower stuffing mixture. Add ⅛ teaspoon salt and mix well to combine. Spread the salted stuffing evenly over one of the disks, but not all the way to the edges—keep a ½-inch (12-mm) margin clear around the circumference of the disk. Place the second disk over the top and press it down evenly with your palms, focusing especially on sealing the circumference.

11. Sprinkle ½ teaspoon dry flour (from the flour plate) evenly over the top of the stuffed disk, then flip it over and sprinkle another ½ teaspoon dry flour over the other side. Roll out the stuffed disk with a rolling pin to a diameter of roughly 7 inches (17 cm), adding more dry flour as necessary. Set the paratha aside and place a piece of wax paper or foil over it.

recipe continues

Gobhi Paratha
· *continued* ·

12. Repeat the process (flattening, seasoning the cauliflower, stuffing, covering, and re-flattening) with the remaining 22 dough balls. Stack each uncooked paratha over the first, with a piece of wax paper or foil between each one. (Mixing the salt with the stuffing will draw moisture out of the cauliflower, so it's ideal to move quickly with the assembly and cooking. If you prefer to take your time, we recommend assembling and cooking the parathas in small batches of 3 to 4 and then repeating the process, rather than working in one large batch.)

COOKING

13. Heat a large pan or griddle over medium heat. Once the pan is hot enough to make a drop of water sizzle, brush any excess flour off the first paratha and place it in the pan. Cook until the bottom layer starts to bubble (as long as 90 seconds when you start cooking, and as quick as 45 seconds once the griddle has heated up). The bubbling can be hard to gauge through the stuffing and second layer of dough—slip a spatula underneath and peel an edge up to peek. If you see small, brown spots starting to appear underneath, go ahead and flip the bread.

14. Apply a thin layer of ghee, about ½ teaspoon, to the cooked side. Press the edges of the paratha down with the back of a spatula to ensure it cooks evenly each time you flip (the edges may pop open while cooking, which is fine, because what seals the disk together is the moisture from the stuffing). Cook until the bottom layer starts to bubble and brown spots begin to appear underneath, another 45 to 90 seconds.

15. Flip and apply another ½ teaspoon ghee to the freshly cooked side. Let cook for about 45 seconds or so before flipping once more and cooking for a final 45 seconds. (The basic idea is to cook each side both without ghee and with ghee, requiring a total of three flips and 3 to 5 minutes on the griddle total.) The final cooked paratha should be golden beige with a generous speckling of brown.

16. Repeat with the remaining 11 parathas. Serve hot.

Serving Tips

→ Parathas are best consumed hot off the stove, but if you're making them in advance, best practice is to store them in a lidded glass or plastic container (or a tortilla warmer) that is large enough that the parathas can sit flat. Line the container with a clean dishcloth, layer a piece of parchment paper over the cloth, and then place the parathas on top of the parchment. (The fabric will help absorb the steam that is released as the flatbreads cool—otherwise, the moisture may compromise the texture of the bottom few.) Keep the container covered. After all of the parathas are cooked, place a paper towel over the top paratha, and then cover the paper towel with foil before placing the lid on the container. Store in the fridge and consume within a couple of days.

→ To reheat, wrap with foil and place them in a preheated 300°F (150°C) oven for 10 minutes. Alternatively, you can reheat them one by one on a griddle over medium heat, cooking each side for up to a minute. We prefer the griddle.

Aloo Paratha

POTATO-STUFFED FLATBREAD

MAKES *12* • **COOK TIME:** *2½ hours (plus time to cook potatoes)* • **PHOTO:** *page 122*

Jyoti Another Punjabi brunch standard: rounds of ghee-fried dough stuffed with a delicious, spiced potato mixture. The technique here involves a stuffed dough ball that is rolled out, in contrast to the Gobhi Paratha (page 194) approach of sandwiching filling between two layers and flattering to seal.

Aloo parathas are an indulgence best served simply, with some Homemade Yogurt (page 40) or Raita (page 238), a bit of Adarak Nimbu Achaar (page 245), and a cup of Masala Chai (page 252).

If you'd like to get some prep out of the way the day before, you can make the dough (Steps 1 through 3) ahead and seal it with foil or plastic wrap before storing it in the fridge. Take the dough out an hour before shaping to allow it to come back to room temperature. Parathas keep well in the freezer once cooked.

Auyon Whether an Indian meal is based on rice, bread, or both is largely dependent on geography. The northern, wheat-producing state of Punjab, nicknamed "The Breadbasket of India," is one of the few regions of India where wheat reigns supreme as the staple starch.

Dough
3¾ cups (490 g) roti or chapati flour (see Roti Flour, page 189)

½ teaspoon salt

¼ teaspoon ground cayenne (optional)

Stuffing + Assembly
2 large russet potatoes (1⅜ pounds // 640 g total), boiled and seasoned (see page 49), and then peeled

½ cup (115 g) finely chopped yellow onion (about ⅔ small onion)

1 fresh Indian green chili (optional; see page 271—jalapeño may be substituted), minced

2 tablespoons finely chopped fresh cilantro, stems and leaves

1½ teaspoons amchoor (ground dried mango, see page 271)

¾ teaspoon garam masala (store-bought or homemade, page 53)

¾ teaspoon salt, plus more to taste

1 cup (130 g) roti or chapati flour

Cooking
½ cup (100 g) unsalted ghee (store-bought or homemade, page 38), warmed

DOUGH

1. Combine the flour, salt, and cayenne (if using) in a large bowl and mix well by hand.

2. Add 2 cups (480 ml) water slowly, a couple of tablespoons at a time, incorporating the liquid into the flour mixture with each addition until you have a slightly tacky, claylike dough that holds together. Use only as much water as you need to get all of the dry flour incorporated. There will usually be a few tablespoons of water left over (save it).

3. Dip your fingertips into the leftover water and make several shallow indentations in the dough (think bowling ball holes) to help hydrate the dough as it rests. Cover with an airtight lid and let rest at room temperature for at least 45 minutes. If you don't have an airtight lid, cover the dough with a damp towel to prevent it from drying out.

recipe continues

Aloo Paratha
· continued ·

STUFFING + ASSEMBLY

4. While the dough rests, mash the potatoes with a potato masher or fork in a large bowl. Add the onion, fresh chili (if using), cilantro, amchoor, garam masala, and salt. Mix well by hand to fully incorporate, then taste for salt.

5. Cover the mixture and set aside. If preparing several hours in advance, store the mixture in the fridge and remove it an hour before assembling the breads to warm it up a bit. There is no need to refrigerate if cooking within a couple of hours.

6. Place the dry flour in a pie pan or a large plate and set aside.

7. Briskly knead the rested dough on a clean, dry work surface until it feels noticeably more tacky and pliable, just a couple of minutes or so. Don't knead for much longer than that, as you don't want the dough to get too sticky. If the dough is sticking to your hands too much, grease your hands with a bit of oil.

8. Divide the dough into 12 equal portions—if you don't have a kitchen scale, an easy way to do this is to divide it in half twice to yield quarters, and then divide each quarter into thirds.

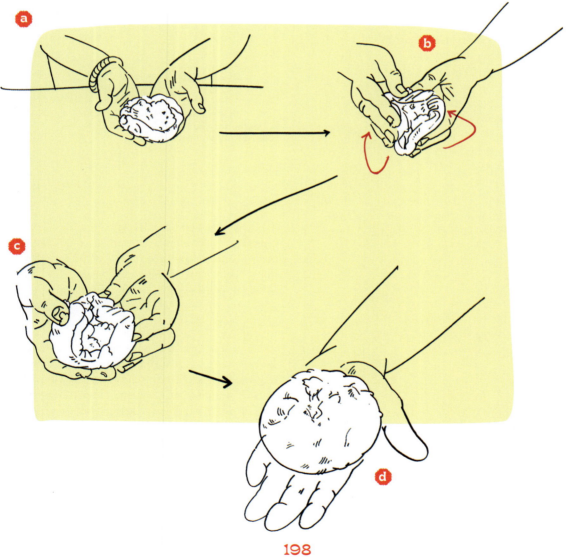

9. Shape each portion into a smooth ball by rolling it between your palms. Place the dough balls back in the large bowl and cover with a damp cloth. Take them out one at a time, keeping the rest covered so that the last few don't dry out by the time you get to them.

10. Take one ball and flatten it into a 3-inch- (7.5-cm-) diameter patty between your palms. Press both sides of the patty into the dry flour on the flour plate, and then roll it out on the clean, dry work surface with a rolling pin until the disk is roughly 4½ inches (11 cm) in diameter.

11. Holding the disc in one hand, place about 2 tablespoons of the chili-potato stuffing into its center ⓐ. Cup your hands together beneath the disc, and use your thumbs to press the potato down while wrapping the dough around the stuffing ⓑ. The idea is to completely cover the stuffing with the dough—think a potato-filled water balloon ⓒ. Seal the dough by pinching it together firmly at the top ⓓ.

12. Gently flatten the stuffed ball into a 3-inch (7.5-cm) patty between your palms, and press both sides of the patty into the dry flour on the flour plate. Place the patty seam-side down (so that in case the seam opens a bit, you won't get potato all over the rolling pin) and roll it out with a rolling pin until the disk is roughly 7 inches (17 cm) in diameter (see Rolling Technique, page 190). Re-flour the disk on the flour plate as necessary. Set the paratha aside and place a piece of wax paper or foil over it.

13. Repeat the process (flattening, stuffing, and re-flattening) with the remaining 11 dough balls. Stack each uncooked paratha over the first, with a piece of wax paper or foil between each one.

COOKING

14. Heat a large pan or griddle over medium heat. Once the pan is hot enough to make a drop of water sizzle, brush any excess flour off the first paratha and place it in the pan. Cook until the bottom starts to bubble (as long as 90 seconds when you start cooking, and as quick as 60 seconds once the griddle has heated up). The bubbling can be hard to gauge through the stuffing—slip a spatula underneath and peel an edge up to peek. If you see small, brown spots starting to appear underneath, go ahead and flip the bread.

15. Apply a thin layer of ghee, about ½ teaspoon, to the cooked side. Press the edges of the paratha down with the back of a spatula to ensure it cooks evenly each time you flip. The bread should puff up a bit as the steam builds. Cook until the bottom starts to bubble and brown spots begin to appear underneath, another 60 to 90 seconds.

16. Flip and apply another ½ teaspoon ghee to the freshly cooked side. Let cook for about 45 seconds or so before flipping once more and cooking for a final 45 seconds. (The basic idea is to cook each side both without ghee and with ghee, requiring a total of three flips and 3 to 5 minutes on the griddle total.) The final cooked paratha should be golden beige with a generous speckling of brown.

17. Repeat with the remaining 11 parathas. Serve hot.

Serving Tips

→ Parathas are best consumed hot off the stove, but if you're making them in advance, best practice is to store them in a lidded glass or plastic container (or a tortilla warmer) that is large enough that the parathas can sit flat. Line the container with a clean dishcloth, layer a piece of parchment paper over the cloth, and then place the parathas on top of the parchment. (The fabric will help absorb the steam that is released as the flatbreads cool—otherwise, the moisture may compromise the texture of the bottom few.) Keep the container covered. After all of the parathas are cooked, place a paper towel over the top paratha, and then cover the paper towel with foil before placing the lid on the container. Store in the fridge and consume within a couple of days.

→ To reheat, wrap with foil and place them in a preheated 300°F (150°C) oven for 10 minutes. Alternatively, you can reheat them one by one on a griddle over medium heat, cooking each side for up to a minute. We prefer the griddle.

Lachhedaar Paratha

FLAKY, BUTTERY FLATBREAD

MAKES 8 • COOK TIME: *2½ hours* • PHOTO: *page 128*

Jyoti These flaky flatbreads, also known as lachha parathas, were my dad's favorite. There is a satisfyingly sculptural element to making them, as each paratha is first rolled into a cone and then flattened to produce spiral layers. Note that the dough preparation is slightly different from the previous flatbread recipes, in that it incorporates a beaten egg and uses all-purpose flour rather than roti flour. The all-purpose flour makes the dough a bit harder to roll out than the roti flour dough, so be prepared to lean into it.

If you'd like to get some prep out of the way the day before, you can make the dough (Steps 1 through 3) ahead and seal it with foil or plastic wrap before storing it in the fridge. Take the dough out an hour before shaping to allow it to come back to room temperature. Parathas keep well in the freezer once cooked.

Auyon Every baking culture seems to have its own way of alternately layering dough and fat to produce a delicate, flaky bread. Southeastern Europe has phyllo, France the croissant, and northern India the lachhedaar paratha. *Lachhedaar*, which means "coiled" or "whorled" in Hindustani, refers to the spiral shape of the layers.

Dough
3 cups (420 g) all-purpose flour

1 egg, beaten

1 teaspoon salt

Assembly + Cooking
1 cup (140 g) all-purpose flour

1 cup (200 g) unsalted ghee (store-bought or homemade, page 38), warmed

DOUGH

1. Combine the flour, egg, and salt in a large bowl. Mix well by hand until all the ingredients are fully incorporated.

2. Add 1 cup (240 ml) water slowly, a couple of tablespoons at a time, incorporating the liquid into the flour-egg mixture with each addition until you have a pliable, slightly tacky dough that holds together. Use only as much water as you need to get the dough soft and uniform. There will usually be a tablespoon or two of water left over (save it).

3. Dip your fingertips into the leftover water and make several shallow indentations in the dough (think bowling ball holes) to help hydrate the dough as it rests. Cover with an airtight lid and let rest at room temperature for at least 45 minutes. If you don't have an airtight lid, cover the dough with a damp towel to prevent it from drying out.

ASSEMBLY + COOKING

4. Place the dry flour in a pie pan or large plate and set aside.

5. Briskly knead the rested dough on a clean, dry work surface until it feels noticeably more tacky and pliable, just a couple of minutes or so. Don't knead for much longer than that, as you don't want the dough to get too sticky. If the dough is sticking to your hands too much, grease your hands with a bit of oil to make things easier.

6. Divide the dough into 8 equal portions and shape each into a smooth ball by rolling it between your palms. Place the dough balls back in the large bowl and cover with a damp cloth. Take them out one at a time, keeping the rest covered so that the last few don't dry out by the time you get to them.

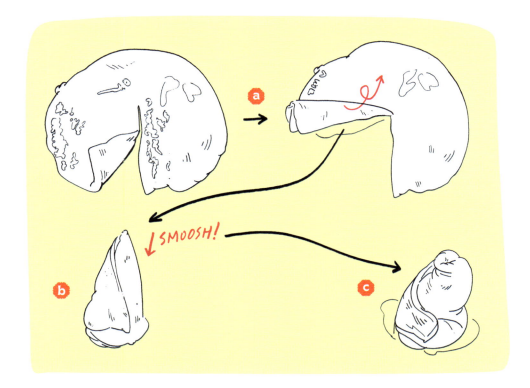

7. Take one ball and flatten it into a 3-inch- (7.5-cm-) diameter patty between your palms. Press both sides of the patty into the dry flour on the flour plate, and then roll it out on the clean, dry work surface with a rolling pin. Roll from edge to edge, until the disk is roughly as thick as a tortilla. Flip and roll out again to a diameter of roughly 7½ inches (19 cm) (see Rolling Technique, page 190). Re-flour the disk on the flour plate as necessary.

8. Apply ½ teaspoon of warmed ghee to the center of the disk, then use your fingers to spread it evenly over the top surface. Liberally sprinkle some dry flour (about ⅛ teaspoon) over the ghee. With a sharp knife, make a single cut from the center to the bottom of the disk.

9. Starting on the left side of the cut, roll the dough clockwise into a tight cone **a**. Place the cone wide-side down (like an upside-down ice cream cone) **b**. Gently flatten it with your palm, pressing the tip down toward the base so that it shortens to about 2¼ inches (5.5 cm) **c**. Store in a covered container.

10. Repeat the process (rolling out, applying ghee, flouring, forming a cone, and squishing) with the remaining 7 dough balls. Place the container with all of the flattened cones into the fridge and chill, covered, until the ghee solidifies, at least 15 minutes. You can also pause here and resume cooking the next day, but if you are leaving the dough for any longer than an hour in the fridge, place a damp cloth or paper towel over the dough balls and make sure the lid is on tight.

11. Remove the container from the fridge and take out one squished cone. Flatten it into a 3-inch- (7.5-cm-) diameter patty. Press both sides of the patty into the dry flour on the flour plate, and then roll it out with a rolling pin again to a diameter of roughly 7½ inches (19 cm). You should be able to see the subtle spiral pattern of ghee and dough as you roll it out.

12. Set the paratha aside and place a piece of wax paper or foil over it. Repeat the flattening process with the remaining 7 cones. Stack each uncooked paratha over the first, with a piece of wax paper or foil between each one.

recipe continues

Lachhedaar Paratha
· continued ·

13. Heat a large pan or griddle over medium heat. Once the pan is hot enough to make a drop of water sizzle, place the first paratha into the pan. Cook until you start to see bubbles form (as long as 60 seconds when you start cooking, and as quick as 30 seconds once the griddle has heated up) and then flip.

14. On the cooked side, which should be sparsely speckled with light brown spots, apply a very thin layer of ghee, about ¼ teaspoon. Once you start to see bubbles form again, flip a second time, applying another ¼ teaspoon ghee to the freshly cooked side.

15. Let cook for about 30 seconds or so before flipping once more and cooking for a final 30 seconds. (The basic idea is to cook each side both without ghee and with ghee, requiring a total of three flips and 2 to 3 minutes on the griddle total.) The flatbread may puff up a bit as it is cooked, which is fine. The final cooked paratha should be golden beige with a generous dappling of cinnamon-brown spots and streaks.

16. Repeat with the remaining 7 parathas. Serve hot.

Serving Tip

→ Parathas are best consumed hot off the stove, but if you're making them in advance, best practice is to store them in a lidded glass or plastic container (or a tortilla warmer) that is large enough that the parathas can sit flat. Line the container with a clean dishcloth, layer a piece of parchment paper over the cloth, and then place the parathas on top of the parchment. (The fabric will help absorb the steam that is released as the flatbreads cool—otherwise, the moisture may compromise the texture of the bottom few.) Keep the container covered. After all of the parathas are cooked, place a paper towel over the top paratha, and then cover the paper towel with foil before placing the lid on the container. Store at room temperature and consume within 24 hours (or keep them in the fridge for a couple of days).

→ To reheat, wrap with foil and place them in a preheated 300°F (150°C) oven for 10 minutes. Alternatively, you can reheat them one by one on a griddle over medium heat, cooking each side for up to a minute. We prefer the griddle.

JYOTI'S MOM

JYOTI'S DAD: LOVER OF LACHHEDAAR PARATHAS

Rice and Bread

Loochi

FRIED BALLOON BREAD

MAKES 18 • **COOK TIME:** 2½ hours • **PHOTO:** page 98

Jyoti This balloon-shaped, deep-fried bread is really a hybrid of two traditional North Indian preparations. The first is the Punjabi puri, which is made from whole wheat roti flour and is rolled slightly thicker. The second is the thinner, crispier Bengali loochi, which is made from all-purpose flour. Our mixed-flour hybrid strikes a balance between the two, combining the nutty flavor of the puri with the delicate texture of the Bengali version.

Loochis are traditionally delivered directly from the frying pan to waiting diners, requiring the cook to labor at the stove while guests indulge at the table. In reference to this expectation of fresh-from-the-stove flatbreads and fried breads (and the time-intensiveness of Indian cooking in general), engineering professor Deb Chachra darkly jokes that the cuisine is "meant to keep women in subjugation." Never hesitate to assign your adult son to run the fryer.

Auyon Since this recipe requires deep-frying, check out the note on deep-frying on page 210 before getting started. The recommended temperature of the frying oil for this recipe (390°F // 196°C) is hotter than what we use for standard deep-frying. This higher temperature is necessary in order for the loochis to puff up properly, but make sure the oil does not get so hot that it starts to smoke.

As my mom mentions above, these breads are best consumed immediately. The air-filled spectacle and crackly, hot-out-of-the-fryer texture are ephemeral treasures. That said, the deflated, made-in-advance variety has its merits too—loochis stay fresh for a couple of days without refrigeration, making them the ideal flatbread for travel or picnics.

Excellent accompaniments include Aloo Tamatar (page 87), Channa Masala (page 74), and Keema Mattar (page 156), along with sides of Homemade Yogurt (page 40) and Adarak Nimbu Achaar (page 245). For a sweet snack, try it with Sooji Halwa (page 258).

Dough

1 cup (130 g) roti or chapati flour (see Roti Flour, page 189)

1 cup (140 g) all-purpose flour

½ teaspoon salt

¼ (60 ml) cup canola oil

Shaping + Frying

2 cups (480 ml) canola oil, plus more as needed

DOUGH

1. Combine the roti flour, all-purpose flour, and salt in a large bowl. Stir well to combine.

2. Add the oil and mix well with your hands to fully incorporate. The mixture should have a lumpy, crumbly texture.

3. Add 1 cup (240 ml) water slowly, a couple of tablespoons at a time, incorporating the liquid into the oily flour with each addition until you have a smooth dough that holds together. Use only as much water as you need to get the dough firm and uniform. There will usually be a few tablespoons of water left over (save it).

4. Dip your fingertips into the leftover water and make several shallow indentations in the dough (think bowling ball holes) to help hydrate the dough as it rests. Cover with an airtight lid and let rest at room temperature for at least 45 minutes, but no longer than a couple of hours. If you don't have an airtight lid, cover the dough with a damp towel to prevent it from drying out. (Unlike the other flatbread doughs, we recommend against refrigerating this dough overnight—it should be made the same day that the loochis are shaped and fried.)

SHAPING + FRYING

5. Briskly knead the rested dough on a clean, dry work surface until it feels noticeably more tacky and pliable, just a couple of minutes or so. Don't knead for much longer than that, as you don't want the dough to get too sticky.

6. Divide the dough into 18 equal portions—if you don't have a kitchen scale, an easy way to do this is to divide it into thirds twice to yield ninths, then divide each ninth in half.

7. Shape each into a smooth ball by rolling it between your palms. Place the dough balls back into the large bowl and cover with a damp cloth. Take them out one at a time, keeping the rest covered so that the last few don't dry out by the time you get to them.

8. Take one ball and flatten it into a 3-inch- (7.5-cm-) diameter patty between your palms. Roll the patty out with a rolling pin on the clean, dry work surface until the disk is roughly 5 inches (12 cm) in diameter. Unlike the other bread doughs in this book, this dough is difficult to rotate with the rolling pin as you roll, so you will have to spin it by hand to get it evenly flattened.

9. Set the loochi aside and place a piece of wax paper or foil over it. Repeat the process with the remaining 17 dough balls. Stack each uncooked loochi over the first, with a piece of wax paper or foil between each one.

10. Heat the oil in a deep wok or Dutch oven over medium-high heat until it gets up to around 390°F (196°C), 5 to 10 minutes depending on the cooking vessel and stove. The oil should be at least 1 inch (2.5 cm) deep, so add more if necessary. If you don't have a thermometer handy, check the oil by dropping in a bit of dough—if it sizzles vigorously and comes up to the surface of the oil almost immediately, the oil is hot enough. If the dough only sizzles a bit or not at all, the oil isn't hot enough, and if the oil starts to smoke, it is too hot. As you wait for the oil to heat up, line a large plate or baking sheet with paper towels and set aside.

11. When the oil is up to temperature, add the first loochi to the pan. It should start to puff up into a balloon after 10 to 15 seconds. Let the first side cook for 20 to 30 seconds, until the underside has cooked and darkened slightly, then flip and cook the other side for another 20 to 30 seconds. Carefully transfer the first loochi to the paper-lined plate with a slotted spoon or spider. The whole process should take no longer than a minute, and the final cooked, inflated flatbread should be a glistening golden beige. Flip once or twice more to get the color right, if necessary. If the loochi does not puff up properly, the oil is either too hot or too cool.

12. Repeat with the remaining loochis, cooking them one at a time. Check the temperature and allow the oil to reheat a bit in between as necessary. Serve immediately (see Auyon's headnote).

CHAPTER SIX

This Is How We Party

Moongphali Aloo Chaat

CITRUS CHILI POTATO with ROASTED PEANUTS

SERVES 6 • **COOK TIME:** *70 minutes* • **PHOTO:** *page 123*

Jyoti This recipe is my own riff on a tried-and-true Indian street food combination—a starchy, creamy base of boiled potatoes with freshly roasted peanuts and a generous garnish of citrus- and chili-spiked Chaat Masala (page 53). The parboiling of the potatoes can be done a day in advance.

We encourage you to buy the peanuts raw and roast them yourself as instructed in the recipe, rather than just buying roasted nuts. You will notice the difference! You should be able to find raw peanuts at any Indian or Asian grocery.

3 large russet potatoes (2⅛ pounds // 960 g total)

1½ tablespoons salt, plus more to taste

½ cup (70 g) raw, shelled peanuts

¼ cup (60 ml) canola oil

1 fresh Indian green chili (optional; see page 271—jalapeño may be substituted), minced

2 tablespoons finely chopped fresh cilantro, stems and leaves

5 teaspoons chaat masala (store-bought or homemade, page 53), plus more to taste

2 teaspoons grated, peeled fresh ginger

2 tablespoons lemon or lime juice

Garnish (optional)
1 tablespoon neutral oil (canola, avocado, etc.)

2 tablespoons finely chopped fresh cilantro, stems and leaves

1. Combine the potatoes and salt with 6 cups (1.4 L) water in a large pot. The water should cover the potatoes with room to spare. Add more if necessary. Bring to a rolling boil over high heat.

2. Reduce the heat to medium, cover, and cook until the potatoes are just slightly underdone, 15 to 20 minutes. They should give some resistance when pierced with a fork or sharp knife.

3. Drain, then run the hot potatoes under cold water to halt the cooking, and allow them to cool to room temperature.

4. In the meantime, heat a medium pan over medium-low heat. Once good and hot, add the peanuts and cook, stirring constantly, until they darken slightly and become fragrant, 5 to 7 minutes. Be vigilant about keeping them moving to avoid blackened hot spots. Remove from the heat and immediately transfer to a plate to cool.

5. Cube the cooled potatoes into ¾-inch (2-cm) chunks. A bit of crumbling is okay, as that will add to the body of the dish, but separate and distinct pieces are ideal.

6. Heat the oil in a large, nonstick pan over medium heat. Once the oil starts to shimmer, add the potato in a single layer. (Work in batches if your pan is not large enough to accommodate all of the pieces.)

7. Cook, undisturbed, until the surfaces in contact with the pan are lightly browned, about 5 minutes. Give a gentle stir, careful to avoid breakage, and then let the potatoes continue to cook, undisturbed. Cook until the potato pieces are lightly browned on a couple of sides for a total of 10 to 12 minutes.

8. Add the chili (if using), cilantro, chaat masala, and ginger. Stir well to combine and remove from the heat.

9. Coarsely crush the cooled peanuts with a mortar and pestle. Just before serving, stir in the citrus juice and crushed peanuts. The dish should taste dazzlingly bright, popping with both chaat masala and citrus. Taste and adjust as necessary (and feel free to use salt instead of chaat masala to up the savoriness, if you'd prefer).

GARNISH

10. Totally optional, but for a slightly more dressed-up presentation, toss the finished dish with the neutral oil (canola, avocado, etc.) to give it a slight sheen. Garnish with cilantro to taste. Serve warm.

• Jhaal Mudhi •

PUFFED RICE with JUNK FOOD and PEAS

SERVES 6 • **THAW TIME:** *30 minutes*
COOK TIME: *35 minutes* • **PHOTO:** *page 100*

Jyoti This preparation is an extremely popular snack in my husband's home state of West Bengal. The dish is simple to construct, but you must resist the temptation to stir everything together until just before you're ready to serve. Mixing at the last minute will ensure the rice stays as crispy as possible. (Although we don't call for it in our recipe, some folks stir in a teaspoon of lemon juice at the very end as well.)

If you don't have mustard oil on hand, hold off on trying this recipe until you do, as its pungent, wasabi-like kick is necessary for the proper flavor. For more on this potentially anxiety-inducing ingredient, see page 171.

4 cups (60 g) puffed rice (available at any Indian grocery)

1 cup (140 g) raw, shelled peanuts

1½ cups (225 g) frozen peas, no need to thaw

1 cup (90 g) Hot Mix (see Notes, right)

½ teaspoon salt, plus more to taste

1 fresh Indian green chili (optional; see page 271—jalapeño may be substituted), minced

½ cup (95 g) finely chopped cucumber (about 1 Persian or mini cucumber, see Cucumber Snobbery, page 56)

½ cup (30 g) finely chopped fresh cilantro, stems and leaves

¼ cup (60 g) finely chopped yellow onion (about ⅓ small onion)

2 tablespoons grated unsweetened coconut (see Frozen Coconut, page 78)

2 tablespoons mustard oil (see Notes, right)

1. Preheat the oven to 250°F (120°C). Spread the puffed rice on a baking sheet and warm it for 20 minutes to crisp it up. Let cool for 10 minutes before handling.

2. While the rice is warming, heat a medium pan over medium-low heat. Once good and hot, add the peanuts and cook, stirring constantly, until they darken slightly and become fragrant, 8 to 10 minutes. Be vigilant about keeping them moving to avoid blackened hot spots. Remove from the heat and immediately transfer to a plate to cool.

3. Combine the peas and ⅔ cup (160 ml) water in a small pot. Bring to a boil over high heat and then drain, reserving the peas. Alternatively, microwave the peas and water for 90 seconds in a microwave-safe container and then drain.

4. Combine the puffed rice, peanuts, Hot Mix, and salt in a large bowl and mix well. Just before serving, add the drained peas, chili (if using), cucumber, cilantro, onion, coconut, and mustard oil. Stir well to incorporate. Taste for salt and serve immediately.

Notes

Hot Mix is an Indian junk food and can be found in the shiny, crinkly bag section of most Indian groceries. You can think of it as a deliciously spicy Chex Mix, with fried besan bits (see Besan, page 81), fried lentils, rice flakes, puffed rice, peanuts, and raisins. It is not to be confused with the identically named asphalt mix.

For all you mustard lovers, try this dish Bengali style with 3 tablespoons mustard oil rather than 2. It will sport a more traditional, sinus-clearing kick.

Turning out perfectly golden, crispy treats without leaving the comfort of one's own kitchen is a true pleasure. First, though, the elephant in the room: deep-frying is unquestionably a bit of a pain. It requires a lot of oil, the immediate environs of the stove will get covered in a thin film of oil that will require some scrubbing, and unless you have a serious hood vent, your kitchen will smell like fried food for a day or so.

That said, we still believe it's worth it. Thankfully, the process itself is really pretty simple. Get the oil up to temperature, then work in batches to avoid crowding the pan. Watch the food carefully and don't wander off. Let the oil return to temperature between batches. Keep in mind that food will continue to brown a bit after coming out of the pan. Serve hot and enjoy.

A few additional things to keep in mind:

- Make sure you have adequate ventilation, in the form of a hood vent or a nearby window.

- If you have one handy, a deep wok is the ideal frying vessel (a Dutch oven will work fine too, but the shape of the wok helps minimize splatter and requires less oil).

- If you don't already have a digital, instant-read thermometer, we recommend acquiring one. Most of our deep-fried recipes call for the oil to be heated to around 375°F (190°C), but a few require the oil to get all the way up to 390°F (196°C), while others are low-and-slow down at 360°F (184°C). While reading the oil without a device is a skill you can and should develop, an instant-read thermometer (with a long probe) is the best way to distinguish between those different temperatures when starting out. You can get a decent one for as little as $20—just buy one with a temperature range that reaches 400°F (200°C).

- Frying does require a lot more fat than other cooking methods, but if you strain the oil after it cools, you can store it in the fridge in a tightly sealed container and reuse it a few times.

- Finally, to dispose of frying oil: never pour it down the drain. Allow it to cool completely, and then pour it into a disposable, sealable container before putting it into the trash. If you want to avoid unnecessary plastic waste, there are plenty of companies that make oil solidifiers for environmentally friendlier disposal.

Chire Bhaja

CRISPY FLATTENED RICE with PEAS

SERVES 4 • **COOK TIME:** *30 minutes* • **PHOTO:** *page 100*

Jyoti This Bengali snack is truly a snap to make. Consider waiting until your guests arrive to finish the final frying steps, as they are worthy of an audience—I love hearing the oohs and aahs when the poha puffs up in my classes! That said, the frying can also be done several hours in advance, in which case the fried (and cooled) poha should be stored in an airtight container until ready to serve.

Since this recipe requires deep-frying, check out the note on deep-frying on page 210 before getting started. The recommended temperature of the frying oil for this recipe (390°F // 196°C) is hotter than what we use for standard deep-frying. The higher temperature is necessary in order for the poha to puff up properly, but make sure the oil does not get so hot that it starts to smoke.

- 1 tablespoon + 2 cups (480 ml) canola oil, plus more as needed
- ¾ teaspoon cumin seeds
- 1 cup (140 g) frozen peas, no need to thaw
- ¼ teaspoon salt, plus more to taste
- ½ fresh Indian green chili (optional; see page 271—jalapeño may be substituted), minced
- 2 tablespoons finely chopped fresh cilantro, stems and leaves
- 1 cup (80 g) poha (roasted and flattened rice, available at any Indian grocery)
- 1 teaspoon chaat masala (store-bought or homemade, page 53; ½ teaspoon salt and several generous grinds of black pepper may be substituted)

1. Heat 1 tablespoon canola oil in a medium pan over medium-high heat. Once the oil starts to shimmer, add the cumin seeds and cook, giving the pan a shake or two, until they darken a couple of shades and become fragrant, about 30 seconds.

2. Add the peas and salt and cook, stirring frequently, until the peas are cooked through and a bit of liquid evaporates, 2 to 3 minutes. Don't overcook the peas to dullness—they should retain their bright green hue.

3. Transfer the peas to a bowl to halt the cooking. Add the minced chili (if using) and cilantro and stir well to combine. Taste for salt.

4. Heat the remaining 2 cups (480 ml) of the oil in a deep wok or Dutch oven over medium-high heat until it gets up to around 390°F (196°C), 5 to 10 minutes depending on the cooking vessel and stove. The oil should be at least 1 inch (2.5 cm) deep, so add more if necessary. If you don't have a thermometer handy, check the temperature by dropping a few grains of poha into the oil—if they sizzle vigorously and puff up immediately, the oil is hot enough. If they sizzle only a bit or not at all, the oil isn't hot enough, and if the oil starts to smoke, it is too hot. As you wait for the oil to heat up, line a large plate or baking sheet with paper towels and set aside.

5. Once the oil is up to temperature, add half of the poha, which should puff up immediately. Reduce the heat to low, then remove with a slotted spoon or spider and transfer to the paper-lined plate.

6. Turn the heat up to medium-high to get the oil back up to temperature, then repeat with the remaining poha. Transfer the puffed poha to a bowl and stir in the chaat masala. Taste for salt.

7. To serve, keep the poha and peas in separate serving dishes and encourage your guests to combine them to taste on their plates (we like three parts poha for every one part peas). Serve warm or at room temperature.

• Paapdi Chaat •

SWEET and SOUR CHICKPEAS with HOMEMADE CHIPS

SERVES 6 • **COOK TIME:** *35 minutes (plus time to cook and chill potatoes)* • **PHOTO:** *page 123*

Jyoti This North Indian street food is a beautiful study in contrasts: sweet-sour, creamy-crunchy, and salty-spicy. It falls under the broad umbrella of *chaat*, which roughly translates to "savory snack foods." The paapdi, or fried chips, would traditionally be made with a fresh dough (a slightly less oily version of samosa dough), but we always use the tortilla shortcut because it works so well.

Since this recipe requires deep-frying, check out the note on deep-frying on page 210 before getting started. The frying can be done as much as a day or two in advance (store the paapdi in a sealed container to keep them fresh), but don't assemble the dish until just before serving, to keep the chips as crispy as possible.

Auyon Some scholars link the prevalence of deep-fried Indian street foods with historical concerns for food safety. Since the temperature of hot frying oil (340° to 390°F // 174° to 196°C) renders food safer (from a pathogenic perspective) than that of boiled or braised foods (212°F // 100°C), deep-fried foods are a friendlier choice in situations with unpredictable hygiene standards.

There is even a relevant legend involving Shah Jahan, the Mughal emperor who built the Taj Mahal, who supposedly moved his empire's capital to New Delhi without having consulted his minister of health. By the time the emperor learned of the pollution of the city's water supply, it was too late to change course. The good people of Delhi were instructed to fry deeply.

- 2 cups (480 ml) canola oil, plus more as necessary
- Six 10-inch (25-cm) flour tortillas, cut into 1-inch (2.5-cm) squares or diamonds
- 3 medium russet potatoes (1⅜ pounds // 600 g total), boiled and seasoned (see page 49), peeled, chilled in the fridge for at least 30 minutes, and then cubed into ½-inch (12-mm) chunks
- 1 cup (195 g) drained Cooked and Seasoned Chickpeas (page 45) or canned chickpeas
- 1½ cups (360 g) whole, unflavored yogurt (store-bought or homemade, page 40), stirred to a smooth consistency
- 1½ cups (415 g) imli chutney (store-bought or homemade, page 243)

Garnish
- 1½ teaspoons cumin seeds, roasted (lightly!) and ground (see page 43)
- 1 teaspoon ground cayenne (optional)
- 1 teaspoon salt, plus more to taste

1. Line a large plate or baking sheet with paper towels and set aside.

2. Heat the oil to 340°F (174°C) in a deep wok or Dutch oven over medium-high heat. The oil should be at least 1 inch (2.5 cm) deep in the cooking vessel, so add more if necessary. If you don't have a thermometer handy, check the oil by dropping in a piece of tortilla—if it sizzles steadily and then comes up to the surface of the oil after a few seconds, the oil is hot enough to fry in. If the tortilla only sizzles a bit or not at all, the oil isn't hot enough, and if the oil starts to smoke, it is way too hot. This is a relatively low-temperature deep-frying process.

3. When the oil is up to temperature, reduce the heat to medium-low and add up to half of the tortilla squares. You can crowd the frying oil a bit more than you normally would for deep-frying—we cook 3 tortillas' worth of chips at a time in a 9½-inch (25-cm) kadhai, or Indian wok, in 2 cups (480 ml) oil, for reference.

recipe continues

Paapdi Chaat
· *continued* ·

4. Stir well to coat, and then continue to stir frequently, keeping an eye on the color. The squares will first go limp, and then start to crisp up and turn golden. Start to stir more frequently, every 30 seconds, once the chips start to crisp up.

5. Cook until the chips are a light golden brown, 8 to 10 minutes, keeping in mind that they will continue to darken a bit outside of the oil. (The frying time can be quicker if you are cooking in smaller batches, so keep a close eye on the color and trust your senses.)

6. Use a slotted spoon or spider to transfer the first batch of chips to the paper-lined plate. Repeat with the remaining tortilla pieces, checking the temperature and allowing the oil to reheat between batches as necessary.

7. To serve, place a generous helping of chips, or paapdi, on six plates. Nestle 2½ tablespoons each of potato and chickpeas into the paapdi. Top with 2 tablespoons each of yogurt and chutney.

GARNISH
8. Garnish with a couple pinches of ground cumin, a pinch of cayenne (if using), and a pinch of salt. Serve immediately.

Dimer Debhil

HARD-BOILED EGG in a SPICY POTATO BLANKET

MAKES 6 • **COOK TIME:** *80 minutes (plus time to cook potatoes)* • **PHOTO:** *page 109*

Jyoti My mother-in-law taught me this recipe, a popular snack from the West Bengali capital of Kolkata. While Western deviled eggs incorporate Satan directly into the yolk, this version features an intact egg nestled inside a layer of deviled, spicy potatoes. Dimer Debhil goes beautifully with Dhania Pudina Chutney (page 242), Imli Chutney (page 243), or ketchup.

Since this recipe requires deep-frying, check out the note on deep-frying on page 210 before getting started. If you have the time, cook the eggs a couple of hours in advance. That should allow plenty of time for them to cool completely (either in the ice bath or in the fridge), which makes peeling a bit easier. If you're looking to prep things even further ahead, everything right up to the frying can be done a day in advance: place a paper towel over the unfried, blanketed eggs (to protect them from any moisture that might condense on the lid), then store them in a sealed container in the fridge.

Auyon Bengali Dimer Debhil and Scotch eggs (a popular British pub food of hard-boiled eggs encased in sausage meat and breadcrumbs) trace a shared ancestry back to nargisi kofta, a Mughlai dish of hard-boiled eggs swaddled in spicy kofta meat. *Nargisi kofta* roughly translates to "narcissus meatballs," a reference to the sliced presentation's resemblance to the narcissus, or daffodil, blossom.

Also, a note on nomenclature: In Bengal, an ellipsoid croquette is known as a *chop*, a colonial-era term that we use in the recipe that follows. Meanwhile, a *cutlet* (another Indian English term for croquettes that we use later in the book) is a flat, patty-shaped fritter. None of this, my Bengali father assures me, is an exact science.

Egg Preparation
6 large eggs + 2 large eggs

Pinch of salt, plus more to taste

Assembly
4 large russet potatoes (2¾ pounds // 1280 g total), boiled and seasoned (see page 49), and then peeled

2 fresh Indian green chilies (optional; see page 271—jalapeños may be substituted), minced

3 tablespoons finely chopped fresh cilantro, stems and leaves

2 tablespoons amchoor (ground dried mango, see page 271)

4½ teaspoons grated, peeled fresh ginger

1 teaspoon garam masala (store-bought or homemade, page 53)

1½ cups (165 g) breadcrumbs

Frying
3 cups (720 ml) canola oil, plus more as needed

EGG PREPARATION

1. Prepare an ice bath by filling a medium bowl half full of ice and then adding water to cover. Set aside.

2. Bring 10 cups (2.4 L) water to a boil in a large, lidded pot over medium-high heat. Carefully lower 6 of the eggs, one by one, into the pot. Leave the heat at medium-high for 30 seconds before reducing the heat to low. Adjust the heat as necessary to keep the water at a low simmer. Cover the pot and cook for an additional 9 minutes (assuming the eggs are fridge-cold; if they are at room temperature, cook for 8 minutes).

3. Immediately remove the eggs with a slotted spoon or spider and place into the ice bath to halt the cooking. Peel when cool.

4. Meanwhile, crack the remaining 2 eggs into a small bowl. Add a pinch of salt and beat well to combine. Set aside.

recipe continues

Dimer Debhil
· *continued* ·

ASSEMBLY

5. Place the potatoes in a large bowl and mash them with a potato masher or fork. Mashing is most easily accomplished if the potatoes are still warm from boiling—if they are cool, we recommend rewarming them in a hot water bath for 10 minutes before attempting to mash.

6. Add the chili (if using), cilantro, amchoor, ginger, and garam masala to the mashed potato and mix well. Taste for salt.

7. Spread the breadcrumbs out on a pie pan or plate and set aside.

8. Divide the mashed potato mixture into 6 equal parts. Flatten a portion to roughly ½ inch (12 mm) thick and place a peeled egg in the center. Wrap the potato mixture around the egg to cover it completely and evenly. Press gently to ensure that the potato jacket is smooth with no cracks, and so that there are no pockets of air between the potato and the egg. Repeat with the remaining eggs.

9. Dip a blanketed egg, or chop, into the beaten egg. Make sure the chop is completely coated, then let any excess drip off and roll it in breadcrumbs to cover uniformly. Repeat with the rest of the chops.

FRYING

10. Heat the oil in a deep wok or Dutch oven over medium-high heat until it gets up to around 375°F (190°C), 5 to 10 minutes depending on the cooking vessel and stove. The oil should be at least 1½ inches (4 cm) deep, so add more if necessary (or use a smaller vessel). If you don't have a thermometer handy, check the oil by dropping in a few breadcrumbs—if they sizzle vigorously and then come up to the surface of the oil after a second or two, the oil is hot enough to fry in. If the breadcrumbs only sizzle a bit or not at all, the oil isn't hot enough, and if the oil starts to smoke, it is too hot. As you wait for the oil to heat up, line a large plate or baking sheet with paper towels and set aside.

11. When the oil is up to temperature, carefully lower the first chop into the wok. Fry until golden brown on all sides, 4 to 6 minutes total, giving it a quarter turn every 60 to 90 seconds. Resist the temptation to fry more than one chop at a time, because they become harder to manipulate (and more likely to break) when the wok is crowded. The oil should come about halfway up the chop, so add more (and let it come up to temperature) if necessary.

12. When done, carefully transfer the first chop to the paper-lined plate using a slotted spoon or spider. Repeat with the remaining chops, cooking them one at a time. Check the temperature and allow the oil to reheat a bit in between as necessary.

13. Allow the chops to rest for 5 minutes or so before serving. To serve, cut each chop in half lengthwise with a sharp knife and serve hot.

Aloo Tikki

PEA-STUFFED POTATO CROQUETTES

MAKES 12 • **COOK TIME:** *2 hours (plus time to cook potatoes)* • **PHOTO:** *page 100*

Jyoti These potato croquettes, known as cutlets in Indian English, are adored across the country. We usually serve them with Dhania Pudina Chutney (page 242) and Imli Chutney (page 243), but finely chopped raw onion and beaten Homemade Yogurt (page 40) are frequent accompaniments too (see Serving Tip, page 219). For a soft, creamy counterpoint to the crispy cutlets, smother the tikki in Ghoogni (page 69) to make the superfood Aloo Tikki Chaat.

Since this recipe requires deep-frying, check out the note on deep-frying on page 210 before getting started. Everything right up to the frying can be done a day in advance. Place a paper towel over the uncooked tikki and store them in a sealed container in the fridge.

Auyon For the sandwich bread, we use Pepperidge Farm white bread. Don't skimp on the amount—the bread is a necessary binding agent that will keep the potato from breaking down while frying. For a gluten-free version, you can replace the bread with 5 teaspoons of cornstarch.

Potatoes
4 large russet potatoes (2¾ pounds // 1280 g total), boiled and seasoned (see page 49), and then peeled

5 slices white sandwich bread (4½ ounces // 130 g total)

½ fresh Indian green chili (optional; see page 271—jalapeño may be substituted), minced

3 tablespoons finely chopped fresh cilantro, stems and leaves

1½ teaspoons amchoor (ground dried mango, see page 271), plus more to taste

¼ teaspoon salt, plus more to taste

Peas
2 tablespoons canola oil

¼ teaspoon cumin seeds

1½ cups (225 g) frozen peas, no need to thaw

¼ teaspoon ground coriander

¼ teaspoon ground cayenne (optional)

¼ teaspoon salt, plus more to taste

Assembly + Frying
1 tablespoon + 2 cups (480 ml) canola oil, plus more as necessary

POTATOES

1. Mash the potatoes with a potato masher or fork in a large bowl.

2. Place ½ cup (120 ml) water in a wide, shallow bowl or plate. Lay a slice of bread flat in the water, then flip the slice to wet the other side. Squeeze the slice between your palms to get rid of excess moisture, then add it to the potato. Repeat with the remaining slices.

3. Add the fresh chili (if using), cilantro, amchoor, and salt. Mix well with your hands to fully incorporate. Make sure the bread gets mashed and mixed evenly into the mixture. Taste for salt and amchoor—it should be pleasantly tart and savory, and enjoyable to eat on its own. Cover and set aside. Do not refrigerate even if making a couple of hours in advance, as refrigeration may compromise the texture.

recipe continues

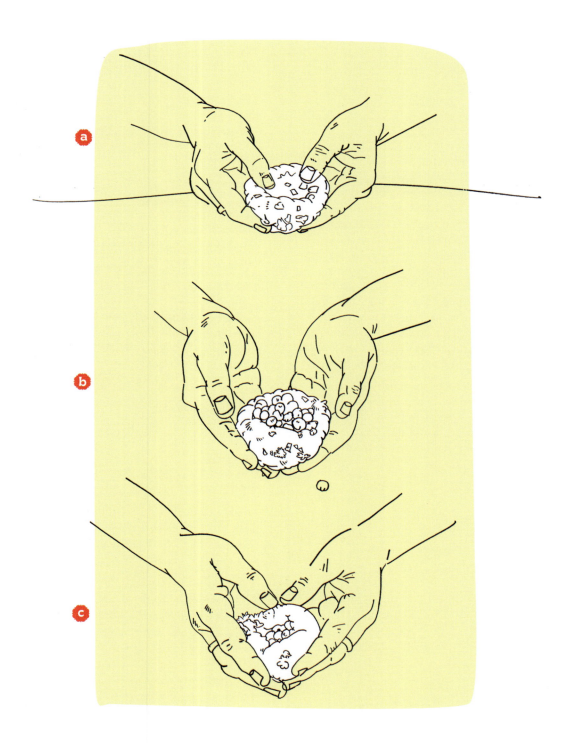

a

b

c

Aloo Tikki
• continued •

PEAS

4. Heat the oil in a medium pan over medium-high heat. Once the oil starts to shimmer, add the cumin. Cook, giving the pan a shake or two, until the seeds darken a couple of shades and become fragrant, about 30 seconds.

5. Add the peas, coriander, cayenne (if using), and salt. Stir well to incorporate, then cook, stirring frequently, until the peas are cooked through, 3 to 4 minutes. Don't overcook the peas to dullness—they should retain their bright green hue. Taste for salt. Transfer to a separate bowl or plate to cool.

ASSEMBLY + FRYING

6. Place 1 tablespoon of oil in a small bowl and use as necessary to grease your hands while working with the potato.

7. Divide the potato-bread mixture into 12 equal portions. If you don't have a kitchen scale, an easy way to do this is to divide it in half twice to yield quarters, and then divide each quarter into thirds.

8. Roll each portion into a ball between your palms. Cup your hands together beneath one of the potato balls and use your thumbs to make a depression in it **a**. Stuff the depression with a few peas short of a full tablespoon of the cumin-pea mixture **b**. Gently press the peas further down while wrapping the potato coating around them **c**. The idea is to completely cover the peas with a smooth layer of potato on all sides. Repeat with the remaining 11 potato balls. You may end up with some peas left over, which make for a great chef snack.

9. Shape each tikki, or stuffed potato ball, into a patty about 3 inches (7.5 cm) in diameter and just over 1 inch (2.5 cm) thick. Set aside.

10. Heat the remaining 2 cups (480 ml) of the oil in a deep wok or Dutch oven over medium-high heat until it gets up to around 375°F (190°C), 5 to 10 minutes depending on the cooking vessel and stove. The oil should be at least 1 inch (2.5 cm) deep, so add more if necessary. If you don't have a thermometer handy, check the oil by dropping in a bit of the potato mixture—if it sizzles vigorously and then comes up to the surface of the oil after a second or two, the oil is hot enough to fry in. If the potato only sizzles a bit or not at all, the oil isn't hot enough, and if the oil starts to smoke, it is too hot. As you wait for the oil to heat up, line a large plate or baking sheet with paper towels and set aside.

11. When the oil is up to temperature, carefully add the first tikki to the oil. (Oil temperature is crucial for this recipe. If the oil isn't hot enough, the tikki will fall apart in the oil.) The tikki should bubble steadily and take on color. Flip once the sides and bottom turn dark golden brown, 3 to 4 minutes. Cook the other side to the same doneness, another 2 to 3 minutes.

12. Transfer the tikki from the oil to the paper-lined plate using a slotted spoon or spider. The whole process should take between 5 and 7 minutes, and the tikki should emerge with a crispy, dark golden brown crust.

13. Repeat with the remaining tikki, checking the temperature and allowing the oil to reheat in between as necessary. Once you get the hang of it, you can try cooking two at a time, but don't overcrowd the wok. Serve hot.

Serving Tip

→ If serving with chutney, which we recommend, gently crush the tikki by lightly squeezing it at opposite ends just before dressing. The pressure should open up a fissure that will allow the good stuff to better penetrate.

Sabudana Vada

TAPIOCA and POTATO CROQUETTES

MAKES 10 • **SOAK TIME:** *5 hours*
COOK TIME: *1¾ hours* • **PHOTO:** *page 115*

Jyoti These deep-fried, tapioca-and-potato Maharashtrian croquettes, or cutlets, feature an impossibly delicate crust. For the full (and intended) experience, you must serve them with a chutney! Serving them naked would be like serving french fries without ketchup, or hot wings without ranch. Dhania Pudina Chutney (page 242) is the traditional option.

Since this recipe requires deep-frying, check out the note on deep-frying on page 210 before getting started. If you're looking to save some time on the day of cooking, everything right up to the frying can be done a day in advance. Place a paper towel over the uncooked vada and store them in a sealed container in the fridge.

Auyon Although sabudana is now synonymous with tapioca pearls (similar to those found in bubble tea and tapioca pudding) within India, it wasn't always so. Sabudana was historically made from sago, an imported starch harvested from the Southeast Asian sago palm. Cassava, a New World tuber and the source of tapioca flour, was not introduced to India until around 1800.

Vada

- ½ cup (85 g) sabudana (see Notes, opposite), rinsed
- ⅓ cup (45 g) raw, shelled peanuts
- 1 large russet potato (11¼ ounces // 320 g), boiled and seasoned (see page 49), and then peeled
- ½ fresh Indian green chili (optional; see page 271—jalapeño may be substituted), minced
- 2 tablespoons finely chopped fresh cilantro, stems and leaves
- 1 tablespoon fresh lemon juice
- 2 teaspoons grated, peeled fresh ginger
- 1 teaspoon cumin seeds, roasted (lightly!) and ground (see page 43)
- ½ teaspoon salt, plus more to taste
- 1 teaspoon cornstarch (see Notes, opposite)

Frying

- 2 cups (480 ml) canola oil

VADA

1. Place the sabudana and ⅓ cup (80 ml) water in a small bowl. Stir well, then soak for 4 to 5 hours, covered. (Now is a great time to prepare the potato if you haven't already.)

2. Heat a small pan over medium-low heat. Once good and hot, add the peanuts and cook, stirring constantly, until they darken slightly and become fragrant, 2 to 4 minutes. Be vigilant about keeping them moving to avoid blackened hot spots. Remove from the heat and immediately transfer to a plate to cool.

3. Mash the potato with a potato masher or fork in a small bowl. Measure out 1 packed cup (235 g) of mashed potato to use in this recipe. Reserve the rest for another use.

4. Coarsely crush the cooled peanuts using a mortar and pestle.

5. Combine the crushed peanuts and 1 cup (235 g) mashed potato with the soaked sabudana (all of the soaking liquid should have gotten absorbed), chili (if using), cilantro, lemon juice, ginger, ground cumin, and salt in a large bowl. Mix well and taste for salt. Add the cornstarch and stir to fully incorporate.

6. Divide the potato mixture into 10 equal portions and shape each into a circular or oval patty about 1 inch (2.5 cm) thick.

FRYING

7. Heat the oil in a deep wok or Dutch oven over medium-high heat until it gets up to around 375°F (190°C), 5 to 10 minutes depending on the cooking vessel and stove. The oil should be at least 1 inch (2.5 cm) deep, so add more if necessary. If you don't have a thermometer handy, check the oil by dropping in a bit of the potato mixture—if it sizzles vigorously and then comes up to the surface of the oil after a second or two, the oil is hot enough to fry in. If the potato only sizzles a bit or not at all, the oil isn't hot enough, and if the oil starts to smoke, it is too hot. As you wait for the oil to heat up, line a large plate or baking sheet with paper towels and set aside.

8. When the oil is up to temperature, carefully add the first vada, or patty, to the oil. (Oil temperature is crucial for this recipe. If the oil isn't hot enough, the vada will fall apart in the oil.) The vada should bubble steadily and quickly take on color. Flip once the sides and bottom turn golden brown, 60 to 90 seconds.

9. Cook the other side to the same doneness, another 60 to 90 seconds. Transfer the first vada to the paper-lined plate using a slotted spoon or spider. The whole process should take between 2 and 4 minutes.

10. Repeat with the remaining vada, checking the temperature and allowing the oil to reheat in between as necessary. Once you get the hang of it, you can try cooking two at a time, but don't overcrowd the wok. Serve hot.

Notes

Sabudana are tapioca pearls and should be available at any Indian or Asian grocery. They look like bits of Styrofoam and are sold in two sizes (large and small). Either type (or a mix) is fine for this recipe. After a few hours of soaking, the pearls will become soft and spongy.

Do not skimp on the cornstarch. Without it, the potato will dissolve into sad, lonely bits in the hot oil.

• Beguni •
BENGALI EGGPLANT FRITTERS

SERVES 4 • COOK TIME: *1 hour* • PHOTO: *page 114*

Jyoti Bengalis rarely eat rice and daal, or kindred dishes like Bengali Khichudi (page 180), without a dry or fried vegetable served on the side as a crispy complement. These fritters often fill that role, but they are just as wonderful as the star of their own show, served with a bit of Dhania Pudina Chutney (page 242). The simple spicing, which highlights the herbal, oniony punch of kalonji, is typical of Bengali cooking. When preparing the batter, don't skimp on the rice flour. It is crucial to this dish's signature crispiness.

Since this recipe requires deep-frying, check out the note on deep-frying on page 210 before getting started. If you'd like to get some prep out of the way the day before, you can refrigerate the batter overnight. Wait to slice the eggplant until immediately before you're ready to batter and fry—if you cut the eggplant in advance, the slices will oxidize and blacken.

Batter
¾ cup (85 g) besan (see Besan, page 81), plus more as needed

¼ cup (40 g) rice flour

¾ teaspoon salt, plus more to taste

¼ teaspoon kalonji (nigella seeds, see page 274)

¼ teaspoon ground cayenne (optional)

Frying
2 cups (480 ml) canola oil, plus more as needed

1 medium eggplant (15 ounces // 430 g), halved lengthwise and then cut crosswise into ⅜-inch- (1-cm-) thick slices

Garnish
1½ teaspoons chaat masala (store-bought or homemade, page 53)

BATTER
1. Combine the besan, rice flour, salt, kalonji, and cayenne (if using) in a large bowl. Stir to incorporate. Add ¾ cup (180 ml) water slowly, a few tablespoons at a time, stirring well after each addition. Stop adding water when the final mixture is slightly thinner than pancake batter, but still thick enough to coat the eggplant pieces without dripping off completely. Adjust the thickness with more water or besan as necessary. Taste for salt.

FRYING
2. Heat the oil in a deep wok or Dutch oven over medium-high heat until it gets up to around 375°F (190°C), 5 to 10 minutes depending on the cooking vessel and stove. The oil should be at least 1 inch (2.5 cm) deep, so add more if necessary. If you don't have a thermometer handy, check the oil by dropping in a bit of batter—if it sizzles vigorously and then comes up to the surface of the oil after a second or two, the oil is hot enough to fry in. If the batter only sizzles a bit or not at all, the oil isn't hot enough, and if the oil starts to smoke, it is too hot. As you wait for the oil to heat up, line a large plate or baking sheet with paper towels and set aside.

3. When the oil is up to temperature, submerge an eggplant slice in the batter to coat, then tap it against the side of the bowl to get rid of any excess. Not every slice will be coated evenly, and that's okay. Avoid thinning the batter with water.

4. Moving quickly, carefully place the beguni, or battered eggplant, in the wok, and repeat with a couple more pieces. Be careful not to overcrowd the wok. Adding too much at once will cool the oil and produce soggy, greasy results.

5. Once in the oil, the beguni should bubble steadily and slowly take on color. Cook for about 8 minutes, flipping two or three times, until they are an even golden brown all over. When done, transfer the first batch to the paper-lined plate using a slotted spoon or spider.

6. Repeat the process (battering and then immediately frying) with the remaining eggplant pieces, checking the temperature and allowing the oil to reheat between batches as necessary.

GARNISH
7. Dust with chaat masala and serve hot.

Gobhi Pakora

CAULIFLOWER FRITTERS

SERVES 4 • **COOK TIME:** *80 minutes* • **PHOTO:** *page 103*

Jyoti Pakoras, also known as bhajji, are a popular fried snack found across the subcontinent and can be prepared using many different vegetables. Dry-spicing cauliflower florets before dipping them in batter was my mother's signature move—it adds an extra dimension of flavor to the dish. We love eating these pakoras with Dhania Pudina Chutney (page 242).

Since this recipe requires deep-frying, check out the note on deep-frying on page 210 before getting started. If you'd like to get some prep out of the way the day before, you can refrigerate the batter overnight.

Auyon Venerated historian K. T. Achaya suggests that the pakora may have been the progenitor of Japanese tempura by way of Portuguese missionaries, merchants, and sailors who had spent time in India.

Masala + Cauliflower

2 tablespoons amchoor (ground dried mango, see page 271)

1 tablespoon ground coriander

2½ teaspoons ground cumin

1 teaspoon salt

¼ teaspoon ground cayenne (optional)

1 medium head (2 pounds // 910 g) cauliflower, cut into 2-inch (5-cm) florets and 1-inch (2.5-cm) stem pieces (see page 90—don't cut them too small, as you need to stuff them)

Batter + Frying

2⅔ cups (300 g) besan (see Besan, page 81)

1 fresh Indian green chili (optional; see page 271—jalapeño may be substituted), minced

2 tablespoons finely chopped fresh cilantro, stems and leaves

1 teaspoon salt

Pinch of baking soda

3 cups (720 ml) canola oil, plus more as needed

MASALA + CAULIFLOWER

1. Combine the amchoor, coriander, cumin, salt, and cayenne (if using) in a small bowl. Amchoor has a tendency to stick together, so stir well to break up any clumps.

2. Scoop up ½ teaspoon of the dry spice mix, or masala, with a small spoon. Holding a cauliflower floret in your other hand, gently tap as much of the masala as possible into the crevices of the floret. Work over the bowl containing the rest of the masala, so that whatever doesn't stay in the vegetable goes back into the bowl. Gently place the spice-stuffed floret onto a large plate or baking sheet, taking care to retain as much of the mixture as possible in the crevices, and repeat the stuffing process with the remaining florets. Set aside any extra masala.

BATTER + FRYING

3. Combine the besan, fresh chili (if using), cilantro, salt, and baking soda in a medium bowl. Stir to incorporate. Add 1¼ cups (300 ml) water slowly, about ¼ cup (60 ml) at a time, stirring well to incorporate after each addition. The final mixture should be slightly thinner than pancake batter, but still thick enough to coat the cauliflower florets without dripping off completely. Adjust the thickness with more water or besan as necessary. Stir in all of the extra masala from the cauliflower stuffing. If you are comfortable tasting raw batter (besan is uncooked), taste for salt.

recipe continues

Gobhi Pakora
· continued ·

4. Heat the oil in a deep wok or Dutch oven over medium-high heat until it gets up to around 375°F (190°C), 5 to 10 minutes depending on the cooking vessel and stove. The oil should be at least 1½ inches (4 cm) deep, so add more if necessary. If you don't have a thermometer handy, check the oil by dropping in a bit of batter—if it sizzles vigorously and then comes up to the surface of the oil after a second or two, the oil is hot enough to fry in. If the batter only sizzles a bit or not at all, the oil isn't hot enough, and if the oil starts to smoke, it is too hot. As you wait for the oil to heat up, line a large plate or baking sheet with paper towels and set aside.

5. When the oil is up to temperature, dip a spiced floret or stem into the batter until evenly coated. Keep as much of the spice stuffing in the cauliflower as possible, and try spooning batter over the cauliflower to see if that works better. Moving quickly, carefully place the pakora, or battered cauliflower, in the wok and repeat with a few more pakoras. Be careful not to overcrowd the wok. Adding too much at once will cool the oil and produce soggy, greasy results.

6. Once in the oil, the pakoras should bubble steadily and slowly take on color. Flip each fritter after 4 to 6 minutes (the pakoras should be golden brown on the cooked side) and fry each for an additional 4 to 6 minutes, or until evenly browned all over.

7. When done, transfer the first batch to the paper-lined plate using a slotted spoon or spider. Repeat the process (battering and then immediately frying) with the remaining cauliflower pieces, checking the temperature and allowing the oil to reheat between batches as necessary. Serve hot.

Samosa

SAVORY POTATO and PEA TURNOVERS

MAKES 10 • **COOK TIME:** 3½ hours (plus time to cook and chill potatoes) • **PHOTO:** page 117

Jyoti These savory, triangular, deep-fried turnovers are perhaps the most universally recognized Indian street food in the West. They are hugely popular in India too, where stuffings and dough preparations vary widely depending on region and tradition. Our version, which exists firmly within the intersection of "snack" and "small meal," is a generous helping of spiced potatoes and peas wrapped in a crispy-chewy dough blanket. The inclusion of peanuts and the boiled potato preparation are both typical of shingharas, or Bengali-style samosas.

Keys to success are careful dough preparation and slow, steady deep-frying. For the dough, take care to fully incorporate the oil into the flour before adding the water. For the deep-frying, start by checking out the note on deep-frying on page 210. If deep-frying is a deterrent, save this recipe for when you are feeling up for an adventure—we don't recommend air-frying or baking. The process will take a bit of practice and patience, but rest assured that the reward is worth it. If you would like to get some prep out of the way beforehand, see Advance Prep, page 228.

Finally, note that our recipe produces a pleasantly savory samosa, but for the full (and intended) flavor experience, you must serve them with a chutney! Serving them naked would be like serving a Manhattan without a cherry, or a hot dog without a bun. Dhania Pudina Chutney (page 242) and Imli Chutney (page 243), either homemade or store-bought, are both excellent options. We also love generously topping our samosas with Ghoogni (page 69) to produce the superfood Samosa Chaat.

Auyon Samosas came to India from the Middle East and Central Asia. Historian Colleen Taylor Sen suggests the term may be a fusion of the Arabic words *se* (meaning three, referring to the traditional triangular form) and *ambos* (a type of bread).

Dough
1½ cups (210 g) all-purpose flour

½ teaspoon salt, plus more to taste

¼ cup (60 ml) canola oil

Filling
¼ cup (35 g) raw, shelled peanuts

3 medium russet potatoes (1⅜ pounds // 600 g total), boiled and seasoned (see page 49), peeled, chilled in the fridge for at least 30 minutes, and then cubed into ¼-inch (6-mm) chunks

⅓ cup (55 g) frozen peas, no need to thaw

2 tablespoons finely chopped fresh cilantro, stems and leaves

1 teaspoon amchoor (ground dried mango, see page 271—this is a crucial ingredient!), plus more to taste

½ teaspoon cumin seeds, roasted (lightly!) and ground (see page 43)

½ teaspoon ground coriander

¼ teaspoon ground cayenne (optional), plus more to taste

Salt, to taste

Assembly + Frying
3 cups (720 ml) canola oil, plus more as needed

DOUGH

1. Combine the flour and salt in a large bowl and stir well to incorporate.

2. Slowly add the oil, about a tablespoon at a time, using your hands to incorporate it into the flour with each addition. Once all the oil is mixed in, you should be able to squeeze a handful of the dough such that when you release it, it remains a single solid piece without cracking.

3. Slowly add ½ cup (120 ml) water, a couple of tablespoons at a time, to the flour-and-oil mixture. Incorporate the liquid with each addition until you have a pliable, slightly tacky dough that holds together. Use only as much water as you need to get the dough soft and uniform. There will usually be 2 or 3 tablespoons of water left over—hold onto it.

recipe continues

Samosa
• continued •

4. Knead the dough with gusto for a minute or two to ensure everything is fully mixed. Unlike with Western pastry doughs, you don't need to worry about over-kneading here.

5. Dip your fingertips into the leftover water and make several shallow indentations in the dough (think bowling ball holes) to help hydrate the dough as it rests. Cover with an airtight lid and let rest at room temperature for at least 45 minutes. If you don't have an airtight lid, cover the dough with a damp towel or plastic wrap to prevent it from drying out.

FILLING

6. While the dough is resting, heat a small pan over medium-low heat. Once good and hot, add the peanuts and cook, stirring constantly, until they darken slightly and become fragrant, 2 to 3 minutes. Be vigilant about keeping them moving to avoid blackened hot spots. Remove from the heat and immediately transfer to a plate to cool.

7. Coarsely crush the cooled peanuts using a mortar and pestle. In a medium bowl, combine the crushed peanuts, boiled and seasoned potato, peas, cilantro, amchoor, ground cumin, ground coriander, and cayenne (if using). Use your hands to mix thoroughly but gently, to avoid breaking up the potato pieces. Taste for salt and flavor—it should be pleasantly tart and savory with just a touch of heat, and enjoyable to eat on its own. Adjust the salt, cayenne, and amchoor (for tartness) as needed. The amount of salt needed will depend on how salty your potatoes are—we typically add a ¾ teaspoon salt when using unseasoned potatoes, for context.

ASSEMBLY + FRYING

8. Briskly knead the rested dough on a clean, dry work surface until it feels noticeably more tacky and pliable, just a couple of minutes or so. Don't knead for much longer than that, as you don't want the dough to get too sticky. Place the reserved water, to be used as a sealant, in a shallow bowl close by.

9. Divide the dough into 5 equal portions and shape each into a smooth ball by rolling it between your palms. Place the dough balls back into the large bowl and cover with a damp cloth. Be vigilant about keeping them covered as you work. Take them out one at a time so that the last few don't dry out by the time you get to them.

10. Take one ball and flatten it into a 3-inch- (7.5-cm-) diameter patty. Use a rolling pin to roll the patty into a disk roughly 8 inches (20 cm) in diameter. The rolling process will take a healthy amount of pressure and a lot of repeated rolling in different directions, as samosa dough is quite elastic and will contract repeatedly. Have faith and patience. Cut the disk in half with a sharp knife.

11. Take one half of the dough disk and use your finger to brush water from the bowl over the cut edge **a**. Bring one corner of the cut edge over the middle of the semicircle, then do the same with the other corner, overlapping the first corner by about ¾ inch (2 cm) to form a cone **b**. Starting from the point, firmly pinch both the inside and the outside of the overlap to seal the cone **c**.

12. Hold the cone by making a C shape with your left hand and drape the cone in to fill it. Line up the seal you just made so that it's the farthest part of the cone from you **d**.

13. Fill the samosa about two-thirds full (roughly 2½ tablespoons of filling) **e**, and then wet the inside of the opening of the cone before pinching the bottom of the samosa shut with your right hand (you are holding it upside down) **f**.

14. Check all the seals again and carefully pinch the dough together where necessary **g**. It is essential that the samosa is well sealed. If there are any holes, the frying oil will seep into the filling and produce an undesirable heaviness.

recipe continues

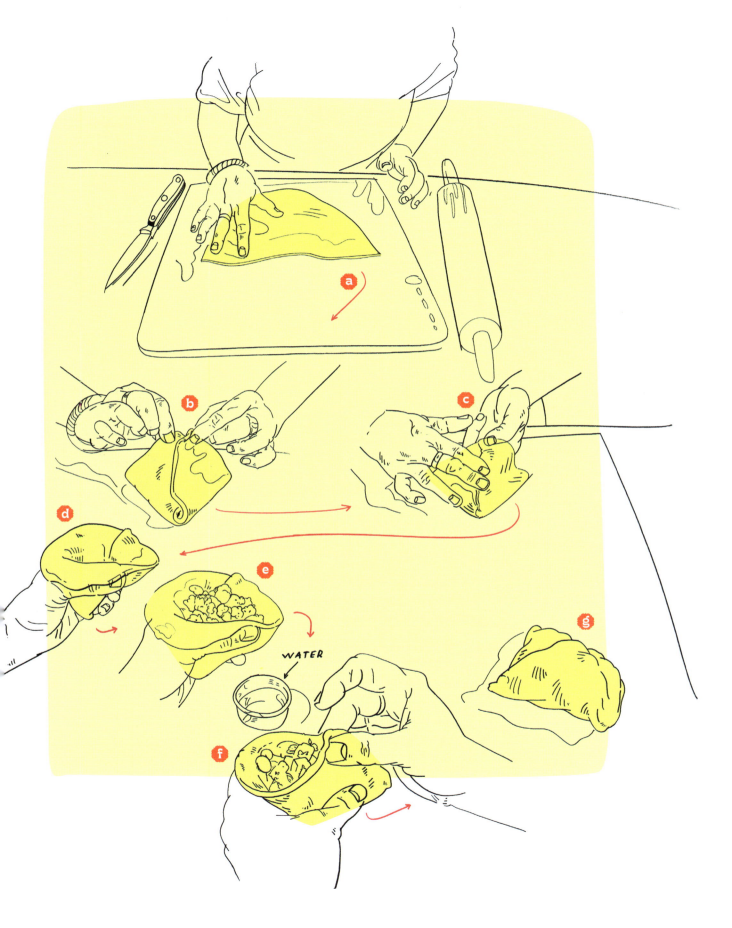

Samosa
• continued •

15. Place the sealed samosa in a covered container, ideally one large enough to accommodate the remaining samosas.

16. Give the other flattened half-circle of dough a quick roll with the rolling pin, as the dough tends to contract with time, and then repeat the sealing and filling process. Repeat the entire process (flattening, sealing, and filling) with the remaining 4 dough balls to produce 10 samosas total. You may have a bit of filling left over—reserve it as a snack.

17. Heat the oil in a deep wok or Dutch oven over medium-high heat until it gets up to around 360°F (184°C), 5 to 10 minutes depending on the cooking vessel and stove. The oil should be at least 1½ inches (4 cm) deep, so add more if necessary. If you don't have a thermometer handy, check the oil by dropping in a bit of dough—if it sizzles vigorously and then comes up to the surface of the oil after a second or two, the oil is hot enough to fry in. If the dough only sizzles a bit or not at all, the oil isn't hot enough, and if the oil starts to smoke, it is too hot. As you wait for the oil to heat up, line a large plate or baking sheet with paper towels and set aside.

18. When the oil is up to temperature, reduce the heat to medium-low and carefully lower the first couple of samosas into the wok. Once the edges start to brown, after a couple of minutes, flip them and continue cooking. Flip once or twice more until golden brown all over, 10 to 12 minutes total. Transfer the first samosa to the paper-lined plate using a slotted spoon or spider.

19. Repeat with the remaining samosas, checking the temperature and allowing the oil to reheat in between as necessary. If the wok is big enough, you can try working in larger batches, but don't overcrowd the wok. Adding too much at once will cool the oil and produce greasy results. Serve hot.

Advance Prep + Serving Tips

→ Although the dough should be made the same day that the samosas are fried, the filling can be prepared a day or two in advance.

→ If you don't think you'll eat a whole batch at once, you can par-fry the remainder until they just start taking on color (just a couple of minutes of frying rather than the 10 to 12 minutes outlined in Step 18) and then store them ready to go in your freezer. To finish off the cooking, thaw the par-fried samosas in the fridge overnight and then re-fry until golden brown all over, another 5 to 10 minutes.

→ To reheat fully cooked samosas, place the samosas in a 250°F (120°C) oven for 10 minutes, uncovered. Cool for at least 5 minutes before serving to restore crispiness.

Sabudana Khichudi

TAPIOCA PEARLS with POTATO, PEAS, and PEANUTS

SERVES 4 • **SOAK TIME:** *4 hours* • **COOK TIME:** *1 hour*
PHOTO: *page 115*

Jyoti Like the similarly tapioca-based Sabudana Vada (page 220), this dish comes from the western state of Maharashtra. Its name remains a mystery to me, as the dish contains neither rice nor legumes (the two otherwise requisite components of khichudi), but the textural interplay between the tapioca pearls, roasted peanuts, and potatoes make it one of my favorites.

We love it as part of a breakfast spread or as a light lunch with a dollop of Homemade Yogurt (page 40) and a bit of Adarak Nimbu Achaar (page 245).

2½ cups (425 g) sabudana (see Note, right), rinsed

1 cup (140 g) raw, shelled peanuts

6 tablespoons canola oil

1 teaspoon cumin seeds

1 teaspoon black or brown mustard seeds

1 large russet potato (11¼ ounces // 320 g), peeled and cubed into ½-inch (12-mm) chunks

1 cup (140 g) frozen peas, no need to thaw

2 fresh Indian green chilies (optional; see page 271—jalapeños may be substituted), minced

¾ teaspoon turmeric

1½ teaspoons salt, plus more to taste

¼ cup (60 ml) fresh lemon juice (from about 1 lemon)

Garnish
3 tablespoons finely chopped fresh cilantro, stems and leaves

1. Place the sabudana and 2½ cups (600 ml) water in a large bowl. Stir well, then soak for 4 to 5 hours, covered.

2. Heat a medium pan over medium-low heat. Once good and hot, add the peanuts and cook, stirring constantly, until they darken slightly and become fragrant, 8 to 10 minutes. Be vigilant about keeping them moving to avoid blackened hot spots. Remove from the heat and immediately transfer to a plate to cool.

3. Heat the oil in a large, lidded (but uncovered for now), nonstick pan over medium-high heat. Once the oil starts to shimmer, add the cumin and mustard seeds. Cook, undisturbed, until the mustard seeds are popping vigorously, about 30 seconds (watch out for oil splatter—use a splatter screen if you have one).

4. Add the potato, reduce the heat to medium, and cover the pan. Cook, stirring occasionally, until the potato pieces are just starting to brown at the edges, about 8 minutes.

5. Stir in the peas, chilies (if using), and turmeric. Cook, stirring frequently, until the peas and potato pieces are cooked through, about 3 minutes.

6. Add the sabudana (all of the soaking liquid should have gotten absorbed), roasted peanuts, and salt. Stir well to incorporate. Reduce the heat to low and cover the pan. Cook undisturbed until the sabudana is heated through, 5 minutes or so.

7. Remove from the heat and stir in the lemon juice. Let rest, covered, for a final 5 minutes to allow the moisture to permeate. Taste for salt. The texture of the sabudana should be akin to that of the tapioca pearls in bubble tea: soft but retaining just a hint of chew.

GARNISH

8. Garnish with cilantro and serve hot.

Note

Sabudana are tapioca pearls and should be available at any Indian or Asian grocery. They look like bits of Styrofoam and are sold in two sizes (large and small). Either type (or a mix) is fine for this recipe. After a few hours of soaking, the pearls will become soft and spongy.

Kaathi Roll

MAKES *8* • PREP TIME: *5 hours* • COOK TIME: *1 hour*
PHOTO: *page 118*

Jyoti This beloved Bengali street food is a kabob, a layered flatbread, and an omelet wrapped into one delicious package. The rolls are perfect on their own as a snack, but one or two accompanied by a simply cooked vegetable or salad makes for a lovely meal.

While the construction is straightforward enough, the dish is a combination of some rather involved recipes (Paratha, page 192, and the tikka portion of Murgh Makhani, page 151), both of which can be made a day or two in advance. If you're making everything on the same day, start by preparing the chicken tikka. While the meat is marinating, prepare the parathas. Immediately after putting the marinated meat into the oven to cook, begin the recipe, starting with the onion marination in Step 1.

It's crucial that the parathas are rolled out big enough (roughly 9 by 9 inches // 23 by 23 cm), or they will not hold all the filling. We also recommend assembling the rolls to order—the individual ingredients all keep well, but the rolls get soggy if they sit for too long after assembly.

In a pinch, the parathas can be swapped out for lightly toasted, large flour tortillas, and the tikka can be replaced by any filling you have on hand—use about ¾ cup (150 g) filling per roll. Ideal fillings tend to be chunky, like pieces of meat or paneer, rather than semisolid like legumes or ground meat. All that said, we highly recommend trying the traditional paratha-murgh makhani format at least once. You'll be glad you did.

Auyon The Kaathi Roll, or Nizam roll, originated at a Kolkata restaurant called Nizam's circa 1930. The *kaathi* designation, which refers to the skewers the kabobs are cooked on, derives from a Bengali word for "stick."

2 cups (235 g) halved, thinly sliced yellow onion (about 1 medium onion)

¼ cup (60 ml) fresh lemon juice (from about 1 lemon)

1½ teaspoons + ¼ teaspoon salt

7 or 8 large eggs, as needed

⅓ cup (20 g) finely chopped fresh cilantro, stems and leaves

½ fresh Indian green chili (optional; see page 271—jalapeño may be substituted), minced

3 tablespoons canola oil

8 parathas (page 192)

3 tablespoons dhania pudina chutney (store-bought or homemade, page 242)

2 pounds (910 g) chicken tikka (see Notes, opposite)

2 teaspoons chaat masala (store-bought or homemade, page 53)

½ teaspoon ground cayenne (optional)

1. Combine the sliced onion, lemon juice, and 1½ teaspoons of the salt in a large bowl. Stir well and set aside to marinate, covered and at room temperature, for at least 30 minutes and up to a couple of hours (it will keep for as long as a couple of days in the refrigerator).

2. Beat 7 eggs with 1 cup (240 ml) water, cilantro, chili (if using), and remaining ¼ teaspoon salt. Pour the mixture into a large measuring cup. You'll need about 3 cups (720 ml) of the egg mixture for this recipe, so make up the rest with a bit more water (or another egg) if you are short.

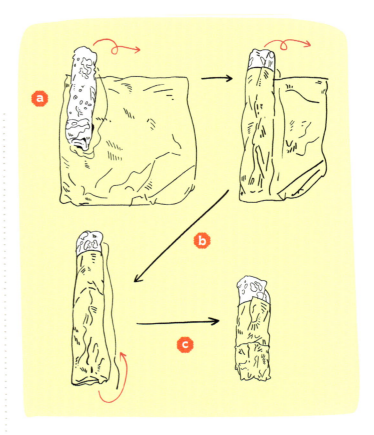

3. Once the onions are done marinating, heat 1 teaspoon of the oil in a large, nonstick pan or skillet over medium-high heat. When the oil starts to shimmer, add ⅓ cup (80 ml) of the egg mixture to the pan and immediately place a paratha over it. Cook for about 90 seconds, using a spatula to gently press the paratha into the egg as it cooks. If any egg pokes out from under the paratha, just gently push it back toward the flatbread. Slide the spatula beneath the egg and carefully flip the paratha egg-side up. The egg should be fully cooked and bound to the paratha. Cook for about 45 seconds to heat the other side, then transfer the paratha, egg-side up, to a clean work surface or large plate.

4. Over the cooked egg, evenly spread 1 teaspoon of the dhania pudina chutney.

5. Line up 4 chicken tikka pieces across the center of the paratha over the chutney, and top with a generous handful of marinated onions (or a small handful if you have any guests who are sensitive to raw onion).

6. Sprinkle ¼ teaspoon of the chaat masala and a pinch of cayenne (if using) over the filling. Carefully roll the paratha and stuffing into an open-ended tube.

7. Place the kaathi roll over the edge of a large (12-inch // 30.5-cm) square of aluminum foil **a**. Position the roll so that as you roll it together with the foil to cover, the top bit of the roll remains exposed **b**. Once all the foil is wrapped around the roll, roll up any excess foil beneath the roll and crimp to seal **c**.

8. Serve immediately. Repeat the process with the remaining 7 parathas, re-oiling the pan with 1 teaspoon of oil before each.

Notes

If the chicken is prepared in advance, don't use it directly out of the fridge. Allow it to warm to room temperature first.

To make the chicken tikka, you'll need to complete Steps 1 through 5 of the Murgh Makhani (page 151) recipe. Note that although we call for a full recipe (2 pounds // 910 g), all of the tikka won't get used for the wraps. Fortunately, leftover tikka is lovely as is. Garnish it with some marinated onions and serve it warm, with a bit of rice and Homemade Yogurt (page 40).

Spiced Liver Toast

MAKES 10 • COOK TIME: *1 hour* • PHOTO: *page 115*

Jyoti I have never been a liver apologist, yet this dish was one of my favorite breakfast treats growing up. The delicate, crispy browned surface makes for a magical contrast with the creamy pâté underneath. For a sumptuous cocktail appetizer, cut each toast into quarters after frying.

Auyon For the sandwich bread, we use Pepperidge Farm white bread, but more rustic loaves will work well too, as long as you don't slice them too thick.

We typically use all of the liver on the toasts, but if you are serving folks who are offal-shy, or if you'd prefer to emphasize the toast component, be a bit less generous when applying the pâté. Leftovers are great as part of a cheeseboard, or better yet, for more toasts the next day.

1 pound (455 g) fresh chicken livers, soaking liquid reserved (if available)

¾ teaspoon salt, plus more to taste

⅓ cup (85 g) chopped yellow onion (¼-inch // 6-mm dice, about ½ small onion)

1 fat clove garlic

1 teaspoon ground coriander

10 slices white sandwich bread

¼ cup (60 ml) canola oil

1. Heat the liver, 6 tablespoons of the soaking liquid (make up the difference with water if you are short, or just use water if the livers were not packaged with liquid), and salt in a medium pan over high heat.

2. Once the liquid comes to a boil, reduce the heat to medium. Cook, stirring occasionally, until the liver is firm throughout and the total amount of liquid has boiled back down to 4 or 5 tablespoons (the liver will release additional liquid as it cooks), about 12 minutes.

3. Remove from the heat and cool to room temperature. Keep covered while cooling to avoid evaporation.

4. Grind the liver, cooking liquid, onion, garlic, and coriander to a thick, smooth paste using a food processor or mortar and pestle. Taste for salt.

5. Line a large plate or baking sheet with paper towels and set aside.

6. Assemble the toasts by spreading an even layer of the liver paste on each slice of bread (for thickness, think cream cheese on a bagel, or somewhere between 1/16 and 1/8 inch // 2 and 4 mm, depending on available surface area).

7. Heat 1 teaspoon of the oil in your largest nonstick skillet or pan over medium-high heat. Once the oil starts to shimmer, carefully place a few liver toasts (as many as will comfortably fit in a single layer), liver-side down.

8. While the liver is cooking, drizzle ½ teaspoon of oil around the perimeter of each slice (i.e., for 4 slices, use 2 teaspoons). Flip the toasts when the liver has a thin, crispy, dark brown layer on top, about 3 minutes.

9. Add another ½ teaspoon of oil around the circumference of each toast to ensure the bread side of each gets browned and crispy. Remove the toasts once the bread side is lightly browned, about 2 minutes, then transfer to the paper-lined plate. Each toast should cook for about 5 minutes total.

10. Repeat with the remaining toasts, working in batches as necessary, and serve hot.

Spiced Watermelon

SERVES 6 • **COOK TIME:** *10 minutes (plus time to chill)*
PHOTO: *page 104*

Jyoti Although it may seem exotic to American palates, seasoned fresh fruit is a part of culinary traditions across the globe—think pineapple with a Mexican treatment of chili, salt, and lime, or Persian-style pomegranate dusted with salt and spice. I came up with this particular preparation back when I started teaching in 2010. I love the way the smoky kalonji spice pairs with the sweet melon. This recipe is only as good as the watermelon you use, so we recommend waiting until the fruit is in season.

1 small seedless watermelon (5 pounds // 2.3 kg), peeled and cubed into 1-inch (2.5-cm) chunks (about 6 cups cut watermelon)

2 tablespoons canola oil

½ teaspoon kalonji (nigella seeds, see page 274)

¾ teaspoon ground coriander

½ teaspoon ground cumin

¼ teaspoon ground cinnamon

½ teaspoon salt, plus more to taste

1. Place the watermelon pieces in a large bowl. Heat the oil in a small pan over medium heat. Once the oil starts to shimmer, add the kalonji and sizzle, giving the pan a shake or two, until the seeds become fragrant, about 20 seconds.

2. Add the coriander, cumin, and cinnamon and swirl for just a couple of seconds to combine.

3. Immediately remove the pan from the heat to prevent the ground spices from scorching (see tadka, page 31). Drizzle the oil and spices over the watermelon. Mix well and chill in the refrigerator, covered, for at least 45 minutes but no longer than 24 hours.

4. Just before serving, stir in the salt—don't do it any sooner, as it will draw moisture out of the fruit. Taste for salt and serve chilled.

Fruit Chaat

SERVES 4 • COOK TIME: 5 minutes • PHOTO: page 115

Jyoti This preparation involves no special cooking techniques nor any complicated processes. Its simplicity makes the unexpected transformation of familiar fruit all the more remarkable—I relish the looks of surprise and delight on my students' faces when they taste their first bite! The not-so-secret ingredient is Chaat Masala (page 53), which contains kaala namak (see page 249), or black salt. The salt has a haunting, sulfurous quality that we absolutely love with fresh fruit, but timid diners should beware.

Auyon A few notes:
- Keep it simple. Less is more is a great rule of thumb. Try to disregard any preconceptions you might have about what a fruit salad should look like. You could make this recipe with only sliced fresh mango (or peaches, or plums) for the fruit component and it would be delightful. Using whatever is in season is a great way to sharpen your focus.
- If you want to get fancy, a variety of textures—juicy, creamy, crunchy, chewy—can be helpful in rounding things out (categorical inspiration courtesy of Stella Parks). Toasted nuts and dried fruit are excellent candidates for creating some of that diversity. One of our favorite combinations is a couple of mangoes (juicy), a banana (creamy), a couple of handfuls of toasted cashews (crunchy), and a few pitted and slivered dates (chewy) garnished with a handful of pomegranate arils.
- If you are including bananas or avocados or anything else that oxidizes or browns, wait to add them until just before serving, along with the chaat masala, lemon, and mint.

Mixed chopped fresh fruit, totaling about 4 cups (680 g)

1 tablespoon fresh mint leaves

2 teaspoons fresh lemon juice, plus more to taste

1 teaspoon chaat masala (store-bought or homemade, page 53), plus more to taste

Toss together the fruit in a large bowl. Just before serving, add the mint, lemon juice, and chaat masala. Mix well. It should be salty and sour and sweet and good. Adjust the lemon juice and masala as needed. Serve at room temperature.

CHAPTER SEVEN

Raitas, Chutneys, and a Pickle

Raitas

AUYON South Asia's great fondness for dairy might be best demonstrated by the ubiquity of yogurt on dining tables across the subcontinent. It serves both as a cooling foil to spicy dishes and as a subtly acidic complement to rich ones. Yogurt is typically offered plain or as a raita, a salted yogurt spiked with vegetables, legumes, and/or nuts. The recipes that follow are three of our favorites.

If you're making any of these in advance, we recommend holding off on adding the salt until you're within an hour or so of serving, to ensure the vegetables and add-ins retain their integrity.

Kheera Tamatar Raita

YOGURT with CUCUMBER and TOMATO

SERVES 6 • PREP TIME: 10 minutes • PHOTO: page 112

2 cups (480 g) whole unflavored yogurt (store-bought or homemade, page 40), stirred to a smooth consistency

½ cup (95 g) finely chopped cucumber (about 1 Persian or mini cucumber, see Cucumber Snobbery, page 56)

½ cup (70 g) finely chopped tomato (about ½ medium tomato)

1 teaspoon cumin seeds, roasted (lightly!) and ground (see page 43)

½ teaspoon salt, plus more to taste

Pinch of ground cayenne (optional)

1 tablespoon finely chopped fresh cilantro, stems and leaves

1. Combine the yogurt, cucumber, tomato, half of the ground cumin, salt, and cayenne (if using) in a large bowl. Mix well and taste for salt. Use immediately, or cover and place in the fridge for no longer than an hour.

2. Garnish with the cilantro and the remaining ground cumin. Serve chilled or at room temperature. Store in the refrigerator and consume within a couple of days.

Paalak Raita

YOGURT with SPINACH and PEANUTS

SERVES 6 • COOK TIME: *20 minutes* • PHOTO: *page 125*

½ cup (70 g) raw, shelled peanuts

5 ounces (140 g) frozen spinach (about 1½ cups when roughly broken up)

2 cups (480 g) whole, unflavored yogurt (store-bought or homemade, page 40), stirred to a smooth consistency

½ teaspoon salt, plus more to taste

Tadka

1 tablespoon canola oil

1 dried red chili, broken into thirds (see page 271)

½ teaspoon black or brown mustard seeds

1. Heat a medium pan over medium-low heat. Once good and hot, add the peanuts and cook, stirring constantly, until they darken slightly and become fragrant, 5 to 7 minutes. Be vigilant about keeping them moving to avoid blackened hot spots. Remove from the heat and immediately transfer to a plate to cool. Set the pan aside but don't wash it.

2. Place the spinach in a small, lidded pot over medium-low heat. Cover the pot and cook for 5 minutes, stirring once or twice. Alternatively, place the spinach in a microwave-safe bowl and zap it in the microwave on high for 4 minutes. Allow the spinach to cool to room temperature, uncovered.

3. Combine the cooled peanuts, spinach, yogurt, and salt with ½ cup (120 ml) water in a large bowl. Mix well and taste for salt.

TADKA

4. To make the tadka (see page 31), in the same pan the peanuts were cooked in, heat the oil over medium heat. Once the oil starts to shimmer, add the chili and cook, giving the pan a shake to distribute the chili pieces evenly, until they darken a shade or two, about 30 seconds.

5. Add the mustard seeds and cook until they are popping vigorously, another 20 seconds or so (watch out for oil splatter—use a splatter screen if you have one).

6. Remove from the heat and pour the tadka over the yogurt. For a more striking presentation, don't stir it in. Serve chilled or at room temperature. Store in the refrigerator and consume within a couple of days.

Boondi Raita

YOGURT with TINY CHICKPEA DUMPLINGS

SERVES 6 • **PREP TIME:** *10 minutes* • **PHOTO:** *page 116*

2 cups (480 g) whole, unflavored yogurt (store-bought or homemade, page 40), stirred to a smooth consistency

½ teaspoon salt, plus more to taste

½ teaspoon cumin seeds, roasted (lightly!) and ground (see page 43)

Pinch of ground cayenne (optional)

1 cup (60 g) salted boondi (see Note, right)

Garnish
1 tablespoon finely chopped fresh cilantro, stems and leaves

1. Beat the yogurt with ½ cup (120 ml) water in a large bowl using a whisk or a fork until fully mixed. Stir in the salt, ground cumin, and cayenne (if using).

GARNISH
2. Just before serving, stir in the boondi and taste for salt. Garnish with cilantro and serve chilled or at room temperature. Store in the refrigerator and consume within a couple of days.

Serving Tip

→ If you have any leftovers, the boondi will soften and the raita will thicken as it sits. Add a bit of milk or water to get it back to the proper consistency.

Note
Boondi is an Indian junk food made from fried chickpea flour and should be available in the shiny, crinkly bag section of most Indian groceries. If all you can find is "boondi masala," that's fine too—it's a more heavily spiced version of the same snack, which lends the raita a lovely tang.

Raitas, Chutneys, and a Pickle

Dhania Pudina Chutney

CILANTRO MINT CHUTNEY

MAKES *roughly 2 cups (480 g)*
PREP TIME: *20 minutes* • **PHOTO:** *page 103*

Jyoti This classic chutney is the quintessential accompaniment to Indian snacks and light meals. The bright acidity, gentle heat, and subtle sweetness make for a wonderfully versatile condiment. It can be used as a dipping sauce, a garnish, or even a pesto-like spread for flatbreads, sandwiches, or tacos. It pairs especially well with soft, fresh cheeses like Paneer (page 46). Double the recipe if you have the ingredients handy—we guarantee you'll find plenty of uses for it. This chutney will keep for about 3 weeks in the fridge or a year in the freezer.

For my favorite variation, try substituting one large green apple for the mint—it makes for a marvelously tart-sweet version. If you're caught in a pinch and you need this chutney for part of another recipe, any cilantro- or mint-based chutney from the store will do as a replacement.

Auyon In the United States and United Kingdom, chutney often connotes a thick, sweet-ish preparation, but in India the term covers broader ground, encompassing thin, thick, sweet, savory, and pickled condiments alike. The term derives from the Hindi word *chatni*, which means "to lick."

- 2½ cups (115 g) roughly chopped, lightly packed fresh cilantro, stems and leaves (around 1½ bunches)
- 1 cup (40 g) lightly packed, roughly chopped fresh mint leaves (around ⅔ bunch)
- ¼ cup (60 g) finely chopped yellow onion (about ⅓ small onion)
- 1 fresh Indian green chili (optional; see page 271—jalapeño may be substituted), finely chopped
- 2 cloves garlic
- 2 tablespoons fresh lemon juice (from about ½ lemon)
- 1 tablespoon canola oil
- 1½ teaspoons cider vinegar (white, rice, or cane vinegar may be substituted), plus more to taste
- ¾ teaspoon sugar
- ½ teaspoon salt, plus more to taste

1. Grind all of the ingredients to a smooth paste using a blender, food processor, or mortar and pestle. (If using a blender, note that it may take scraping down the sides of the blender and stirring between attempts—a silicone spatula is handy here—to get everything properly incorporated.) Resist the temptation to add any liquid. It may take some effort, but your patience will be rewarded with a thick, delicious chutney.

2. Taste for salt and vinegar. Store in a sealable container in the fridge and serve chilled.

Imli Chutney

TAMARIND CHUTNEY

MAKES roughly 1½ cups (360 g)
COOK TIME: 35 minutes (plus time to cool)
PHOTO: page 103

Jyoti While this preparation is superb in its own right, it also serves as an excellent counterpoint to Dhania Pudina Chutney (opposite) in a condiment lineup. In contrast to the bright green puree, tamarind chutney is more akin to molasses in color and texture, with a sweetness that is balanced by sour tamarind and zingy ginger rather than vinegar and chili.

As with our other chutney recipes, this recipe scales up well. We like it with some texture, so we recommend chopping whole dates rather than using date paste. That said, feel free to mince the whole dates more finely if you would prefer a smoother, more restaurant-like consistency. Imli chutney will keep for a couple of months in the fridge (we don't recommend freezing).

Auyon This condiment's sweet-sour profile makes it a great substitute for barbecue sauce or ketchup in sandwiches or alongside fried treats. I also love it over vanilla ice cream.

My mom and I have different sweetness preferences—the recipe that follows is to my taste, whereas my mom prefers it with an additional ¼ cup (50 g) of sugar (or more!).

1 tablespoon tamarind paste (see page 277)

½ cup (100 g) sugar, plus more to taste

¼ cup (40 g) finely chopped pitted dates (raisins, or a mix of raisins and dates, may be substituted)

1 teaspoon ground dried ginger

½ teaspoon cumin seeds, roasted (lightly!) and ground (see page 43)

¼ teaspoon salt, plus more to taste

1. Bring 1¼ cups (300 ml) water to a rolling boil in a medium pot over high heat. Reduce the heat to medium and add the tamarind. Stir to dissolve.

2. Reduce the heat to low and add the sugar, dates, ginger, ground cumin, and salt. Simmer, uncovered, stirring once or twice to dissolve the sugar, for about 25 minutes, to slightly thicken the chutney. It should end up roughly the consistency of maple syrup. Keep an eye on the pot and reduce the heat (or transfer to a larger pot) if it threatens to boil over.

3. Cool to room temperature, ideally covered to avoid further evaporation. If you are pinched for time, cool the chutney uncovered but make sure to cover it as soon as it is cool enough to refrigerate. Taste for sugar and salt.

4. Store in a sealable container in the fridge and serve chilled or at room temperature.

Serving Tip

→ The mixture will thicken more as it cools, but it should remain pourable. If it solidifies, stir in a bit of boiling water to thin it out.

Tamatar Khajoor Chutney

TOMATO DATE CHUTNEY

MAKES *roughly 1½ cups (360 g)*
COOK TIME: *50 minutes (plus time to cool)*
PHOTO: *page 101*

Jyoti As I mentioned in my introduction at the beginning of the book, I was introduced to a slew of Bengali traditions that were unfamiliar to me when I married my husband, Jhulan. My mother-in-law once explained, for example, that any time one invites a Bengali family over for a meal, it is an essential cultural duty to prepare a sweet chutney to cleanse the palate before dessert. Not doing so, she told me, is a sign of disrespect.

Tamatar Khajoor Chutney is one such sweet chutney, and it features a characteristically Bengali combination of spices and sugar. This recipe will keep for about 3 weeks in the fridge or a year in the freezer.

Auyon This condiment traditionally pairs with Bengali Khichudi (page 180), but we encourage you to think about ways to use it outside of Indian fare too. A well-regarded British restaurant group called Dishoom uses a similar spread in their signature Bacon Naan Roll, which features streaky bacon, cream cheese, and tomato jam wrapped up in a flatbread and served for breakfast. All to say, double the recipe to allow for some experimentation.

My mom and I have different sweetness preferences—the recipe that follows is to my taste, whereas my mom prefers it with an additional ¼ cup (50 g) of sugar (or more!)

1 tablespoon canola oil

1 dried red chili, broken into thirds (see page 271)

½ teaspoon panch phoron (see Note, right)

1¾ cups (425 g) canned crushed (or diced) tomatoes

2 tablespoons grated, peeled fresh ginger

⅓ cup (65 g) sugar, plus more to taste

¼ cup (40 g) finely chopped pitted dates

¼ cup (35 g) raisins

¼ teaspoon salt, plus more to taste

1. Heat the oil in a medium, lidded (but uncovered for now) pot over medium heat. Once the oil starts to shimmer, add the chili and cook, giving the pan a shake to distribute the chili pieces evenly, until they darken a shade or two, about 30 seconds.

2. Add the panch phoron and cook, undisturbed, until the mustard seeds are popping vigorously, another 30 seconds or so (watch out for oil splatter—use a splatter screen if you have one).

3. Add the tomato and ginger and stir well. Reduce the heat to low and cover the pot. Cook at a gentle boil, stirring occasionally, for about 25 minutes to thicken the mixture and infuse the tomato with the spices.

4. Add the sugar, dates, raisins, and salt. Stir well and cover. Cook, stirring once or twice, until the dates start to break down and the flavors begin to meld, about 10 minutes. Taste for sugar and salt.

5. Cool to room temperature, ideally covered to avoid evaporation. If you are pinched for time, cool the chutney uncovered but make sure to cover as soon as it is cool enough to refrigerate.

6. Store in a sealable container in the fridge and serve chilled or at room temperature.

Note

Panch phoron, which translates to "five spice" in Bengali, is a blend of equal parts black mustard seeds, cumin seeds, fennel seeds, kalonji (nigella) seeds, and a half-part of fenugreek seeds. Unlike most other Indian spice mixes, panch phoron is always made with whole seeds, never ground. It is available ready-made at any Indian store, but it is also a breeze to make at home if you have the ingredients handy.

Adarak Nimbu Achaar

GINGER LEMON PICKLE

MAKES *roughly 2 cups (480 g)*
PREP TIME: *15 minutes* • **PICKLING TIME:** *48 hours*
PHOTO: *page 122*

Jyoti This was my dad's favorite achaar, or Indian pickle, and it was on our dining table at every meal while I was growing up. It is (relatively) quick and easy to make, and the perfect gateway into the magical, salty-sour world of achaars. For more on the oil-fermented styles that we typically buy at the Indian store, see pages 29 and 279.

Note that you'll need to start this two days in advance of when you want to eat it.

Auyon For this recipe, you'll need whole, fresh turmeric root (as opposed to the dried powder), which can usually be found near its cousin ginger in both Indian groceries and, increasingly, most supermarkets. There is no need to peel it, but consider wearing gloves when cutting it, as it will turn anything it touches orange.

Another color-related concern: if you happen to use young ginger, it may turn pink as it sits in the lemon juice, which is totally fine. The color change is the result of anthocyanins (a class of compounds responsible for the dark color of eggplant skins and blackberries) responding to the citric acid of the lemon juice.

¾ cup (80 g) julienned, peeled fresh ginger (cut into short, thin matchsticks)

¼ cup (25 g) julienned fresh turmeric root

1 fresh Indian green chili (optional; see page 271—jalapeño may be substituted), halved lengthwise

2 teaspoons salt

1 cup (240 ml) fresh lemon juice (from about 4 lemons), plus more as necessary

1. Mix the ginger, turmeric, chili (if using), and salt in a clean glass jar that is large enough to hold the mixture.

2. Pour the lemon juice over to cover, then stir again to combine. If not all of the ingredients are fully submerged, add more lemon juice.

3. Leave on a sunny windowsill or countertop for 48 hours, covered. You will know it is pickled enough when the ginger and turmeric are spicy, tart, and pleasantly salty.

4. Store in a sealable container in the fridge and serve at room temperature. This achaar will keep for at least a month in the fridge.

JULIENNED GINGER

JULIENNED TURMERIC

CHAPTER EIGHT

Drinks and Sweets

WHEN THE HIMALAYA GIVE YOU LEMONS...

Auyon The progenitors of modern citrus trees appeared about eight million years ago in the southeast foothills of the Himalaya, a region that comprises neighboring portions of Myanmar, the Indian state of Assam, and the Chinese province of Yunnan. As the climate shifted over successive millennia, the fruits slowly advanced out of the mountains and across the globe.

Circa 8000 BCE, long after the lemon trekked its way out of the Himalaya, sugarcane was cultivated in New Guinea, a large island off the coast of Australia. The perennial grass soon spread to Southeast Asia, India, and China. As early as the sixth century BCE, Indians developed the process of refining the juice into granulated sugar. Tellingly, the words *sugar* and *candy* are both Sanskrit derivatives, via the terms *sarkara* ("sugar," and originally, "sand or gravel") and *khanda* ("fragment," or "to crush"), respectively.

Nimbu Pani

INDIAN LEMONADE

SERVES 6 • PREP TIME: *10 minutes (plus time to chill)*
PHOTO: *page 120*

Jyoti Although lemonade now seems as American as peanut butter and baseball, the beverage has Indian roots. As demonstrated on the opposite page, the histories of citrus and sugar are both intertwined with the subcontinent. A cold glass of nimbu pani was almost always on offer when I visited friends' homes when I was young. The tangy, refreshing concoction remains a favorite treat of mine now, especially in the heat of Kansas City summers.

1 cup (200 g) sugar, plus more to taste

5 tablespoons fresh lemon juice (from about 1¼ lemons), plus more to taste

½ teaspoon kaala namak (black salt, see Kaala Namak, below)

½ teaspoon cumin seeds, roasted (lightly!) and ground (see page 43)

Garnish
2 tablespoons fresh mint leaves

1. Combine the sugar with 6 cups (1.4 L) water in a pitcher or large jug. Stir to dissolve.

2. Add the lemon juice, kaala namak, and ground cumin. Stir to incorporate and taste for lemon and sugar. Chill in the refrigerator for at least 30 minutes and no longer than a few days.

GARNISH
3. Garnish each glass with a few mint leaves and serve chilled.

Kaala Namak

Kaala namak, or black salt, has a haunting, sulfurous quality that we love in this sweet-tart lemonade. That said, we recommend you taste some before adding it in. If it seems like it might be a bit much (or if you are preparing it for folks with less adventurous palates), replace some or all of it with regular table salt.

Aam Lassi

MANGO LASSI

SERVES 8 • PREP TIME: *10 minutes (plus time to chill)*
PHOTO: *page 120*

Jyoti Growing up, my exposure to lassi was limited to two varieties: sweetened with sugar, or savory with salt and roasted cumin powder. I wasn't introduced to mango lassi until adulthood, but I quickly fell for it. The acidity of the yogurt plays beautifully with the fruity and floral mango, which we've highlighted with a bit of cardamom and mint.

We recommend using a good-quality canned mango pulp for this recipe, as the fresh mangoes that are available stateside are inconsistent at best. Canned pulp varieties almost always come sweetened (and to differing degrees), so wait to taste before adding any sugar. For reference, we usually add about ¼ cup (50 g) sugar to the full recipe when using Swad's Sweetened Kesar Mango Pulp.

4 cups (960 ml) whole milk (nondairy milk alternatives may be substituted)

2 cups (480 g) whole, unflavored yogurt (store-bought or homemade, page 40), stirred

2 cups (530 g) sweetened Alfonso or Kesar mango pulp

2 pinches of salt

Sugar, to taste

Fresh lemon juice, to taste

Garnish
2 whole green cardamom pods

2 tablespoons fresh mint leaves

1. In a blender, combine the milk, yogurt, mango pulp, and salt and puree to a smooth consistency. Taste for flavor. Adjust the sweet-tart balance by adding sugar or more lemon juice as necessary. Chill in the refrigerator for at least 30 minutes and no longer than a couple of days.

GARNISH

2. Smash and peel the cardamom pods. Coarsely grind the seeds using a mortar and pestle or rolling pin (see Note, page 43) and discard the peels.

3. Serve chilled, and garnish each glass with a few mint leaves and a pinch of cardamom powder.

Masala Chai

SWEET and SPICY MILK TEA

SERVES 4 • **COOK TIME:** *20 minutes* • **PHOTO:** *page 98*

Jyoti For those of you who drink a lot of carefully brewed tea, the idea of steeping tea in boiling water for almost 10 minutes might seem like a heretical over-brew, but that's actually what we're going for. The slightly bitter, tannic taste that results from a longer brew is necessary for properly made chai, as it ensures that the flavor will stand up to the sugar, spices, and dairy.

Masala chai is consumed widely across the subcontinent, but the spicing and flavoring vary widely from region to region and even from home to home. This is our preferred recipe, but you can and should adjust it as you wish. Most traditional preparations also include much more sugar than we use, so sweeten to taste.

If you don't drink dairy, nondairy milk alternatives may be substituted.

Auyon The tea that's traditionally used for chai in India is the lowest grade stuff, the tiny bits that are left after the whole leaves and large leaf pieces are sorted out. Due to the high surface area to volume ratio of these tea bits (known as fannings or dust), they impart flavor and color much more quickly than the more expensive whole leaves. In the spirit of authenticity, we recommend using cheap supermarket brands like Lipton (cheap decaf is fine too). Save the loose-leaf first flush Darjeelings for unadulterated brewing.

- 4 cloves
- 4 black peppercorns
- 6 green cardamom pods
- ¼ cup (30 g) thinly sliced ginger (peeling optional)
- One 3-inch (7.5-cm) cinnamon stick
- 1 teaspoon fennel seeds
- 4 teaspoons loose-leaf black tea or 4 single-serving tea bags
- 1 cup (240 ml) whole milk (plant-based milk alternatives may be substituted, see Note, right), or more to taste
- ¼ cup (50 g) sugar, or to taste

1. Use a mortar and pestle to coarsely crush the cloves and black peppercorns. Add the cardamom pods to the mortar and crack them open so that the seeds are exposed. (The goal is to maximize the exposed surface area of the pods and seeds, not pulverize anything.)

2. Combine the crushed cloves, peppercorns, and cracked cardamom pods, seeds and all, with the ginger, cinnamon, fennel, and 4 cups (960 ml) water in a large, lidded (but uncovered for now) pot. (Use a cooking vessel with plenty of headroom—the milk shouldn't boil over, but the extra space is good insurance just in case.) Bring to a rolling boil over high heat. Cook for 3 minutes.

3. Meanwhile, if using loose-leaf tea, put it in a cheesecloth sachet or a tea bag. If using commercial tea bags, snip off the labels or any extraneous paper bits so that you can add the whole bags in without worrying about the dye from the labels steeping with the tea.

4. Add the tea and milk to the pot, then bring the mixture back to a boil. Reduce the heat to low. Partially cover the pot, leaving the lid cracked open ½ inch (12 mm) or so, and simmer for about 8 minutes until the flavors meld. Keep an eye on it so nothing boils over.

5. Remove the sachet/tea bags with a slotted spoon or spider. Add the sugar and stir to dissolve.

6. Taste for milk and sugar and then strain into individual mugs. Serve hot.

Serving Tip

→ Chai unfortunately doesn't keep well, so we recommend consuming it within 12 hours of brewing. We usually don't bother refrigerating it for such a short time span.

Note

If using a nondairy milk, add it in at the end with the sugar and reheat gently if necessary. Don't bring the mixture all the way up to a boil, as plant-based milks have a propensity to curdle.

A NOTE ON MASALA CHAI

Auyon Purveyors of masala chai often chronicle the drink's ancient roots in Ayurveda, or Indian traditional medicine. It's a lovely story, but like most great marketing schemes, it's also nonsense. Although the tea plant is native to parts of northeastern India, its consumption (both as an infusion and as a fermented pickle) was historically limited to just that region.

Brewed tea as we know it today is Chinese in origin. The British began commercially cultivating the plant in India in the early nineteenth century in order to break the Chinese monopoly, but the bulk of what they grew was shipped directly back to Britain. Tea drinking within India remained largely limited to the British and Anglicized elites until the 1930s, when international tea prices dropped sharply due to ripple effects of the Great Depression.

Early attempts to market the stuff to Indians were stymied by the vehement opposition of prominent Indian nationalists, including Mahatma Gandhi, who cited the industry's association with colonial overlords and objectionable labor practices among their grievances. It wasn't until the British departure in 1947, and the accompanying Indianization of the tea industry in the early 1950s, that tea truly became the drink of the Indian masses (albeit in a milk-and-spice-doctored form that may have been all but unrecognizable to a British tea propagandist).

For historical reference, contemporary phenomena in the United States include Kraft Cheez Wiz (1952) and Eggo Frozen Waffles (1953).

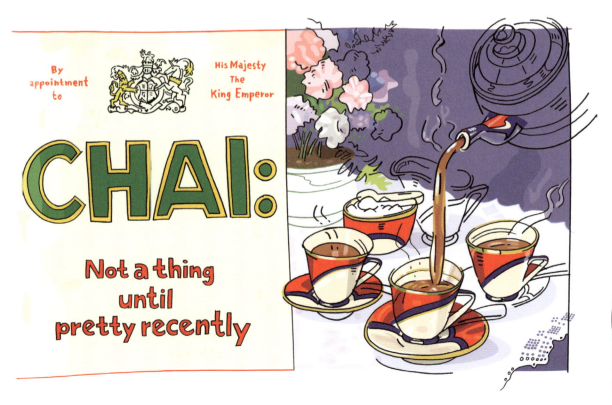

Aam Panna

CUMIN and SOUR MANGO CORDIAL

SERVES 4 • **COOK TIME:** *1 hour (plus time to cool the mango after roasting)* • **PHOTO:** *page 120*

Jyoti This classic, tangy summer tonic derives its restorative properties from a healthy dose of antioxidant-rich roasted raw mango. The concentrate will keep for at least a couple of weeks in the fridge or a year in the freezer.

Auyon The unripe green mango necessary for this recipe is not something you'll find in a standard Western grocery store. You're looking for a hard, unyielding fruit, picked well before ripening, with a sour, nutty taste. You should be able to find it at most Indian markets, either fresh or frozen.

If you find fresh ones, we recommend buying an extra and trying it as a crudité. Cut around the seed like you would a normal mango (but be careful, since it will be less forgiving). Remove the peel, slice it into sticks, and then sprinkle with salt and lime. You can also cut it into long spears to use as an alternate garnish for this recipe or Aam Panna Punch (page 257).

1 large unripe green mango (14½ ounces // 410 g, see Note, right)

1 tablespoon fresh mint leaves

1 teaspoon kaala namak (black salt, see Kaala Namak, page 249)

¾ teaspoon whole cumin seeds, roasted (lightly!) and ground (see page 43)

Serving + Garnish
Sugar, to taste

Fresh mint leaves

1. Preheat a toaster oven to 425°F (220°C) (a full-size oven is fine too if that's all you have), and adjust the top rack so that the top of the mango sits 2 to 3 inches (5 to 7.5 cm) below the top heating element. Once the oven is up to temperature, put the mango on a baking sheet or piece of foil (on the top rack) and cook to soften, about 25 minutes.

2. Switch the oven to broil and cook for 10 minutes to lightly char the fruit on one side.

3. Flip the mango over and broil the other side for a final 10 minutes.

4. Remove from the heat and let cool to room temperature.

5. Carefully peel the mango, scraping as much flesh as possible from the peel using a spoon or a knife.

6. Slice the mango open to remove the seed, and then cut the flesh into chunks. Discard the peel and seed.

7. Using a blender, food processor, or mortar and pestle, grind the mango flesh, mint leaves, kaala namak, ground cumin, and ½ cup (120 ml) water to a smooth puree. This puree is the unsweetened aam panna concentrate.

SERVING + GARNISH

8. To serve, add 2 tablespoons concentrate to 1 cup (240 ml) water, multiplied by as many servings as you need. Stir well and sweeten to taste. We like a 1:1 sugar-to-concentrate ratio (2 tablespoons of sugar for 2 tablespoons of concentrate).

9. Garnish each glass with a few mint leaves and serve chilled.

Note

If fresh green mangoes are unavailable, frozen green (unripe) mango may be substituted. Instead of roasting, though, you'll be boiling the fruit—an equally common method for making aam panna. Start with 10 ounces (285 g) frozen green mango (about 2½ cups of 1-inch // 2.5-cm mango cubes). Sometimes frozen mango is sold with the peel on—there's no need to remove it unless someone in the household is sensitive to mango skin (not uncommon, as the fruit is in the same family as poison ivy). Place the mango in a small pot and add just enough water to cover. Bring the mixture to a rolling boil, cover, and cook for 8 minutes. Allow the mixture to cool to room temperature. Using a blender or food processor, grind the cooked mango, its cooking liquid, an additional ½ cup (120 ml) water, cumin, kaala namak, and mint to a smooth puree. This puree is the unsweetened aam panna concentrate, which should be used as directed in Steps 8 and 9.

• Thandai •

ALMOND, FENNEL, and CARDAMOM CORDIAL

MAKES *roughly 3 cups (720 ml) of concentrate* • **SOAK TIME:** *6 hours* • **COOK TIME:** *20 minutes*
PHOTO: *page 121*

Auyon Thandai is the essential refreshment of Holi, the Hindu festival of colors: a celebration of both the arrival of spring and the triumph of good over evil. Although our recipe is family friendly, the drink is traditionally spiked with bhang, or cannabis. Other features of the holiday include smearing brightly colored powder on friends and neighbors, live music, and lighting an effigy of a demon on fire. It is an enjoyable festival.

This recipe produces just shy of 3 cups (720 ml) of syrup, so you should have plenty to play with. Try a splash to liven up unsweetened oats or granola, or use it as a nutty, aromatic sweetener for hot chocolate or tea. Cocktail aficionados can think of it as a spiced orgeat. The syrup will keep for at least a couple of weeks in the fridge, or up to a year in the freezer.

¼ cup (40 g) raw almonds

4 green cardamom pods

1 tablespoon white poppy seeds

1 tablespoon fennel seeds

½ teaspoon black peppercorns

1 cup (200 g) sugar

¼ teaspoon almond extract

4 drops kewra water (see page 275)

2 pinches of salt

Garnish + Serving

2 pinches of saffron

Pinch of sugar

Whole milk, chilled (nondairy milk alternatives may be substituted), about 1 cup (240 ml) per serving

1. Combine the almonds, cardamom pods, poppy seeds, fennel seeds, and peppercorns with ¾ cup (180 ml) water in a small bowl. Soak overnight, or for at least 6 hours.

2. Using a blender, food processor, or mortar and pestle, grind the soaked mixture to a smooth paste.

3. Line a large bowl with a large square of butter muslin or fine cheesecloth.

4. Carefully pour the blended mixture into the center. Pull up the edges of the cheesecloth and bring them together to make a pouch. Suspend the pouch over the bowl, twisting and squeezing it to extract as much liquid as possible from the blended mixture. Try working at different angles to maximize yield.

5. Gently open the cheesecloth and scrape the solids back into the blender, food processor, or mortar. Add another ½ cup (120 ml) water, then re-grind and re-strain into the same bowl, again extracting as much liquid as possible. Discard the solids.

6. Combine the sugar and 1 cup (240 ml) water in a medium pot. Prepare a simple syrup by warming the mixture for a couple of minutes over medium heat, stirring, until fully dissolved.

7. Remove from the heat and stir in the almond extract, kewra water, salt, and freshly extracted almond-and-spice liquid.

GARNISH + SERVING

8. Combine the saffron and sugar in a mortar and pestle. Crush the mixture to make a pale pink saffron sugar, which will turn brilliant crimson, orange, and gold when you sprinkle it over the drink in Step 10.

9. To serve, pour as many servings of chilled milk into a pitcher or large bowl as you need and add syrup to taste. We enjoy a roughly 1:4 ratio (1 cup // 240 ml of thandai syrup in 4 cups // 960 ml of milk).

10. Divide the thandai among individual glasses and sprinkle some of the garnish over each glass. Wait for a few seconds for the garnish to bloom and change color. Serve chilled.

HOLD YOUR BREATH

Auyon Some religiously biased historians would have you believe that alcohol was not a significant part of the subcontinental diet of antiquity. The record demonstrates otherwise, especially if you subscribe to the idea that a high specificity of punishment implies a high frequency of misdeed.

The Dharmasutras, a series of Sanskrit texts that date back to the first millennium BCE, prescribed the following punishments for members of the priestly class: if alcohol was deliberately consumed, the offender must drink liquid from a boiling hot glass; if alcohol was consumed by accident, the inadvertent wrongdoer must subsist on hot milk, hot ghee, hot water, and hot air for 72 hours each (presumably in direct succession); if alcohol was merely smelled on the breath of an acquaintance, the hapless cleric must practice yoga, eat ghee, and control his breathing.

In keeping with the straightforwardly misogynistic conventions of the time, a woman from the priestly class who drank alcohol was simply doomed to be reborn as a leech or an oyster.

We encourage you to celebrate the centuries-old Indian traditions of rule-flouting and shameless indulgence by incorporating Aam Panna (page 254) concentrate or Thandai (page 255) syrup into a cocktail at your next boozy get-together.

Aam Panna Punch

MAKES 1 cocktail • **PHOTO:** page 121

Small handful of fresh mint leaves, plus an optional sprig for garnish

Pinch of sugar

¼ cup (60 ml) white rum

1 tablespoon unsweetened aam panna (page 254) concentrate

2 tablespoons simple syrup (1:1 water to sugar by volume), plus more to taste

1 tablespoon fresh lime juice

½ cup (120 ml) chilled seltzer water

1. Muddle the mint leaves and sugar in a highball or Collins glass. Cover the muddled mint with ice (crushed, ideally) to half-fill the glass, and set aside.

2. Combine the rum, aam panna concentrate, simple syrup, and lime juice in a mixing glass. Stir briskly to mix.

3. Pour the rum mixture into the prepared highball or Collins glass. Add the seltzer and stir once to combine. Sweeten to taste. Garnish with a sprig of mint, if using, and serve immediately.

Thandai Old-Fashioned

MAKES 1 cocktail • **PHOTO:** page 121

¼ cup (60 ml) bourbon or rye whiskey

5 teaspoons thandai concentrate (page 255)

Orange peel coin (optional; to make, cut a quarter-sized coin out of the rind of a fresh orange)

2 to 3 dashes of aromatic bitters (optional)

1. Combine the whiskey and thandai concentrate with several cubes of ice in a mixing glass. Stir briskly to chill the mixture.

2. Fill a rocks glass with a few cubes of fresh ice (or, preferably, one large ice cube). Strain the chilled whiskey mixture into the rocks glass. Add the aromatic bitters (if using).

3. Express the oil from the orange peel coin (if using) by holding the peel with your thumb and forefinger about 4 inches (10 cm) over the glass, so that the outside of the peel points toward the surface of the drink. Gently squeeze the peel by pinching your fingers together. You should see (and smell) a spritz of orange oil as the coin buckles toward the drink. Discard the spent peel, or cut a small slit into it and perch it on the rim of the glass to garnish. Serve immediately.

Sooji Halwa

SWEET ROASTED SEMOLINA with GHEE

SERVES 4 • COOK TIME: *25 minutes* • PHOTO: *page 98*

Jyoti Sooji halwa is one of the most frequently prepared sweets in Punjabi homes. It is also often distributed as prasad, or blessed food, at religious festivals and temples. We included it here as much for cultural significance as for its remarkable flavor and texture—the rich, buttery beads of wheat combine marvelously with the acidic punch of the softened raisins. This recipe makes a lightly sweet dish, but you should feel free to add an extra 2 tablespoons of sugar for a sweeter, more traditional preparation.

We love the dish served warm, but if you choose to serve it at room temperature, bear in mind that the halwa takes on a pleasantly gelatinous quality as it cools. You can also serve it as a solid sweet by cooking off more of the liquid. For a truly decadent (and starchy!) treat, try it Punjabi style with Loochi (page 204).

Auyon This dairy-free dessert falls under the broad umbrella of *halwa*, an Arabic loanword that spans flour-, fruit-, vegetable-, nut-, and legume-based confections within India. Outside of India and especially in the Levant and surrounding areas, the term *halwa* (or *halva*) often refers specifically to tahini-based preparations.

¾ cup (150 g) sugar, plus more to taste

2 tablespoons unsalted ghee (store-bought or homemade, page 38)

½ cup (95 g) fine sooji (see Note, right)

1 tablespoon raisins

1 tablespoon slivered almonds

Pinch of salt

Garnish
2 teaspoons slivered almonds

1. Combine the sugar with 2 cups (480 ml) water in a small pot. Prepare a syrup by warming the mixture for a couple of minutes over medium heat, stirring, until fully dissolved. Remove from the heat and set aside.

2. Heat the ghee in a medium, lidded (but uncovered for now) pan over medium heat. Once the ghee is good and hot, add the sooji. Cook, stirring constantly, until it becomes fragrant and browns just slightly, about 5 minutes.

3. Add the syrup, raisins, slivered almonds, and salt. Stir well, reduce the heat to low, and cover the pan. Cook, stirring occasionally, until all the water is absorbed and the halwa thickens to where it is barely pourable, 5 to 7 minutes. Taste for sweetness.

GARNISH
4. Garnish with the slivered almonds. Serve hot or warm.

Note
Sooji is an Indian semolina, or milled wheat product. It's ideal to buy it from an Indian grocery, where it is sold in both coarse and fine varieties—the fine version is what you want for this dish. Semolina flour (like the kind you use for pasta; we tested with Bob's Red Mill brand) will do in a pinch, but because it's ground finer than fine sooji, the resulting halwa will be a bit more gooey.

Mishti Doi

BAKED SWEET YOGURT

SERVES 6 • COOK TIME: *2 hours (plus time to chill)*
PHOTO: *page 127*

Jyoti The traditional mode of preparing this Bengali delicacy requires both overnight fermentation and the use of terra cotta cookware. Neither is necessary for our baked adaptation. If you have terra cotta at your disposal, though, by all means use it. It will imbue the dish with an authentic earthiness.

The flavor sits somewhere in the tempting intersection of melty ice cream, tangy yogurt, and dulce de leche. Visually, however, mishti doi does not rank among the most aesthetically pleasing of sweets. Fortunately, it takes well to (nontraditional) garnishes. Tart berries are a standby in our house. We also love saffron sugar (see page 277)—sprinkle the pale pink powder over the mishti doi a few minutes before serving and you will be rewarded with brilliant patterns of orange, crimson, and gold.

Auyon Bengal's reverence for sweets is a defining feature of the region. Historian Chitrita Banerji writes: "Traditional Bengalis of my grandmother's generation firmly believed that it was unhealthy to drink water on an empty stomach. The remedy was to pop a sweet into your mouth before lifting the glass of water."

Cookware note: To ensure an evenly set result, you'll need an oven-safe baking dish that will comfortably hold 3½ cups (840 ml) of liquid at a depth of at least 2 inches (5 cm).

1⅓ cups (320 g) whole, unflavored yogurt (store-bought or homemade, page 40), stirred

1⅓ cups (320 ml) whole milk

¾ cup (180 ml) sweetened, condensed milk

Pinch of salt

1. Make sure you have a suitably sized oven-safe ceramic or glass baking dish (see Auyon's headnote). Prepare a water bath by placing ½ inch (12 mm) of water in a roasting tray or rimmed baking sheet that will comfortably accommodate the baking dish. Place the water bath (without the baking dish inside it) on the lowest rack of the oven. Preheat the oven (with the water bath inside it) to 250°F (120°C).

2. Combine the yogurt, whole milk, sweetened condensed milk, and salt in a large bowl. Using an immersion blender or whisk, blend the mixture to fully incorporate. Scrape the sides and bottom of the bowl to ensure all of the condensed milk combines.

3. Pour the mixture into the baking dish. Once the oven is up to temperature, place the dish into the water bath in the oven and bake until the doi has set, about 1 hour. When you gently tip the pan, you should see the doi jiggle rather than flow. (There's no need to make sure the water bath is up to temperature beforehand, as long as it warmed up with the oven.)

4. Turn off the heat and let the dish rest undisturbed in the unopened oven for an additional 45 minutes to ensure an even set.

5. Remove from the oven and let cool to room temperature. The mishti doi will firm up to the texture of regular yogurt as it cools. Cover and refrigerate for 8 hours, or ideally overnight. Serve chilled.

Doodh Seviyan

CARDAMOM MILK PUDDING with NOODLES

SERVES 4 • **COOK TIME:** *30 minutes* • **PHOTO:** *page 127*

Auyon Although noodles exist in both sweet and savory forms within Indian gastronomy, they do not often feature as a staple starch (unlike across much of the rest of Asia).

This traditional North Indian winter dessert is essentially a noodled version of a rice pudding. I love the intricate, Magic Eye–like patterns created by the wavy, overlapping golden vermicelli on the surface of the finished dish.

Roasted vermicelli is readily available at most Indian stores, either precut or in long strands. Sometimes the "roasted" descriptor is left off, but if the vermicelli is golden brown (as opposed to the pale yellow of raw pasta), then you've got the right stuff. Using pre-roasted noodles prevents them from clumping up.

- 4 green cardamom pods
- 2 cups (480 ml) whole milk
- ½ cup (33 g) bite-size roasted vermicelli pieces
- 2 tablespoons sugar, plus more to taste
- 1 tablespoon raisins (optional)
- 1 tablespoon sliced almonds
- Pinch of salt
- Boiling water (optional)

Garnish
- 1 tablespoon coarsely crushed pistachios

1. Smash and peel the cardamom pods. Discard the peels, then coarsely grind the seeds using a mortar and pestle or a rolling pin (see Note, page 43).

2. Rinse a medium, heavy-bottomed pot with cold water, leaving just enough water to coat the bottom of the pot. This step will help prevent the milk from scorching.

3. Add the milk and ground cardamom to the pot. Cook over medium-high heat, stirring constantly, until it just starts to boil, about 5 minutes.

4. Reduce the heat to medium-low so the milk simmers and add the vermicelli. Cook, continuing to stir constantly, for about 3 minutes. The noodles should completely soften quickly, and the continued cooking will help thicken the mixture slightly via evaporation (although the change in texture will be hard to discern when the milk is still hot).

5. Add the sugar, raisins (if using), almonds, and salt. Cook, stirring once or twice, until the seviyan starts to bubble again, which should be quite quick, then remove from the heat.

6. Let rest, covered, for 10 minutes before serving. The final texture of the dish is difficult to describe—thicker than heavy cream, but still pourable, with a slightly gelatinous quality because of the noodles. It's a forgiving dish, though, so if yours came out a bit thinner or thicker, it will still taste great. You can always adjust the texture by adding a bit of boiled milk to thin it out, or by cooking it further to thicken it via evaporation. Taste for sweetness.

GARNISH

7. Serve warm, at room temperature, or transfer to the refrigerator and chill for an hour or two (and consume within a couple of days). Garnish with pistachios before serving.

Salted Caramel Almond Flan

SERVES 8 • **SOAK TIME:** *8 hours*
COOK TIME: *1¾ hours (plus time to chill)*
PHOTO: *page 126*

Jyoti When I was growing up, breakfast was often accompanied by a bowl of almonds that had been soaked overnight, leaving the nuts beautifully soft but still with some bite. Fond memories of that morning treat inspired me to try blending a healthy dose of soaked almonds into a custard base for a crème caramel. The resulting recipe has now become one of the most requested desserts in my classes.

One point of caution: Watch closely when the sugar liquefies to make sure it doesn't burn. Once it gets going, it all happens very quickly. And if the sugar does burn, just like with spices, it's better to throw it out and start fresh rather than risk ruining the whole dish.

Auyon The popularity of Indian fare in Britain is well known, but the gastronomical exchange went both ways. Holdovers from the colonial period, like crème caramel, are still part of the collective culinary repertory of the homes, canteens, and wayside hotels of West Bengal, a former seat of British power. Other examples of crossover fare include two of my mom's childhood favorites: Spiced Liver Toast, page 232, and Fruit Cream, page 263. A more complete translation of Anglo-Indian cuisine can be found within the menus of Anglo-Indian restaurants and members-only clubs of cities like Kolkata, New Delhi, Chennai, and Mumbai.

A great number of these Anglo-Indian establishments demonstrate authenticity in not only fare, but also in old-fashioned British pomposity. My father was once not allowed entry into a lunch event in the dining room of the hallowed Calcutta Club, as he was not properly attired in a collared shirt. The lunch was in his honor.

Almonds
50 almonds (about ⅓ cup // 55 g)

Caramel
½ cup (100 g) sugar
¼ teaspoon salt

Flan
1 cup (240 ml) + 1 cup (240 ml) whole milk (nondairy milk alternatives may be substituted, see Note, page 262)

4 large eggs
½ cup (100 g) sugar
1 teaspoon vanilla extract

Garnish
3 tablespoons sliced almonds

ALMONDS

1. Combine the almonds with 2 cups (480 ml) water in a bowl. Soak overnight, or for at least 8 hours.

CARAMEL

2. Prepare a water bath by filling a rimmed baking sheet or roasting tray (large enough to hold the baking pan you'll use for the flan, see Step 3) with ½ inch (12 mm) of water and placing it on the lowest rack of the oven. Preheat the oven to 325°F (165°C).

3. Keep a 9½-inch (24-cm) round baking pan, or a baking pan with a roughly equivalent surface area, within arm's reach of the stove. (For an alternate presentation, you can also use individual ramekins with a roughly equivalent combined surface area.)

4. Heat the sugar and the salt in a small pan over high heat and stir constantly. Lumps will start to form after a minute or so, and the sugar will start to melt and brown. Soon you will be left with a few lumps of sugar swimming in a golden brown pool of caramel.

5. As soon as the last of the lumps dissolves, after about 4 minutes of cooking, pour the mixture into the baking pan and rotate to evenly coat the bottom of the pan with caramel. We like to use a spatula to make sure the entire surface gets coated. If the caramel starts to harden in the pan, reheat it for a minute to make it pourable again.

recipe continues

Drinks and Sweets

Salted Caramel Almond Flan
· continued ·

6. Set the coated baking pan aside. As the caramel cools and hardens, it will crack (which is fine).

FLAN

7. Drain and peel the soaked almonds—the peel should slide right off when you press one end of the nut. Discard the peels and soaking liquid.

8. Combine the peeled almonds and 1 cup (240 ml) of the milk in a blender and grind until completely smooth.

9. Add the eggs, sugar, vanilla, and remaining 1 cup (240 ml) milk to the blender and blend again to incorporate. (We find the two phases of blending are necessary to ensure the almonds get evenly ground.) Pour the mixture over the cooled caramel.

10. Carefully place the pan into the water bath once the oven is at temperature and bake for 45 minutes, until just set. When you gently tip the pan, you should see the flan jiggle rather than flow.

11. Turn the oven off and let the dish sit undisturbed in the unopened oven for an additional 30 minutes to ensure an even set.

12. Remove the flan from the oven (and water bath) and transfer to a cooling rack to cool to room temperature to firm up. Store in the fridge, uncovered, for at least 3 hours to fully set. Cover once set.

13. To serve, carefully run a pie server or butter knife between the edge of the flan and the pan to release the sides. Place a large serving plate upside down over the top of the pan and then, moving quickly, invert the pan and the plate together. When you remove the pan, the caramel layer will be on top.

GARNISH

14. Garnish with the sliced almonds. Serve chilled.

Note

If using a plant-based milk alternative, use a substitute that has a bit of body to it, such as oat milk, and increase the baking time to 1 hour.

Fruit Cream

SERVES 6 • **PREP TIME:** *15 minutes (plus time to chill)*
PHOTO: *page 126*

Jyoti When I was a little girl, I knew we were expecting special guests whenever I heard my mother order cream from the milkman. This simple preparation was, and remains, my absolute favorite of my mother's desserts.

Auyon If you like, you can replace the apples, pears, and grapes with a roughly equivalent volume of other fruit (1½ cups, or 250 g, in total). Raspberries, blueberries, strawberries, and pitted cherries are all lovely. Avoid fresh pineapple, melon, papaya, and guava, though, because they all contain enzymes that can react with dairy and turn bitter. (Canned pineapple, which this recipe calls for, is fine.) Increase the sugar by a couple of tablespoons if the fruit you are using is especially tart.

2 cups (480 ml) heavy cream

⅓ cup (65 g) sugar, plus more to taste

1 navel orange, cubed into 1-inch (2.5-cm) chunks

1 apple or pear (or half of each), cubed into ½-inch (12-mm) chunks

½ cup (80 g) halved grapes

½ cup (115 g) drained, canned crushed pineapple

1 banana, left unpeeled until just before serving

1. Combine the cream and sugar in a large bowl. Beat with an immersion blender (or a whisk and some elbow grease if you're feeling plucky) until the cream starts to thicken and increases in volume, as quick as 10 seconds by machine. All you want to do is introduce some air, not make whipped cream, so stop well before soft peaks start to form.

2. Fold in all of the fruit except for the banana. Taste for sweetness.

3. Cover the mixture and refrigerate for at least 1 hour or up to 24 hours.

4. Just before serving, thinly slice the banana and stir it in. Serve chilled.

Kulfi

JYOTI   This popular frozen dessert traces its lineage back to the Mughals of sixteenth-century Delhi, who likely acquired the recipe from the Persians. Unlike ice cream and gelato, kulfi is never churned, which accounts for its signature creamy-crumbly mouthfeel and satisfying density.

The traditional preparation involves a lengthy boiling process, scraping and stirring the pan until the milk is reduced to less than half of its original volume. Our recipes, adapted from Meera Sodha's *Made in India*, cut the cooking time down to just 10 minutes or so. Kulfi is typically served with thin glass noodles called falooda, but we prefer a simple garnish of nuts or mango puree.

AUYON   *Kulfi* gets its name from the conical, metal molds that are used to make it. We use lidded aluminum molds that are about 3 inches (7.5 cm) long and can be found at most any Indian grocery. The increased surface area of the conical molds is important, so avoid wider, rounder molds like ramekins (although longer popsicle molds are fine).

Aam Kulfi

CREAM POPS with MANGO

MAKES 12 • **COOK TIME:** *40 minutes*
FREEZE TIME: *4 hours (ideally overnight)*
PHOTO: *page 127*

- 1½ cups (375 g) evaporated milk
- 1½ cups (360 ml) heavy cream
- ¼ cup (50 g) sugar, plus more to taste
- Pinch of salt
- 1½ cups (400 g) sweetened Alfonso or Kesar mango pulp (see Note, right)

Garnish
- ½ cup (135 g) sweetened Alfonso or Kesar mango pulp

1. Rinse a medium, heavy-bottomed pot with cold water, leaving just enough water to coat the bottom of the pot. This step will help prevent the milk from scorching.

2. Add the evaporated milk, cream, sugar, and salt to the pot. Cook over medium heat, stirring constantly, until the mixture just starts to boil, about 10 minutes.

3. Remove from the heat and partially cover the pot. Set aside to cool, stirring every few minutes to prevent a skin from forming over the milk.

4. Once the mixture has cooled to room temperature, add the mango pulp and stir well to incorporate—if you add the pulp too early while the dairy is still hot, you risk curdling the milk. Taste for sweetness.

5. Divide the mango-milk mixture among individual kulfi molds, making sure to leave at least ½ inch (12 mm) of headroom in each to allow for expansion. Screw on the lids, if applicable, and freeze upright, narrow end down, for at least 4 hours, until fully frozen and set (overnight is ideal).

GARNISH

6. When ready to plate and serve, fill a small pot with water and heat until lukewarm. Make a small puddle with a couple teaspoons of mango pulp in the center of each plate.

7. Remove the molds from the freezer and quickly dip the first mold, narrow end down, into the warm water. Unscrew the lid, then tap the inverted mold over the plate to deliver the kulfi into the middle of the puddle. Repeat (and individually plate) the remainder of the kulfi. Serve immediately.

Note

As with the mango pulp for Aam Lassi (page 250), we recommend plumping for a good-quality canned version (and resisting the temptation to puree fresh fruit). Commercial varieties are sweetened to different degrees, so be sure to taste for sweetness after incorporating.

KULFI MOLDS

Pista Kesar Kulfi

CREAM POPS with PISTACHIO and SAFFRON

MAKES *12* • **COOK TIME:** *40 minutes*
FREEZE TIME: *4 hours (ideally overnight)*
PHOTO: *page 127*

¼ cup (35 g) unsalted pistachios

Pinch of saffron threads

1½ cups (375 g) evaporated milk

1½ cups (360 ml) heavy cream

5 tablespoons sugar, plus more to taste

Pinch of salt

Garnish
2 tablespoons unsalted pistachios

1. Combine the pistachios with the saffron threads using a spice grinder or a mortar and pestle. Grind the mixture to a powder. Set aside.

2. Rinse a medium, heavy-bottomed pot with cold water, leaving just enough water to coat the bottom of the pot. This step will help prevent the milk from scorching.

3. Add the evaporated milk, cream, sugar, and salt to the pot. Cook over medium heat, stirring constantly, until the mixture just starts to boil, about 10 minutes.

4. Remove from the heat and add the pistachio-saffron powder to the dairy mixture. Stir well to incorporate, then partially cover the pot.

5. Set aside to cool, stirring every few minutes to prevent a skin from forming over the milk. Once the milk mixture has cooled to lukewarm, taste for sweetness.

6. Divide the mixture among individual kulfi molds, making sure to leave at least ½ inch (12 mm) of headroom in each to allow for expansion. Screw on the lids, if applicable, and freeze upright, narrow end down, for at least 4 hours, until fully frozen and set (overnight is ideal).

GARNISH

7. When ready to plate and serve, coarsely grind the pistachios using a mortar and pestle or a spice grinder. Set aside.

8. Fill a small pot with water and heat until lukewarm. Remove the molds from the freezer and quickly dip the first mold, narrow end down, into the warm water. Unscrew the lid, then tap the inverted mold over the center of a small plate to release. Repeat (and individually plate) the remainder of the kulfi.

9. Garnish each plate with the coarsely ground pistachios. Serve immediately.

Cardamom Rose Kulfi

Keep in mind that our kulfi recipes are variations on a theme—feel free to try some substitutions. One of our favorite riffs is a Cardamom Rose Kulfi. Replace the pistachio-saffron mixture from Step 1 with ½ teaspoon freshly ground green cardamom seeds, to be added in Step 4. Once the cardamom-dairy mixture is cool, add in 1 teaspoon rose water (see page 276) before tasting for sweetness in Step 5. Then proceed with the recipe as written. Edible flower petals are a great alternative garnish.

Sesame Jaggery Brittle

SERVES *plenty* • **COOK TIME:** *1 hour (plus time to cool)*
PHOTO: *page 126*

Auyon This preparation is my lone nonalcoholic recipe contribution to our book. The initial inspirations were a nut-based Indian sweet called chikki and an excellent crumble made by the Vermont-based confectioner Battenkill Wholesome Foods.

The recipe that follows makes a delicate brittle that I love using as granola and as a topping for ice cream. My standby is the plain version, but the recipe accommodates ground spices well. Turmeric, black pepper, green cardamom, ginger, and cinnamon are all excellent additions (both on their own and in combination).

Finally, note that the nomenclature may be a bit misleading. This brittle is light and just sweet enough to offset the bitterness of the roasted sesame seeds—a far cry from the beloved, hypersweet peanut brittle of American candy stores. If you're looking for something more indulgent, up the jaggery and ghee by 1 tablespoon (or more) each.

- 1 teaspoon canola oil (ghee or a spritz of cooking spray may be substituted)
- 1 cup (120 g) raw pecans
- 2 cups (400 g) raw, hulled sesame seeds (see Note, right)
- 1½ cups (200 g) raw sunflower seeds
- ¾ cup (120 g) raw pumpkin seeds
- 2 generous pinches of salt (kosher or other coarse salts are great)
- 2½ tablespoons unsalted ghee (store-bought or homemade, page 38)
- 3 tablespoons jaggery (broken into small pieces or powdered; see Jaggery, page 133)
- 2½ tablespoons maple syrup

1. Preheat the oven to 300°F (150°C). Grease a half sheet pan (13 by 18 inches // 33 by 46 cm) with the canola oil. (Any oven-safe pan with a roughly equivalent area will be fine, although using glass will likely necessitate a longer cook time.)

2. Using a food processor or mortar and pestle, grind the pecans to a meal.

3. Combine the pecan meal, sesame seeds, sunflower seeds, pumpkin seeds, and salt in a large bowl. Stir well to combine, then set aside.

4. Place the ghee in a small pot over low heat for a minute and cook until just melted.

5. Add the jaggery and maple syrup to the ghee and stir well to combine. Cook, stirring frequently, until the jaggery melts completely. The process should be quick, but will vary depending on whether you are using powdered or solid jaggery.

6. Remove the pot from the heat and add 1 tablespoon water (the mixture shouldn't be hot enough to spit, but be careful just in case). Pour the sweetened ghee over the pecan-and-seed mixture. Stir well to combine.

7. Spread the mixture into the prepared pan. The back of a spatula or large spoon can be helpful in getting it evened out. It may feel a bit crumbly, which is fine—as long as the ghee mixture is evenly incorporated into the seeds, the brittle will firm up and stick together as it cooks. The thickness in the pan should be between ¼ inch and ½ inch (6 mm and 12 mm).

8. Once the oven is up to temperature, bake undisturbed for about 50 minutes, until the brittle has darkened a few shades and feels firm when you press it gently (and carefully!) with your finger.

9. Remove the pan from the oven and allow it to cool completely to room temperature in the pan. Pry the brittle out of the pan with a spatula (twisting the pan gently is helpful here). Break it up to taste—I like having both bigger chunks to eat plain and smaller crumbles to use as granola. Store in an airtight container for up to a week.

Note
Hulled sesame seeds are slightly less bitter and have a more pleasant texture (in this context) than their unhulled counterparts. It's worth seeking them out.

Spices and Sundry

Spices

Perhaps the greatest hallmark of Indian cuisine is its use of spices, which add flavor, texture, and pigment. Spices are an affordable way to elevate simple dishes, which is especially important in a country where the majority of the population lives off less than seven dollars a day. Spices also contain antibiotic compounds that help curb bacterial and fungal growth—chronic concerns in a tropical climate.

The botanical world of spices is wide-ranging, and includes fruits, leaves, barks, minerals, resins, underground stems, seeds, kernels, arils, and flower bits. Our guide includes basic facts, along with shopping and usage tips. We listed the spices and ingredients in alphabetical order by how you're most likely to find them (and how we listed them in the recipes): Hindustani first for items that will most likely be labeled in Hindustani at the Indian store, like amchoor and anardana, and English first for more familiar spices like ginger and garlic.

(As with any generalization about a subject as vast as the cooking of India, there are anomalies. Some of the hill tribes of northeast India, for example, historically did not have access to cooking oil, so the technique of tempering, and the use of spices more broadly, are notably absent from traditional cuisines of the region.)

Amchoor
GROUND DRIED MANGO

Amchoor is what you get when green, unripe mangoes (*Mangifera indica*) are peeled, cut into strips, sun-dried, and then ground. Sharply sour yet fruity, it is particularly useful when you want to add an acidic or sour component to a dish without introducing any liquid. Indian stores sell both dried slices and the ground stuff—we generally buy the powder. It can clump up, so crush it between your fingers before adding it to a dish. Try it on toasted nuts and buttered popcorn, ideally in concert with Kaala Namak (see page 249).

Anardana
DRIED POMEGRANATE

Made from dried pomegranate (*Punica granatum*) arils, anardana is a subtle mix of sweet and earthy, with just a hint of acidity. If you purchase whole, dried seeds (and you want to use it as a powder), you may need to dry the seeds in a low-temperature oven to firm them up before grinding them with a spice grinder or mortar and pestle. Experiment with anardana in homemade jams and fruit leathers—it plays especially well with citrus, warm spices, and stone fruit.

Black Pepper
KAALI MIRCH

Black peppercorns are the dried berries of *Piper nigrum*, a flowering vine native to South India's Malabar Coast. Before the arrival of chilies to India, black pepper and a related fruit called pipli, or long pepper, were the primary sources of heat in Indian food. The chemical compound responsible for black pepper's spiciness is called piperine.

Note that although the name Tellicherry is an anglicization of Thalassery, a city in the South Indian state of Kerala, the "Tellicherry peppercorn" designation denotes a larger size rather than a geographic point of origin. Always buy whole peppercorns and grind as needed.

Cardamom, Black
KAALI ELAICHI/BADI ELAICHI

Black cardamom, also known as Bengal cardamom, comes from *Amomum subulatum*, a member of the ginger family. The dark brown seedpods are dried over an open fire, lending the spice a deep, smoky flavor. Try adding a whole pod to homemade barbecue sauce, bean-based chili, or meat marinades. Black cardamom is rarely used in sweet dishes and should never be used as a substitute for its green cousin (nor vice versa). When used whole to flavor a dish, black cardamom pods are not meant to be eaten.

Cardamom, Green
HARI ELAICHI

Green cardamom pods are the dried seedpods of *Elettaria cardamomum*, another ginger family member native to India. The spice has a sweet, floral quality that works well in both savory and sweet dishes. It should be used sparingly, as it can easily overpower.

To make cardamom powder, extract the seeds by pinching or crushing the pods, then dispose of the husks and grind the seeds. Try a sprinkle of ground green cardamom over granola with yogurt (or vanilla ice cream), or stirred into your morning coffee. We love eating cooked cardamom pods when they are served as part of a dish, but the flavor can be too much for some people. Raw whole pods can also be chewed as a breath freshener.

Chili (Red, Green, and Kashmiri)
MIRCH

Native to the Americas, *Capsicum annuum* arrived in India sometime in the early sixteenth (or very late fifteenth) century, courtesy of Portuguese traders. Over the next couple hundred years, it established itself as a culinary mainstay across the subcontinent, unseating black pepper (and the related long pepper) as the main source of heat in Indian cuisine. Most of the recipes in this book involve whole dried red chilies, dried chili powder, or fresh green chilies.

continues

Although we tend to keep ours intact, seeding whole chilies (fresh or dried) is always an option to reduce heat.

For whole dried chilies, buy bags labeled generically as "whole chilies" or "whole red chilies" at Indian grocers. Ground cayenne works well for the powdered version. If shopping in non-Indian grocery stores, beware of the confusingly monikered "chili powder," a spice mix laced with cumin and other extraneous spices (à la the eponymous bean-and-meat stew).

Fresh green chilies can be found in the vegetable section at Indian grocers, where there are often a couple of kinds available. We suggest buying the long (4- to 6-inch // 10- to 15-cm), slim, green ones, appropriately nicknamed "finger chilies." Jalapeños are a fine substitution. Avoid the shorter (2-inch // 5-cm or so) green chilies available at Indian stores, as those are spicier in our experience.

Finally, a few of our recipes also call for dried Kashmiri chilies, a mild-flavored chili known for its eye-poppingly red color. These are also available at Indian grocers, both whole and ground. We highly recommend seeking out the real thing, but you can substitute paprika (a powder made from sweeter pepper varieties) with a dash of cayenne for ground Kashmiri chili in a pinch.

Cilantro
HARA DHANIYA

Coriandrum sativum, a Mediterranean native and a member of the carrot and fennel family, is the source of both coriander seeds and cilantro leaves. The plant is umbelliferous, meaning the flowers shoot out in little firework-esque arrangements. When harvesting the leaves, there's no need to waste time plucking them off the stems—the stems are just as bright and flavorful as the leafy bits. The herb will wilt and lose flavor when heated, so it's best to add just before serving. Cilantro tastes like soap to some people with unfortunate genetics, so it might be worth checking in with your guests before making a lawn all over the food.

Cinnamon
DAALCHINI

Most of the cinnamon we buy in the United States is actually the inner bark of the cassia plant, *Cinnamomum aromaticum*, a Chinese evergreen species that is different from (but related to) *Cinnamomum verum*, or true cinnamon, native to South India and Sri Lanka. Cassia has a sweeter, spicier flavor, while true cinnamon is more floral and complex. You can distinguish between these two spices when buying them in stick form—cassia bark is made up of a single thick layer, whereas true cinnamon bark is made up of many thin layers and breaks up more easily. Buy whatever you can get your hands on. When used whole, cinnamon sticks are not meant to be eaten.

Clove
LAUNG

Native to the Moluccas, or Spice Islands, of Indonesia, cloves are the dried flower buds of *Syzygium aromaticum*, a tropical evergreen in the same family as guava, eucalyptus, and allspice. The primary aromatic component is called eugenol, and it is also found in nutmeg, cinnamon, basil, and bay leaves. The English name derives from the Latin *clavus*, or "nail," due to the dried bud's resemblance. We love eating cooked cloves when they are served as part of a dish, but some people find them unpleasant and prefer to push them off to the side of the plate. Try adding whole cloves to soups, stews, and braises (or for a pleasantly intense experience, chew a couple raw as a breath freshener!).

Coconut
NAARIYAL

The coconut is the fruit of *Cocos nucifera*, a member of the palm tree family whose geographic origins trace back to the Indian subcontinent and Southeast Asia. The recipes in this book mostly call for the grated, unsweetened stuff. Frozen and fresh are both fine, but avoid desiccated. If you're feeling determined, you can also buy a whole fruit and smash it open yourself.

Coriander Seed
DHANIYA KE BEEJ

The coriander seed's greatest claim to Americana fame might be that its oil was (allegedly) listed as one of the flavorings in the original Coca-Cola recipe (in concert with nutmeg oil, lemon oil, orange oil, cinnamon oil, neroli oil, alcohol, and coca). The small, tan orbs are the dried seeds of *Coriandrum sativum*, the cilantro plant: a member of the cumin and carrot family and a Mediterranean native. Dry-roasting the seeds deepens their grassy, citrusy flavor.

The spice is often paired with cumin in Indian cooking, but it works nicely with sweets too. Try adding whole seeds to any baked good with lemon or orange peel, or sprinkle lightly crushed seeds over vanilla ice cream and hot fudge for a surprisingly citrus-forward crunch.

Cumin Seed
JEERA

If we had to recommend just one spice to begin your Indian culinary adventures, cumin would be our pick. The dried seeds of the Mediterranean native *Cuminum cyminum* (yet another member of the plant family that includes celery, carrot, and cilantro) are a key component of an immense number of Indian dishes. Toasting unlocks a warm, smoky flavor that plays especially well with coriander seed. The ancient Greeks kept a box of cumin powder as part of their table setting, much as we do today with black pepper. Try toasted cumin with creamy pasta dishes, or folded into scrambled eggs with fresh herbs and a bit of chili.

Curry Leaf
KARI PATTA

Murraya koenigii, also known as sweet neem, is a tropical (and subtropical) tree. It grows freely throughout India and is part of the citrus family. Its small, slender leaves are ubiquitous in South Indian cooking, where they add a sharp, tangy, herbal dimension. Their bright flavor pairs nicely with the nuttiness of black mustard seeds.

You can strip the fresh leaves from the stem in one fell swoop by quickly running your pinched fingers up the stalk, starting from the base. Some folks also like to give the individual leaves a quick rub between their fingers before frying to release the natural oils. As with all vegetation, we recommend rinsing curry leaves before use, but make sure to dry them completely with a paper towel before adding them to hot oil to reduce splatter.

Curry leaves are often unlabeled at Indian markets, either in open bins at the back of the store or in clear plastic bags in the corner of a cooler. Each sprig usually contains somewhere between twelve and twenty leaves, and there is a lot of variability in leaf size. We kept our recipe recommendations purposely vague (in small sprigs rather than a specific number of leaves), and you can always increase or decrease the amount depending on how much you like the aroma. For reference, our small sprigs are 5 to 6 inches (12 to 15 cm) in length, with leaves no longer than 1 inch (2.5 cm).

We always eat the cooked leaves, but you should feel free to push them to the side of your plate if the flavor is too intense. Try them in savory stir-fries (tempered in a bit of oil or ghee first) or pulverize them with some water before adding the puree to desserts or baked goods with a citrus component.

Fennel Seed
SAUNF

Fennel seeds are one of the last things you see on your way out of an Indian restaurant, offered up in a bowl as a postprandial breath freshener and usually spiked with brightly colored candied bits and sugar crystals. The sweet, licorice-flavored seeds come from the *Foeniculum vulgare* plant, indigenous to the Mediterranean and yet another umbelliferous member of the cumin, carrot, and caraway family. Add the seeds to your favorite homemade granola recipe, or use them raw as a crunchy topping for ice cream or peanut butter toast.

Garlic
LAHASUN

A bulbous plant that originated in Central Asia, *Allium sativum* is a member of the same genus as onions, chives, and leeks. Devout Hindus regard it with suspicion due to its supposed aphrodisiac properties. Its English name derives from *gārlēac*, Old English for "spear-leek," due to the tapered shape of its cloves. Only buy fresh heads, which should be dense and unyielding.

Ginger
ADARAK

Zingiber officinale is a flowering herbaceous perennial in the same family as turmeric, galangal, and cardamom and is likely native to South and Southeast Asia. The bit we eat is the rhizome, or subterranean plant stem. The skin can easily be scraped off with a knife or spoon edge. At the store, look for pieces with shiny, taut skin. Ginger is refreshingly spicy and sharp, and its carminative qualities make it an important ingredient in many legume-based dishes. If you ever need a pick-me-up on a caffeine-free morning, chewing a few slices of raw ginger will do the trick (be sure to keep a chaser of cut fruit close by).

Heeng (Hing)
ASAFOETIDA

Like all organized religions, Hinduism has many extraordinarily weird bits. One of them is an apparent fear of thirsty clergymen and horny widows. In some Hindu communities, Brahmins (individuals who belong to the priestly class of the deplorable and antiquated caste system) and surviving wives alike are supposed to avoid any foods that are thought to induce lust. Meat is therefore taboo, as are alliums like garlic and onion.

Fortunately, there is a chaste workaround for the forsaken alliums in the form of heeng, a resin derived from the dried sap of a fennel-like plant called *Ferula asafoetida*, native to Western and Central Asia. Although it's extremely pungent when raw, tempering a small amount in oil unlocks a beautiful allium-like aroma. It's an especially useful ingredient when cooking for folks who are digestively sensitive to garlic and onion (low-FODMAP dieters, etc.).

You can purchase heeng in chunks or as a powder; if using the former, grind into a powder just before using. The nicknames it has inspired—"devil's dung" and "food of the gods" among them—are a testament to its potency.

Indian Bay Leaf
TEJ PATTA

The Indian bay leaf comes from a member of the laurel family called *Cinnamomum tamala*. Western bay leaves, on the other hand, come from a different but related plant called *Laurus nobilis* (also laurel leaf or bay laurel), which is native to the Mediterranean and was used to make the laurel wreaths that crowned the winningest naked athletes in ancient Greece. The easiest way to distinguish the two is that the (often larger) Indian leaf has three parallel stem-to-tip veins, whereas *Laurus nobilis* has just one central vein. The Indian version should be available at any Indian grocery. Bay leaves should be bought dried rather than fresh.

Kaala Namak
BLACK SALT

Also known as Himalayan black salt, this mineral salt is mined from volcanic rock and kiln-fired. It contains trace amounts of sulfur compounds, which lend it a distinctive, eggy quality. It works beautifully with fresh fruit (page 235), buttery popcorn, and lemonade (page 249).

Kalonji
NIGELLA

Confusingly referred to as black caraway, black onion seed, black cumin, Roman coriander, fennel flower, and nutmeg flower, *Nigella sativa* is a member of the buttercup family and thereby unrelated to any of its purported appellative cousins. The plant, native to Eastern Europe and Western Asia, produces seeds with an earthy, oniony flavor and a peppery bite. The spice has a close association with Bengali cooking, but is also used for pickling across the subcontinent. Outside of Indian fare, toast the seeds before adding them to grilled cheese sandwiches—kalonji are a featured ingredient in tel banir, a delightful Armenian string cheese—or grind the toasted seeds to a powder for a meat marinade addition (credit to Anita Jaisinghani's *Masala*).

Kewra Water
KEVADA JAL

A South and Southeast Asian analog of rose water, kewra water is a flavoring derived from the male flowers of the fragrant screwpine, *Pandanus odorifer*. The plant is native to Asia and Oceania. (*Pandanus amaryllifolius*, whose fragrant leaves are the source of the pandan flavor in Southeast Asian cooking and confectionery, is a close relative.)

Kewra is one of the primary flavorings in Rooh Afza, a beloved ruby syrup used to flavor drinks and sweets across the subcontinent. The flavor of kewra water itself is somewhere at the intersection of rose, lychee, and cedar. As with rose water and other floral hydrosols, it should be used sparingly. Try adding a few drops to coconut-, rice-, or dairy-based desserts.

Mace
JAVITRI

Myristica fragrans is a tropical evergreen tree hailing from the Moluccas, or Spice Islands, of Indonesia. Its fruit gives us two spices: nutmeg from the seed, and mace from the fleshy aril, or seed covering. Fresh mace is a dazzling vermilion (and worth an image search), but once flattened and dried, it dulls to a muddy orange. Mace and nutmeg have similar flavor profiles, but mace is both sharper and more expensive. Buy it in whole pieces (blades) rather than ground. When used whole, mace blades are not meant to be eaten. For experimentation ideas, see Nutmeg (page 276).

Mango
AAM

Native to South Asia, *Mangifera indica* is the national fruit of both India and Pakistan and the national tree of Bangladesh. There are roughly fifteen hundred varieties grown in India, but only a handful make their way to the United States due to the short growing season, importation difficulties, and the fruit's propensity to bruise. If you see them available, the Alphonso, Kesar, and Chaunsa varieties are all worth grabbing fresh. A few recipes in this book also call for canned, sweetened mango pulp—if you have any left over, we highly recommend trying it over vanilla ice cream.

Mango skin contains a small amount of urushiol, the offending compound in poison ivy, which is in the same plant family. It's not a problem for most people, but check with guests about mango sensitivities just in case.

Methi
FENUGREEK SEEDS AND LEAVES

The *Trigonella foenum-graecum* plant, a member of the bean and legume family, produces both fragrant, angular seeds and leafy, spinach-like greens. The leaves have a briny, bitter flavor reminiscent of radicchio or endive, while the nutty seeds have a much more pronounced bitterness. Both leaf and seed also contain an aromatic compound called sotolone, one of the primary flavorings in artificial maple syrup and the chief culprit in causing people to smell like a faintly sweet curry days after eating Indian food.

The tan seeds (which can also be sprouted) turn intensely bitter if cooked too long, so roast or fry briefly, only until they turn golden brown. The leaves may be purchased fresh, frozen, or dried. The dried version is sometimes labeled as Kasuri methi, which historically would have indicated that the leaves were an export of Kasur, a city in the Pakistani province of Punjab famed for its fenugreek. As with the New York of strip steaks, however, the Kasuri designation no longer specifies a geographic point of origin.

Try adding a small amount of fenugreek leaves to tomato-based sauces, or experiment with using toasted, ground seeds to add a subtle layer of bitterness to bean-based dishes. (If you're into spiced butters, Ethiopian niter kibbeh is a clarified butter that often incorporates fenugreek seeds.) Folks with peanut or chickpea allergies sometimes react to fenugreek, so check in with guests before serving.

Mustard Seeds and Powder
RAI, SARSON

When heated in oil until they pop, the black seeds of *Brassica nigra* and the brown seeds of *Brassica juncea* trade their sharpness for a round, earthy nuttiness. Staples of South Indian cooking, they make for a crunchy, toasty complement to the bright, citrusy flavor of curry leaves. Tempered mustard seeds (ideally with a squeeze of lemon) are also an excellent garnish for pureed vegetable soups.

Yellow mustard powder comes from *Sinapis alba*, a related (and less potent) member of the mustard and cabbage family. The three plants are native to Europe and Asia. For more on mustard oil, a potentially anxiety-inducing ingredient, see page 171.

Nutmeg
JAAYAPHAL

Nutmeg is the seed kernel of *Myristica fragrans*, a tropical evergreen tree from Indonesia. The tree bears an edible, apricot-like fruit that splits in two once mature, revealing a crimson seed covering (which is removed, dried, and flattened to produce mace) around a shiny brown seed. The seed is dried in the sun for several weeks until the seed kernel shrinks and separates from the hard seed coat, at which point the shell is broken and the nutmeg is harvested. Like mace, nutmeg has a warm, sweet, nutty flavor, and like mace, nutmeg is a narcotic when consumed in large quantities. Buy whole and grate as needed. We love it grated over peanut butter toast, mixed into whipped cream and citrus-flavored desserts, and as a subtle addition to creamy pasta dishes.

Pomegranate
ANAAR

Pomegranates are the vaguely six-sided fruits of *Punica granatum*, a fruiting bush or small tree native to West Asia but cultivated throughout the Mediterranean, Arabian Peninsula, and South Asia since antiquity.

Our favorite way to isolate the juicy, ruby arils is to quarter the whole fruit and then fill a large bowl halfway with water. Submerge one quarter and carefully separate the arils from the papery pith and leathery skin underwater. Applying a little pressure to invert the hard outer skin often helps release the arils. Discard the spongy white bits as you work. The pith and skin will float, the arils will sink, and the water will mostly protect you from the inevitable juice spurts (but it's still worth wearing an apron for insurance). Repeat with the remaining quarters. Drain the water, discard the skin and pith, and enjoy the gem-like arils.

Poppy Seeds
KHASKHAS

The seeds of the opium poppy *Papaver somniferum*, a plant native to the Mediterranean but naturalized across Europe and Asia in ancient times, can be dark blue, gray, or creamy white. White seeds are the traditional choice for Indian cooks. The seeds are often roasted and then ground to make a paste, which can be used to thicken sauces or to add a nutty flavor. Outside of Indian cooking, poppy seeds are often paired with lemon in both savory and sweet contexts (salad dressings, scones, etc.).

Take note: Although it is the unripe seedpods (rather than the seeds themselves) that are used to make opium, the seeds do contain trace amounts of opiates—enough to be detected on a drug test.

Rose Water
GULAAB JAL

Rose water is a by-product of the steam distillation of rose petals (genus *Rosa*), although a homemade version can be made by steeping rose petals in water. When shopping, look for bottles with just a single ingredient (distilled rose water)—try to avoid anything with extraneous flavorings or preservatives.

In moderation, rose water introduces a subtle, floral complexity, but too much can make a dish taste like soap. Use sparingly, and err on the side of restraint when introducing it to a recipe, as brands can vary in strength. We love it in rhubarb and stone fruit desserts, and as a subtle addition to whipped cream.

Saffron
KESAR

Crocus sativus, which originated in western Asia but has been cultivated across Europe and Asia since ancient times, is a member of the iris family. Aromatic saffron threads are the dried, red stigmas of its flowers. The threads are employed both for their honeyed, earthy flavor and for the rich, golden color they lend to dishes.

It takes around 75,000 blossoms (the stigmas of which must be carefully removed by hand) to produce a single pound (455 g) of saffron, which accounts for the high price point. Buy whole threads, never ground, as the powdered stuff is often adulterated.

To bloom saffron, first grind several threads to a powder using a small mortar and pestle (or by crushing them with your fingers, but beware of staining). Warm about ¼ cup (60 ml) water to 175°F (80°C) and pour it over the powder. Allow it to steep for a few minutes to produce a fragrant saffron water that you can employ in sweet and savory dishes alike. (Some folks suggest sprinkling the powdered saffron over ice cubes for a slower "cold bloom," but we find the warm water method to be much more potent.) You can also add crushed saffron threads directly to dishes with a high moisture content like stews or risottos.

To make saffron sugar, grind a few saffron threads with a pinch of sugar using a small mortar and pestle. The pale pink powder will turn brilliant orange, crimson, and gold when sprinkled over yogurt or vanilla ice cream, and adds a beautiful floral note to boot. (Wait a minute or two after adding the saffron sugar for the full color change to take effect.)

Sesame Seed
TIL KE BEEJ

Sesamum indicum is one of the world's oldest oilseed crops and has been cultivated widely since antiquity, although its precise origin is still debated. Toasting the raw seeds unlocks their sweet, nutty flavor, which pairs well with savory and sweet dishes alike—try the toasted seeds in savory rice dishes, or add them to chocolate-based desserts. For the purposes of this book, the white, hulled seeds are ideal, but the slightly more assertive black seeds are worth having around the pantry as well.

Tamarind
IMLI

Although *Tamarindus indica* is native to tropical Africa, Indians have been using it for so long that the Arabs deemed it the "date of India," *tamr hindi*. The leguminous tree is a member of the bean family, and the pulp surrounding its seeds is used across the globe as a souring agent. Tamarind is a key ingredient in Worcestershire sauce, which supposedly traces its lineage back to colonial-era Bengal.

You can find tamarind in stores as a ready-made paste, as a concentrate, and in compressed blocks. We usually buy it as a paste for simplicity and consistency, and Tamicon is our preferred brand. If using the blocks, you'll need to soak it in boiling water (the water-to-paste volume ratio should be 2:1) for 15 to 20 minutes before forcing the pulp through a sieve to remove the fibrous bits. You should be left with a paste with the consistency of applesauce.

Tamarind's sweet-sour flavor is a pleasure to play with in the kitchen. Try tamarind alongside ginger in meat marinades, in concert with citrus juice in rum cocktails, or as a sour addition to fruit leather.

Turmeric
HALDI

Curcuma longa might sport the greatest breadth of use of all Indian spices, as it is employed as a food coloring, a seasoning, a cosmetic, a dye plant, and a medicine. The plant is native to South Asia. As with its cousins ginger and galangal, the bit we use is the rhizome, or subterranean plant stem. The turmeric rhizome is most often found boiled, dried, and then ground into a powder, but can also be used fresh.

Turmeric has a warming, slightly bitter, earthy flavor. Try adding it to rice dishes, baked goods, and stews. As with ginger, its carminative properties make it an important component of lentil and bean dishes. The myriad health benefits of turmeric are usually pinned on the antioxidant curcumin, the effects of which are thought to be enhanced when consumed alongside either fat or piperine, the spicy compound in black pepper.

SAMPLE MENUS

Loochi Brunch
LOOCHI (page 204)

ALOO TAMATAR (page 87)

CHANNA MASALA (page 74)

SOOJI HALWA (page 258)

Punjabi Paratha Lunch
GOBHI PARATHA (page 194)
or **ALOO PARATHA** (page 197)

HOMEMADE YOGURT (page 40)

ADARAK NIMBU ACHAAR (page 245)
or **STORE-BOUGHT PICKLE** (page 29)

From Bengal with Love
MACHHER JHOL (page 169)
or **SHORSHE CHINGRI** (page 171)

KALONJI BROCCOLI (page 95)

JEERA PULAO (page 177)

MISHTI DOI (page 259)

Aroop's Favorite Snack
LEMON RICE (page 179)

PAALAK RAITA (page 240)

MASALA CHAI (page 252)

Summertime Street Food
PAAPDI CHAAT (page 213)

SPICED WATERMELON (page 233)
or **BHUTTA CHAAT** (page 139)

ALOO TIKKI (page 217) with
DHANIA PUDINA CHUTNEY (page 242)
and **IMLI CHUTNEY** (page 243)

GHOOGNI (page 69)

NIMBU PANI (page 249)

Moti Mahal Special
MURGH MAKHANI (page 151)

DAAL MAKHANI (page 63)

GOBHI ALOO (page 91)

GHEE BHAAT (page 44)
or **ROTI** (page 189)

AAM KULFI (page 265)
or **PISTA KESAR KULFI** (page 266)
or **ROSE CARDAMOM KULFI** (page 266)

Key
This dish can be made up to a day in advance. Some of the prep for **this dish** can be done in advance (see relevant headnote for further instruction).

RESOURCES

Retailers

Burlap & Barrel (www.burlapandbarrel.com)

Diaspora Co. (www.diasporaco.com)

Kalyustan's (www.foodsofnations.com)

Penzeys Spices (www.penzeys.com)

Pure Indian Foods (www.pureindianfoods.com)

The Reluctant Trading Experiment (www.reluctanttrading.com)

Spicewalla (www.spicewallabrand.com)

For achaar (Indian pickle), we buy the *Achar Pachranga* (Mixed Pickle) flavor by Pachranga Foods by the can. Other companies like Deep and Priya make great products too—we encourage you to buy a few and experiment.

For yogurt starter cultures, we recommend the *Traditional Flavor Yogurt Culture* from the website Cultures for Health (www.culturesforhealth.com).

Further Reading: Books We Lean On or Otherwise Love

Botany in a Day by Thomas J. Elpel (HOPS Press, 2013)

The Calcutta Cookbook by Minakshie Das Gupta, Bunny Gupta, and Jaya Chaliha (Penguin, 1995)

City of Djinns by William Dalrymple (Penguin, 1993)

Curry by Lizzie Collingham (Oxford University Press, 2006)

Dishoom by Shamil Thakrar, Kavi Thakrar, and Naved Nasir (Bloomsbury, 2019)

The Drunken Botanist by Amy Stewart (Algonquin, 2013)

Eating India by Chitrita Banerji (Bloomsbury, 2008)

Feasts and Fasts by Colleen Taylor Sen (Reaktion, 2015)

Flavours of Delhi by Charmaine O'Brien (Penguin, 2003)

The Food Lab by J. Kenji López-Alt (Norton, 2015)

A Historical Dictionary of Indian Food by K. T. Achaya (Oxford University Press, 1998)

My Bombay Kitchen by Niloufer Ichaporia King (University of California Press, 2007)

On Food and Cooking by Harold McGee (Scribner's, 1984)

Salt Fat Acid Heat by Samin Nosrat (Simon & Schuster, 2017)

A comprehensive list of sources and citations can be found at the *Heartland Masala* page on our publisher's website (see "Resources").

INDEX

Page numbers in *italics* refer to photographs

A

Aam Kulfi, *126*, 265
Aam Lassi, *120*, 250
Aam Panna, *120*, 254
   Aam Panna Punch, *120*, 257
Adarak Nimbu Achaar, *122*, 245
alcohol, 256
almonds
   Salted Caramel Almond Flan, *126*, 261–62
   Thandai, *120*, 255
   Thandai Old Fashioned, *120*, 257
Aloo Baingan, *128*, 129
Aloo Paratha, *122*, 197–99
Aloo Tamatar, *87*, 98
Aloo Tikki, *100*, 217–19
amchoor, 271
anardana
   about, 271
   Channa Masala, 74–75, *99*
arhar
   about, 61
   Arhar Daal with Green Mango, 67–68, *105*
asafoetida, 274

B

Baghare Baingan, *108*, 132–33
Baingan Bharta, *96*, 113
beans, 61. *See also* daals; *individual varieties*
beef, 158
Beguni, *114*, 222
Bengali Khichudi, *114*, 180–81
besan
   about, 81
   Beguni, *114*, 222
   Gobhi Pakora, *103*, 223–24
   Kadhi, 79–81, *102*
Bharva Baingan, *97*, 130
Bharva Bhindi, 88–89, *102*
Bhuna Gosht, *125*, 162–63

bhunaoing, 162
Bhutta Chaat, *104*, 139
biryanis
   about, 183
   Kacchi Hyderabadi Biryani, *125*, 186–87
   Mushroom Dum Biryani, *125*, 184–85
boondi
   about, 241
   Boondi Raita, *116*, 241
bourbon
   Thandai Old Fashioned, *120*, 257
bread
   Aloo Paratha, *122*, 197–99
   Aloo Tikki, *100*, 217–19
   Gobhi Paratha, *122*, 194–96
   Lachhedaar Paratha, *128*, 200–2
   Loochi, *98*, 204–5
   Paratha, *113*, 192–93
   Roti, *106*, 189–91
   Spiced Liver Toast, *115*, 232
Brittle, Sesame Jaggery, *126*, 267
broccoli
   cutting, 90
   Kalonji Broccoli, 95, *110*
   Murgh Hariyali, *102*, 146–47
   Saag Paneer, *116*, 136–37
Brussels Sprouts, Masala, 93, *105*
butter. *See* Ghee

C

cardamom
   black, 271
   green, 271
cashews
   Lemon Rice, *109*, 179
   Murgh Rezala, *113*, 148–50
cauliflower
   Bengali Khichudi, *114*, 180–81
   cutting, 90
   Gobhi Aloo, 91, *107*
   Gobhi Pakora, *103*, 223–24
   Gobhi Paratha, *122*, 194–96
Chaat Masala, 53

Chai, Masala, *99*, 252–53
channa. *See* chickpeas
cheese
   Mattar Paneer, *106*, 134–35
   Paneer, 46–47, *107*
   Saag Paneer, *116*, 136–37
chicken
   Chicken Tikka, 231
   Kaathi Roll, *118*, 230–31
   Kacchi Hyderabadi Biryani, *125*, 186–87
   Murgh Do Pyaaza, *105*, 144–45
   Murgh Hariyali, *102*, 146–47
   Murgh Kaali Mirch, *119*, 142–43
   Murgh Makhani, *128*, 151–53
   Murgh Rezala, *113*, 148–50
   Spiced Liver Toast, *115*, 232
chickpeas. *See also* besan; boondi
   Channa Masala, 74–75, *99*
   Cooked and Seasoned Chickpeas, 45
   Ghoogni, 69, *100*
   Lauki Channa Daal, 72–73, *113*
   Narkol Cholar Daal, 70–71, *101*
   Paapdi Chaat, *123*, 213–14
   Sukha Kaala Channa, 76–77, *116*
   Sundal, 78, *109*
   varieties of, 45, 76
chilies
   about, 271–72
   heat content of, 20–21
Chire Bhaja, *100*, 212
chutneys
   Dhania Pudina Chutney, *102*, 242
   Imli Chutney, *103*, 243
   Tamatar Khajoor Chutney, *114*, 244
cilantro
   about, 272
   Dhania Pudina Chutney, *102*, 242
   Jhaal Mudhi, *100*, 209
   Kacchi Hyderabadi Biryani, *125*, 186–87
   Murgh Hariyali, *102*, 146–47
   Murgh Makhani, *128*, 151–53
cinnamon, 272

cloves, 272
coconut
   about, 272
   Baghare Baingan, *108*, 132–33
      frozen, 78
      Goan Machhli, *124*, 168
      Narkol Cholar Daal, *101*, 70–71
      Shorshe Chingri, *110*, 171–73
      Sundal, 78, *109*
cooking times, 33
coriander, 272–73
corn
   Bhutta Chaat, *104*, 139
courses, 57
cow protection movement, 158
cucumbers
   about, 56
   Jhaal Mudhi, *100*, 209
   Kachumbar, 56, *119*
   Kheera Tamatar Raita, *113*, 239
cumin, 273
curries
   about, 42, 50
   Bhuna Gosht, *125*, 162–63
   Ghoogni, 69, *100*
   Goan Machhli, *124*, 168
   Kadhi, 79–81, *102*
   Machher Jhol, *101*, 169–70
   Murgh Do Pyaaza, *105*, 144–45
   Murgh Hariyali, *102*, 146–47
   Murgh Kaali Mirch, *119*, 142–43
   Murgh Rezala, *113*, 148–50
   Mutton Aloo Korma, *97*, 159–61
   Rajma, 82–83
   Rogan Josh, *111*, 164–65
   Shorshe Chingri, *110*, 171–73
   Vindaloo, *124*, 166–67
curry leaves, 273
curry powder, 42

D

daals
   about, 61
   adding water to, 34
   Arhar Daal with Green Mango, 67–68, *105*
   Bengali Khichudi, *114*, 180–81
   cooking, 66
   Daal Makhani, 63–64, *128*
   Daal Paalak, 59, *119*
   Lauki Channa Daal, 72–73, *113*
   Narkol Cholar Daal, 70–71, *101*
   Sukhi Moong Daal, 62, *107*
   Tomato, Red Lentil, and Ginger Soup, 58, *123*
dates
   Imli Chutney, 243, *103*
   Tamatar Khajoor Chutney, *114*, 244
deep-frying, 210–11, 213
desserts. *See* sweets
Dhania Pudina Chutney, *103*, 242
Dimer Debhil, *109*, 215–16
Doodh Seviyan, *126*, 260
drinks
   Aam Lassi, *120*, 250
   Aam Panna, *120*, 254
   Aam Panna Punch, *121*, 257
   Masala Chai, *98*, 252–53
   Nimbu Pani, *120*, 249
   Thandai, *121*, 255
   Thandai Old Fashioned, *121*, 257

E

eggplant
   Aloo Baingan, *128*, 129
   Baghare Baingan, *108*, 132–33
   Baingan Bharta, *96*, 113
   Beguni, *114*, 222
   Bharva Baingan, *97*, 130
eggs
   Dimer Debhil, *109*, 215–16
   Kaathi Roll, *118*, 230–31
equipment, 24

F

fennel seeds, 273
fenugreek, 275
fish
   Goan Machhli, *124*, 168
   Machher Jhol, *101*, 169–70

Flan, Salted Caramel Almond, *126*, 261–62
fox nuts. *See* phool makhana
fruit. *See also* individual fruits
   Fruit Chaat, *115*, 235
   Fruit Cream, *126*, 263

G

Garam Masala, 53
garbanzo beans. *See* chickpeas
garlic
   about, 273
   Murgh Kaali Mirch, *119*, 142–43
   Vindaloo, *124*, 166–67
Ghee, 38–39
   amount of, 20
   Ghee Bhaat, 44, *101*
   substituting for, 28
Ghoogni, 69, *100*
ginger
   about, 274
   Adarak Nimbu Achaar, *122*, 245
   Channa Masala, 74–75, *98*
   Gobhi Aloo, 91, *107*
   Jeera Mattar, *97*, 138
   Masala Chai, *98*, 252–53
   Saag Paneer, *116*, 136–37
Goan Machhli, *124*, 168
goat
   about, 159
   Mutton Aloo Korma, *97*, 159–60
Gobhi Aloo, 91, *107*
Gobhi Pakora, *103*, 223–24
Gobhi Paratha, *122*, 194–96

H

heeng (hing), 274
Hot Mix
   about, 209
   Jhaal Mudhi, *100*, 209
Hung Curd, 41

I

Imli Chutney, *103*, 243
Indian bay leaves, 274
Indian cooking
    authenticity and, 17
    diversity of, 17
    history of, 17
    Mexican cooking and, 188
    tips for, 19, 32–35

J

jaggery, 133
Jeera Mattar, *97*, 138
Jeera Pulao, *105*, 177
Jhaal Mudhi, *100*, 209

K

kaala namak (black salt), 249, 274
Kaathi Roll, *118*, 230–31
Kacchi Hyderabadi Biryani, *125*, 186–87
Kachumbar, 56, *119*
Kadhi, 79–81, *102*
kalonji
    about, 274
    Kalonji Broccoli, 95, *110*
kedgeree, 182
Keema Mattar, *113*, 156–57
kewra water, 275
Kheera Tamatar Raita, *113*, 239
khichudi
    about, 180
    Bengali Khichudi, *114*, 180–81
kidney beans
    about, 82
    Daal Makhani, 63–64, *128*
    Rajma, 82–83, *97*
kormas
    about, 159
    Mutton Aloo Korma, *97*, 159–61
kulfis
    about, 264
    Aam Kulfi, *126*, 265
    Pista Kesar Kulfi, *126*, 266
    variations, 266
Kundan Lal Jaggi and Gujral, 154–55

L

Lachhedaar Paratha, *128*, 200–2
lamb
    Bhuna Gosht, *125*, 162–63
    Rogan Josh, *111*, 164–65
lassi
    about, 250
    Aam Lassi, *120*, 250
lauki
    about, 72
    Lauki Channa Daal, 72–73, *113*
lemons
    about, 248
    Adarak Nimbu Achaar, *122*, 245
    Lemon Rice, *109*, 179
    Nimbu Pani, *120*, 249
lentils
    about, 61
    Tomato, Red Lentil, and Ginger Soup, 58, *123*
Liver Toast, Spiced, *115*, 232
Loochi, *98*, 204–5

M

mace, 275
Machher Jhol, *101*, 169–70
mangoes
    about, 275
    Aam Kulfi, *126*, 265
    Aam Lassi, *120*, 250
    Aam Panna, *120*, 254
    Aam Panna Punch, *120*, 257
    amchoor, 271
    Arhar Daal with Green Mango, 67–68, *105*
marinades, 34
Masala Brussels Sprouts, 93, *105*
Masala Chai, *98*, 252–53
masalas
    about, 17, 52
    Chaat Masala, 53
    Garam Masala, 53
masoor
    about, 61
    Tomato, Red Lentil, and Ginger Soup, 58, *123*
Mattar Paneer, *107*, 134–35
measurements, 19, 22

menus, sample, 278
methi, 275
milk, 28. See also cheese; yogurt
mint
    Aam Panna Punch, *120*, 257
    Dhania Pudina Chutney, *103*, 242
    Kacchi Hyderabadi Biryani, *125*, 186–87
mise en place, 32
Mishti Doi, *127*, 259
moong
    about, 61
    Bengali Khichudi, *114*, 180–81
    Daal Paalak, 59, *119*
    Sukhi Moong Daal, 62, *107*
Moongphali Aloo Chaat, *123*, 208
Murgh Do Pyaaza, *105*, 144–45
Murgh Hariyali, *102*, 146–47
Murgh Kaali Mirch, *119*, 142–43
Murgh Makhani, *128*, 151–53
Murgh Rezala, *113*, 148–50
Mushroom Dum Biryani, *125*, 184–85
mustard greens
    Saag Paneer, *116*, 136–37
mustard oil, 16, 171
mustard seeds and powder, 275–76
Mutton Aloo Korma, *97*, 159–61

N

Narkol Cholar Daal, 70–71, *101*
nigella. See kalonji
Nimbu Pani, *120*, 249
nonstick pans, 16, 92
noodles
    Doodh Seviyan, *127*, 260
nutmeg, 276

O

oils
    amount of, 20
    reading, 33
    storing, 30
    types of, 16, 30, 171

okra
  Bharva Bhindi, 88–89, *102*
  Goan Machhli, *124*, 168
  shopping for, 88
onions
  about, 25, 144
  cooking, 32–33
  Kacchi Hyderabadi Biryani, *125*, 186–87
  Pyaaz Pulao, *119*, 178

P

Paalak Raita, *125*, 240
Paapdi Chaat, *123*, 213–14
pakoras
  about, 223
  Gobhi Pakora, *103*, 223–24
  Kadhi, 79–81, *102*
Paneer, 46–47, *107*
  Mattar Paneer, *107*, 134–35
  Saag Paneer, *116*, 136–37
Paratha, *113*, 192–93
  Aloo Paratha, *122*, 197–99
  Gobhi Paratha, *122*, 194–96
  Kaathi Roll, *118*, 230–31
  Lachhedaar Paratha, *128*, 200–2
peanuts
  Baghare Baingan, *108*, 132–33
  Jhaal Mudhi, *100*, 209
  Lemon Rice, *109*, 179
  Moongphali Aloo Chaat, *123*, 208
  Paalak Raita, *125*, 240
  Sabudana Khichudi *115*, 229
  Sabudana Vada, *115*, 220–21
  Samosa, *117*, 225–28
peas
  Aloo Tikki, *100*, 217–19
  Bengali Khichudi, *114*, 180–81
  Chire Bhaja, *100*, 212
  Jeera Mattar, *97*, 138
  Jhaal Mudhi, *100*, 209
  Keema Mattar, *113*, 156–57
  Mattar Paneer, *107*, 134–35
  Sabudana Khichudi, *115*, 229
  Samosa, *117*, 225–28
pecans
  Sesame Jaggery Brittle, *126*, 267

peppercorns, black, 271
phool makhana
  about, 150
  Murgh Rezala, *113*, 148–50
pickles
  Adarak Nimbu Achaar, *122*, 245
pistachios
  Pista Kesar Kulfi, *127*, 266
pomegranates
  about, 276
  anardana, 271
  Channa Masala, 74–75, *98*
  Kachumbar, 56, *119*
poppy seeds, 148, 276
pork
  Vindaloo, *124*, 166–67
potatoes
  about, 25
  Aloo Baingan, *128*, 129
  Aloo Paratha, *122*, 197–99
  Aloo Tamatar, 87, *98*
  Aloo Tikki, *100*, 217–19
  Boiled and Seasoned Potatoes, 48
  cooking, 49, 92
  Dimer Debhil, *109*, 215–16
  Gobhi Aloo, 91, *107*
  Masala Brussels Sprouts, 93, *105*
  Moongphali Aloo Chaat, *123*, 208
  Murgh Hariyali, *102*, 146–47
  Murgh Kaali Mirch, *119*, 142–43
  Mutton Aloo Korma, *97*, 159–61
  Paapdi Chaat, *123*, 213–14
  Rajma, 82–83, *97*
  Sabudana Khichudi, *115*, 229
  Sabudana Vada, *115*, 220–21
  Samosa, *117*, 225–28
  Shorshe Chingri, *110*, 171–73
  varieties of, 49
pressure cooking, 27
pulaos
  about, 176
  Jeera Pulao, *105*, 177
  Pyaaz Pulao, *119*, 178
pumpkin seeds
  Sesame Jaggery Brittle, *126*, 267
Pyaaz Pulao, *119*, 178

R

raisins
  Imli Chutney, *102*, 243
  Tamatar Khajoor Chutney, *114*, 244
raitas
  about, 238
  Boondi Raita, *116*, 241
  Kheera Tamatar Raita, *113*, 239
  Paalak Raita, *125*, 240
Rajma, 82–83, *97*
rice
  basmati, 44
  Bengali Khichudi, *114*, 180–81
  Chire Bhaja, *100*, 212
  Ghee Bhaat, 44, *101*, 110
  Jeera Pulao, *105*, 177
  Jhaal Mudhi, *100*, 209
  Kacchi Hyderabadi Biryani, *125*, 186–87
  Lemon Rice, *109*, 179
  Mushroom Dum Biryani, *125*, 184–85
  Pyaaz Pulao, *119*, 178
  rinsing, 33
  tips for cooking, 44
Rogan Josh, *111*, 164–65
rose water, 276
Roti, *107*, 189–91
rum
  Aam Panna Punch, *120*, 257
rye whiskey
  Thandai Old Fashioned, *121*, 257

S

Saag Paneer, *116*, 136–37
sabudana
  about, 221, 229
  Sabudana Khichudi, *115*, 229
  Sabudana Vada, *115*, 220–21
saffron, 276–77
salads
  about, 56
  Kachumbar, 56, *119*
salt, 20. *See also* kaala namak (black salt)
Samosa, *117*, 225–28
serving sizes, 22

sesame seeds
    about, 277
    Baghare Baingan, *108*, 132–33
    Sesame Jaggery Brittle, *126*, 267
shrimp
    Shorshe Chingri, *110*, 171–73
sooji
    about, 258
    Sooji Halwa, *98*, 258
Soup, Tomato, Red Lentil, and Ginger, 58, *123*
spices. *See also* masalas; *individual spices*
    dry-roasted and ground, 43
    guide to, 270–77
    shopping for, 28, 29
    storing, 28, 30
    tempering (tadka), 31
spinach
    Daal Paalak, 59, *119*
    Murgh Hariyali, *102*, 146–47
    Paalak Raita, *125*, 240
    Saag Paneer, *116*, 136–37
sugar, 133, 248
Sukha Kaala Channa, 76–77, *116*
Sukhi Moong Daal, 62, *106*
Sundal, 78, *109*
sunflower seeds
    Sesame Jaggery Brittle, *126*, 267
sweets
    Aam Kulfi, *126*, 265
    Doodh Seviyan, *126*, 260
    Fruit Cream, *126*, 263
    Mishti Doi, *127*, 259
    Salted Caramel Almond Flan, *126*, 261–62
    Sesame Jaggery Brittle, *126*, 267
    Sooji Halwa, *98*, 258

T

tadka, 31
tamarind
    about, 277
    Baghare Baingan, *108*, 132–33
    Imli Chutney, *103*, 243
Tamatar Khajoor Chutney, *114*, 244
tandoor, 151, 155
tapioca. *See* sabudana

tea
    Masala Chai, *98*, 252–53
Thandai, *121*, 255
    Thandai Old Fashioned, *121*, 257
tomatoes
    Aloo Baingan, *128*, 129
    Aloo Tamatar, 87, *98*
    Baingan Bharta, 96, *113*
    Bhuna Gosht, *125*, 162–63
    Daal Makhani, 63–64, *128*
    Goan Machhli, *124*, 168
    Kachumbar, 56, *119*
    Keema Mattar, *112*, 156–57
    Kheera Tamatar Raita, *112*, 239
    Machher Jhol, *101*, 169–70
    Mattar Paneer, *106*, 134–35
    Murgh Do Pyaaza, *105*, 144–45
    Murgh Makhani, *128*, 151–53
    Mushroom Dum Biryani, *125*, 184–85
    Mutton Aloo Korma, *97*, 159–61
    Rajma, 82–83, *97*
    Saag Paneer, *116*, 136–37
    Sukhi Moong Daal, 62, *106*
    Tamatar Khajoor Chutney, *114*, 244
    Tomato Puree, 83
    Tomato, Red Lentil, and Ginger Soup, 58, *123*
tortillas
    Kaathi Roll, *118*, 230–31
    Paapdi Chaat, *123*, 213–14
turkey
    about, 156
    Keema Mattar, *113*, 156–57
turmeric
    about, 277
    Adarak Nimbu Achaar, *123*, 245

U

urad
    about, 61
    Daal Makhani, 63–64, *128*

V

vegetables. *See also individual vegetables*
    cooking, 94
    prepping, 25
Vindaloo, *124*, 166–67

W

Watermelon, Spiced, *104*, 233

Y

yogurt. *See also* raitas
    about, 28
    Aam Lassi, *120*, 250
    Homemade Yogurt, 40, *123*
    Hung Curd, 41
    Mishti Doi, *127*, 259

ACKNOWLEDGMENTS

Jyoti and Auyon This book would not have been possible without our marvelous team: Amy Treadwell, Angela Engel, Rachel Lopez Metzger, and the rest of the Collective Book Studio crew; illustrator Olivier Kugler; designer Laura Palese; publicist Carrie Bachman; photographer Kevin J. Miyazaki, photo stylist Trina Kahl, and prop stylist Abby J. Campbell. We are indebted to you all for not only your expertise, but also for your willingness to invest precious time and energy into our passion project. It has been an honor to work with each of you. Thank you.

Jyoti This book is a collective effort, and there are many to whom I am grateful: the late Nirmal Sehgal, Sumana Mukharji, and Mayme DiMaggio D'Agostino (my mother, mother-in-law, and Italian mother, respectively) from whom I learned both the joy of shared family meals and the magic of a well-run kitchen; Auyon Mukharji, my co-author, for his many agencies: grit, determination, attention to detail, literary skill, research, and most importantly, a willingness to accept the prodigious burden of putting it all together while working with his mother; Aroop Mukharji, for 14 years of constant remote clerical support, between minor distractions advising the US government and instructing graduate students on International Relations; Arnob Mukharji for days spent shopping for ingredients, and for evenings spent assisting me in post-class clean-up; my wonderful husband Jhulan Mukharji, for urging me to start teaching many years ago (and for his judicious insight to stay out of the kitchen while I did so); Deepak Sehgal, Sumita Banerjea, Chitra Raghavan, and Harminder Gill for their enduring encouragement and recipe suggestions; Karan Sehgal for consistent and sustained technical assistance; Murari Lal, our family chef in India, and his sous chef Israel Safi, for their tireless problem-solving and for their wealth of practical culinary tips; Artir Halili for neighborly supplementation; the fifty-five hundred (and counting!) folks who have attended my classes, many now friends, for the motivation to keep going; and finally, Kimberly Winter Stern, Jill Silva, Vivien Jennings, Roger Doeren, Darren Mark, Mary Pepitone, and Judith Fertig for spreading the word and otherwise partnering in this labor of love.

Auyon Additional thanks to: Rosemary Macedo and the Thomas J. Watson Foundation for the time to get lost; Billy and Dodee Crockett, and the rest of the Occupy Blue Rock team, for a pivotal week in Texas Hill Country; The Mastheads in Pittsfield, MA and my dream of a cohort there—Danny Lavery, Elisa Gonzalez, Julia Mounsey, and Kristina Gaddy—for inspiring the first public reading of (portions of) this text; Ariel Bernstein, Katie Schmidt, Will Schmidt, and Ellie Schmidt for the space to think and write; Dennis Davis, Arjun Prasad Ramadevanahalli, and Rohan Rupani for friendship and legal counsel; our esteemed league of recipe testers for their labor, care, and judgment; Monojit DasGupta, Prodipto Banerjea, and Deb Mukharji for cogitations on tea, Anglo-Indian cuisine, and many Indias; Emily Stephenson, Jenn Sit, Frances Baca, Alice McBride, Eugenie Du, Vasudha Viswanath, Faith Kramer, Mary Bailey, Kara Mae Harris, Charlie Burt, Ananda Burra, Priya Krishna, and Dorothy Smith for their generosity and guidance; Tse Wei Lim, Diana Kudajarova, Tu Le, Mark Forsyth, Arnab Chakladar, Niloufer Ichaporia King, Samin Nosrat, and Wendy MacNaughton for the inspiration to push boundaries and get a little messy; Sally Ekus, Katherine Conaway, and Chloe Feldman Emison for their help in considering the many shapes this book could take; Dave Senft, Don Mitchell, Harris Paseltiner, and Sam Kapala for teaching me to think carefully and critically about writing and making; Abby McBride for encouraging me to step outside; and finally, to my beloved mother for bringing me along on this wild, wonderful, and occasionally ill-advised ride—what a gift.

RECIPE TESTERS

Alexander & Shira Kopynec
Amy Persechini
Anagha Prasad & Alex Schultz
Ananda Burra
Angela Consani
Anita Hegde
Ann Levin & Maggie Weis
Annie O'Sullivan
Aron Chang & Alexandra Stokes
Beth Bader & Kurt Becker
BethAnne Flynn
Bob Volpi
Catherine & Eric Jonash
Chip & Kendall Schellhorn
Chris Lee
Chris Offensend & Jill Duncan
Clarissa Randolph
Conner & Richard McDowell
Cortney Tunis
Dan Cardinal & KC Roddy
Daniel & Avery Eisenson
Daniel Wollin & Eugenie Du
David D DeVaughn & Camila Gómez Cualla
David, Diane, & Ellie Burke
Diana Kudajarova & Tse Wei Lim
Elizabeth Haff & Suzanne Ainslie
Ellen & Scott Paseltiner
Eva Mrak (Spoondrift Kitchen)
Evelyn Otsuka-Davis
Gala Bauer & Tracy Fairley

Georgia Crump & Robert Ratcliffe
Harris Paseltiner & Hannah Ratcliffe
Ina & James Trotta
Janis Knorr
Jen & Colin Pespisa
Josh Cantor & Lisa Present
Judith Evnen
Kate Nolfi & Eugene Korsunskiy
Katherine Conaway
Katie Fleming & Don Mitchell
Katie Sanghvi
Lisa & the Little Moss Restaurant Team
Liz Kodela
Mark Danforth & Molly McManus
Martin Earley & Callie Peters
Melissa Dresselhuys
Michele & Marc Sopher
Molly Milroy & Daniel Shearin
Nancy Leazer
Rosemary Macedo
Sarah Dewey
Sean & Shelbi McCarthy
Sheila Hegde
Steve Stollman
Steven Danforth
Susan Garcia
Trent & Amanda Skaggs
Valerie Eisenson & Aroop Mukharji
Zack Brewer & Maryn Juergens